DATE			

STRATEGIC THINKING
for the
NEXT ECONOMY

STRATEGIC THINKING
for the
NEXT ECONOMY

Michael A. Cusumano

Constantinos C. Markides

Editors

MITSloan
Management Review

JOSSEY-BASS
A Wiley Company
San Francisco

Published by

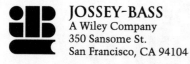

JOSSEY-BASS
A Wiley Company
350 Sansome St.
San Francisco, CA 94104

www.josseybass.com

Jossey-Bass books and products are available through most bookstores. To contact Jossey-
Bass directly, call (888) 378-2537, fax to (800) 605-2665, or visit our website at
www.josseybass.com.

Substantial discounts on bulk quantities of Jossey-Bass books are available to corporations,
professional associations, and other organizations. For details and discount information,
contact the special sales department at Jossey-Bass.

We at Jossey-Bass strive to use the most environmentally sensitive paper stocks available to us.
Our publications are printed on acid-free recycled stock whenever possible, and our paper
always meets or exceeds minimum GPO and EPA requirements.

Library of Congress Cataloging-in-Publication Data

Strategic thinking for the next economy / sponsored by MIT Sloan
management review ; Michael A. Cusumano, Constantinos C. Markides,
editors.— 1st ed.
   p. cm.
  ISBN 0-7879-5729-1 (alk. paper)
  1. Decision making. 2. Industrial management. I. Cusumano,
Michael A., 1954- II. Markides, Constantinos C. III. Sloan
management review.
  HD30.23 .S768 2001
  658.4'012—dc21
2001001015

FIRST EDITION
PB Printing   10 9 8 7 6 5 4 3 2 1

The Jossey-Bass
Business & Management Series

CONTENTS

Kathleen M. Eisenhardt

Successful strategy emerges from a decision process in which executives develop collective intuition, accelerate constructive conflict, maintain decision pacing, and avoid politics.

PART THREE THE STRATEGY-MAKING PROCESS

Richard T. Pascale

Treating organizations as complex adaptive systems provides powerful insights into the nature of strategic work.

Eric D. Beinhocker

Managers can form populations of strategies by using lessons learned from complexity theory and evolution.

Peter J. Williamson

In the face of uncertainty and rapid change, companies must reengineer their strategy processes to create a portfolio of options on the future and integrate planning with opportunism.

PART FOUR STRATEGIC INNOVATION AND GROWTH

Gary Hamel

What will catalyze the emergence of new, viable strategies in a successful but complacent company?

STRATEGIC THINKING
for the
NEXT ECONOMY

MICHAEL A. CUSUMANO
CONSTANTINOS C. MARKIDES
EDITORS

Behind every successful company there is a strategy that works. Managers may have developed this strategy through formal analysis, trial and error, intuition, or even pure luck. No matter how it has emerged, strategy underpins the success of any company. Of course, companies must develop or acquire the knowledge and skills they need to make their strategies work. Nonetheless, as a start for understanding why some firms perform better than others, we believe it is useful to try to understand why some strategies or strategy-making processes seem to work better than others.

Even when "luck" seems to play an important role in determining the success of a particular company's strategy, we believe that there still is an underlying logic—a set of principles—that helps explain this success. Even in cases where managers readily admit that they arrived at their successful strategy through intuition or made the "right" choice on a hunch, we believe that at least in retrospect it is possible to identify a logic behind the success.

There seems to be little argument that strategy is important to the success of any organization. But despite decades of academic research on the subject, there is surprisingly little agreement as to what strategy really is or what the ideal process should be to develop a good strategy. Within both business and academic circles, it would be quite miraculous if you could identify two people who shared the same definition of strategy. Several possible definitions fight for legitimacy, ranging from notions of "strategy as positioning" to "strategy as visioning." The lack of an acceptable definition has opened up the field to an invasion of "sexy" slogans and faddish terms, all of which add to the confusion over what strategy is or should be. No wonder that a recent editorial in *The Economist* made the claim that "nobody really knows what strategy is."[1]

Similar confusion and disagreements exist regarding the process by which organizations develop good strategies. We are all experts after the fact in identifying companies with superior strategies, but we have little to say on how companies created these superior strategies in the first place or how other companies could develop similarly successful or innovative strategies in a systematic manner. For example, the big debate that has been raging in the field for the past twenty years is whether a company can choose its strategy through a "rational" planning process or whether successful strategy really "emerges" through a process of experimentation.

To make matters worse, it is not unusual to hear academics and consultants give conflicting and contradictory advice. For example, following the success of the book *In Search of Excellence*, many strategy experts advised companies to "stick to their knitting."[2] Yet within four years, another consultant from the same firm, in his study of technological innovations, suggested that the last thing a company should do is continue with the same old thing as a business matures![3] In times of technological upheavals or fast-paced change, sticking to one's knitting can be a quick path to bankruptcy. Similarly, in 1960, Harvard professor Ted Levitt argued in his influential article, "Marketing Myopia," that companies should define their businesses broadly—*not* according to the product they are selling but according to the underlying functionality of their products.[4] Yet a second prominent academic, Hermann Simon, in his study of German success stories (*Hidden Champions*), found that these companies succeeded exactly because they were careful not to define their markets broadly. Instead, they focused on narrowly defined markets (which they defined according to the product they were selling) and then proceeded to dominate these markets worldwide.[5] Another example: A well-known dictum from the field of marketing says that companies should stay close to and listen to their customers. How many times have you heard the saying, "the customer is always right!" Yet the article that won the 1995 McKinsey award for the best article in *Harvard Business Review* argued that companies that pay *too much* attention to their existing customers in times of technological change will fail.[6] What are managers to believe?

These examples show that no advice, however sound and practical, will apply to all firms all the time. What a firm should do depends on its particular circumstances, which in turn reflect the company's stage of evolution. Strategic advice that fails to put an organization in its proper historical and environmental context runs the risk of being dangerous advice.

THE BOOK

It is from these thoughts that we came up with the idea for a special collection of *Sloan Management Review* articles on strategy and the strategy-making process. We first published a special issue of *SMR* on this topic in Spring 1999. We are now following with the current volume, which includes most of the articles from the special issue as well three additional articles published in *SMR* between 1998 and 2001. We continue to feel that the field of strategy has reached a defining moment in its evolution and that a collection of articles from some of the best thinkers in the field can help pave the way for the debates of the next twenty years.

The chapters in this volume fall into four categories. Part One (two chapters, one by Ghoshal, Bartlett, and Moran and one by Mintzberg and Lampel) deals primarily with strategy and value creation in the next economy. Part Two (one chapter by Hax and Wilde and one by Eisenhardt) talks about flexibility in a volatile world. Part Three (three chapters, by Pascale; Beinhocker; and Williamson) continues on this theme but focuses on strategy and the strategy-making process in times of uncertainty. Finally, Part Four (five chapters, by Hamel; Kim and Mauborgne; Markides; Prahalad and Oosterveld; and von Krogh and Cusumano) concentrates on strategic innovation and strategies for growth, particularly in fast-paced markets.

The authors of the chapters in this book chose their own topics. Nonetheless, the chapters share a common belief, a common theme, and a common view of what constitutes the biggest strategic challenge for companies in this fast-changing, Internet economy. The common *belief* is that it *is* possible for a company to design a superior strategy; and it *is* possible for others to learn the art of crafting superior strategies. But designing a successful strategy is not a science—it is an art. It is the art of asking intelligent questions, exploring possible answers, experimenting with possible solutions, and starting the thinking process all over again by questioning the answers arrived at a year or two before. Effective strategic thinking is a process of continuously asking questions and thinking through the issues in a creative way. Hence, correctly formulating the questions is often more important than finding a "solution." Thinking through an issue from a variety of angles is often more productive than collecting and analyzing unlimited data. And actually experimenting with new ideas is often more critical than scientific analysis and discussion.

The common *theme* through this book is that designing a successful strategy is a never-ending quest. Just because Dell or Wal-Mart have superior strategies and are successful *today* is no guarantee that they will be successful tomorrow. To be successful tomorrow, they will need to build a superior strategy for tomorrow's market; and to be able to do so, they must understand the underlying principles of their successful strategies of today. Even successful companies need to understand the logic behind their strategies. This is especially the case if they arrived at their strategic positions through intuition, trial and error, or luck. It is highly unlikely that the same companies will be "lucky" twice. But if they understand the building blocks of successful strategies, they are more likely to craft a superior strategy when their current approach runs its course.

Finally, although the authors in this book focus on different strategic questions and discuss different challenges facing the modern firm, there appears to be a common strategic *issue* that all the chapters raise: How can a firm achieve "fit" between what it does and what its industry environment requires today, while also preparing itself to stretch capabilities and evolve its culture to tackle the new environment that tomorrow might bring? This has always been a challenge for firms, but the speed with which environments and markets change in today's world makes this an even more pressing concern.

We are all familiar with the story of the frog: When a frog is put in a pot of boiling water, it jumps out. When instead the same frog is put in a pot of cold water and the water is slowly brought to a boil, the frog stays in the pot and boils to death. In the same manner, if a company does not understand and react to the constant and sometimes subtle changes taking place in its environment, it might find itself "boiled to death." Companies can also become like the proverbial deer, paralyzed in the headlights of an oncoming car, unable to move.

Companies need strategies and capabilities that are appropriate for their *current* environment while remaining flexible enough to respond to (or even create) changes in their environment. But what does it mean when we say that a firm "must remain flexible?" The trouble is that managers do not know for sure how the environment will change or when. How, then, can they prepare for the unknown in advance? What competencies do they need to develop today to prepare for this uncertain future and what investments should they undertake today to be prepared when this unknown future arrives? The chapters in this book try to provide answers to these questions.

It is often said that learning takes place *not* when we are provided with answers and solutions but when we are confronted with serious questions and problems that force the mind to start thinking. This is what the *MIT Sloan Management Review* tries to do in general: force managers to think more deeply as well as more broadly about what they are doing. In this spirit, we hope that this book raises more questions than answers and provides some perspective on the current state of thinking on strategy and the strategy-making process.

NOTES

1. *The Economist,* March 20, 1993, p. 106.
2. Thomas J. Peters and Robert H. Waterman, *In Search of Excellence* (New York: Harper & Row, 1982).
3. Richard J. Foster, *Innovation: The Attacker's Advantage* (New York: Summit Books, 1986).
4. Theodore Levitt, "Marketing Myopia," *Harvard Business Review,* July-August 1960.
5. Hermann Simon, *Hidden Champions* (Boston: Harvard Business School Press, 1996).
6. Joseph L. Bower and Clayton M. Christensen, "Disruptive Technologies: Catching the Wave," *Harvard Business Review,* January-February 1995, pp. 43–53.

PART ONE

Strategy and Value Creation

CHAPTER ONE

A New Manifesto for Management

SUMANTRA GHOSHAL
CHRISTOPHER A. BARTLETT
PETER MORAN

Why do corporations elicit such powerful love-hate responses? On the one hand, amid the decay of influence and legitimacy of other institutions—such as states, political parties, churches, monarchies, or even families—the corporation has emerged as perhaps the most powerful social and economic institution of modern society. Versatile and creative, the corporation is a prodigious amplifier of human effort across national and cultural boundaries. Corporations, not abstract economic forces or governments, create and distribute most of an economy's wealth, innovate, trade, and raise living standards. Historically, they have served as a pervasive force for civilization, promoting honesty, trust, and respect for contracts. As the market sphere has grown to annex areas such as health and sports, companies loom even larger in the lives of individuals. People look to them for community and identity as well as economic well-being.

Yet, in the closing year of the century, corporations and managers suffer from a profound social ambivalence. Hero-worshipped by the few, they are deeply distrusted by the many. In popular mythology, the corporate manager is Gordon Gecko, the financier who preaches the gospel of greed in Hollywood's *Wall Street*. Corporations are "job killers." There is so much uncertainty about what companies represent that Bill Clinton in the United States and Tony Blair in the United Kingdom set up reviews of companies' roles. Big business arouses big suspicion in France, Korea, and Germany. Even in the United States, executive salaries have caused a public furor, while the equally astronomical remuneration of entertainers, entrepreneurs, and bond traders raises scarcely an eyebrow. When asked by pollsters to rank professionals by ethical standing, people consistently rate managers the lowest of the low—below even politicians and journalists.

People are *right* in their intuition that something is wrong. But this is not because large corporations or management are inherently harmful or evil. It is because of the deeply unrealistic, pessimistic assumptions about the nature of individuals and corporations that underlie current management doctrine and that, in practice, cause managers to undermine their own worth.

It has been said that every living practitioner is a prisoner of the ideas of a dead theorist. Obsessed though they are with the "real world," managers are no exception. Ironically, in their day-to-day actions and choices, the hardest driving of today's managers are conforming to theories to which the real "real world" no longer corresponds. To the extent that conformity is unconscious and the assumptions behind the theories untested, the theories are self-fulfilling and therefore doubly debilitating. It is time to expose the old, disabling assumptions and replace them with a different, more realistic set that calls on managers to act out a positive role that can release the vast potential still trapped in the old model. The new role for management breaks from the narrow economic assumptions of the past to recognize that

▼ Modern societies are not market economies; they are organizational economies in which companies are the chief actors in creating value and advancing economic progress.

▼ The growth of firms and therefore economies is primarily dependent on the quality of their management.

▼ The foundation of a firm's activity is a new "moral contract" with employees and society, replacing paternalistic exploitation and value appropriation with employability and value creation in a relationship of shared destiny.

BETWEEN A ROCK AND A HARD PLACE

To understand why rethinking is necessary, start by looking at what happened to the corporate world in the 1980s. Driven by vociferous shareholders and global competition, managers have concentrated on enhancing competitiveness by improving their operating efficiencies. Managers have enlisted an array of techniques such as total quality, continuous improvement, and process reengineering to this end. Firms have cut costs, eliminated waste, focused, outsourced, downsized, let go, and generally pared themselves to the bone. The result has been victory—of a sort. Shareholder returns (and senior executives' pay) have, in many cases, soared. Value has been extracted, but at what price?

Explicit or implicit past contracts with both employees and suppliers were broken. Employee loyalty and commitment have been shattered. So has management confidence in its ability to create instead of cut; witness the vogue of high-growth companies like Reuters handing back cash to shareholders via share buy-backs and special dividends instead of investing it to pursue emerging opportunities. Michael Porter expressed alarm that the obsession with operating efficiencies was "leading more and more companies down the path of mutually destructive competition."[1] Stephen Roach, chief economist of Morgan Stanley, reversed his previous enthusiasm for downsizing and warned that if cutting labor costs and hollowing companies were all there was to the productivity-led recovery, "the nation could well be on a path toward industrial extinction."[2] Perhaps he was thinking of Scott Paper, which was reengineered, restructured, and retrenched until, to the dismay of its remaining workforce, the rump was sold to its traditional enemy, Kimberly Clark. "Chainsaw" Al Dunlap, Scott's CEO, stoutly defended the process by using what might be called the Vietnam justification of management: To save the company for shareholder value, we must destroy it.

Some companies, however, have never accepted this logic of auto-dismemberment. In the United States, companies like HP, 3M, Disney, and Microsoft have shown no fear of diversity, no timidity about growth. Continuously proliferating new products and technologies, they seem unfazed by the things that most companies find so difficult: innovation, organic expansion, creating new businesses. In Europe, ABB doubled its size in six years, despite the slow growth of its businesses. These companies have created more shareholder wealth than most break-up artists by marching to a drum that the downsizers can't hear. They have also grown, expanded their geographic reach and global market share, and created an internal environment and external reputation that have made them the preferred employers of the best human talent.

Are these exceptions that just prove the rule? Or do these companies know something that others don't? The answer is that they have escaped the deadly pincer of dominant theory and practice in which other companies are crushing themselves to bits.

Geneen's Monkey

The top jaw of the pincer is the doctrine by which managers run their companies. Two generations of top managers have learned to frame their task through the viewfinder of the three Ss: crafting *strategy*, designing the *structure* to fit, and locking both in place with supporting *systems*. In its time, the strategy-structure-systems trilogy was a revolutionary discovery. Invented in the 1920s by Alfred Sloan and others as a technology to support their pioneering strategy of diversification, it served companies well for decades. It supported vertical and horizontal integration, the wave of conglomer-ate diversification in the 1960s, and the start of globalization in the 1970s and 1980s. But then it began to break down. However sophisticated their structure and systems, the great companies that had been bidding fair to inherit the earth—a French intellectual warned in the early 1980s that IBM had everything it needed to become a world power—were suddenly transformed into stumbling giants. The decline of excellence is well known. So what went wrong?

What happened was that the "real world" changed. The strength—and fundamental weakness—of the classic strategy-structure-systems model was the primacy it gave to control. As Frederick Tay-lor had made complex assembly repeatable by breaking it down to its simplest component tasks, so the new doctrine, the managerial equivalent of Taylorism, aimed to make the management of com-plex corporations systematic and predictable. Once strategy had been set at the top, structures and systems would banish trouble-some human idiosyncrasy, thus enabling large, diversified compa-nies to be run in the same machine-like ways. Like the workers on Henry Ford's assembly lines, all employees were replaceable parts. Harold Geneen, the accountant who ran the quintessential 1970s conglomerate ITT, used to boast that he was building a system that "a monkey will be able to run when I'm gone."

Famous last words. In the world that today's companies oper-ate in—a world of converging technologies and markets, swirling competition, and innovation that can outdate established industry structures overnight—machine-like systems of control aren't help-ful. In a situation where the most important corporate resources are not the financial funds in the hands of top management but the knowledge and expertise of the people on the front lines, they are downright unhelpful. To say that they stifle initiative, creativity, and diversity is true—but that was their point. They were designed for an organization man who has turned out to be an evolutionary dead end.

The Tyranny of Theory

The second jaw of the pincer in which companies are gripped is theory. Instead of providing remedies, academic prescriptions mostly have tightened the squeeze on managers and companies. They are part of the problem. Consider two strands of theory that have dominated managerial discourse, both academic and practical, for the past decade.

The first is Michael Porter's theory of strategy, grounded in industrial organization economics.[3] Crudely, under Porter's theory, the essence of strategy is competition to appropriate value. Companies strive to seize and keep for themselves as much as they can of the value embodied in the products and services they deal with, while allowing as little of this value as possible to fall into the hands of others. Employees, customers, suppliers, and direct or potential competitors are all trying to do the same thing. In short, strategy is positioning to grab all you can, while preventing anyone else from eating your lunch.

The difficulty is that, in this view, the interests of the company are incompatible with those of society. For society, the freer the competition among companies the better. But for individual firms, the purpose of strategy is precisely to restrict the play of competition to get as much as possible for themselves. To do their jobs, managers must prevent free competition, at the cost of social welfare. The destruction of social welfare is not just a coincidental by-product of strategy; it is the fundamental objective of profit-seeking firms and, therefore, of their managers.

The second influential strand of theory addresses a very basic question. Why do companies exist? The answer provided by most economists is so straightforward that it appears compelling; companies exist simply because markets fail. Accept this and it's only a short step toward the dangerously misleading belief that markets represent some sort of ideal way to organize all economic activities. According to "transaction-cost economics," the dominant branch of theorizing on this subject, a company is an inferior substitute for markets. Oliver Williamson, a key contributor to one strand of this theory, refers to companies as the organizing means "of last resort, to be employed when all else fails."[4] Markets fail, Williamson presumes, because people are weak. It is only because we, as humans, are limited in our ability to act rationally and because at least some of us are prone to acting "opportunistically" that we need organizations to save us from ourselves. In some of our dealings with others, particularly those requiring complex coordination of tasks, our opportunity to behave strategically is too great for markets to restrain. In these cases, companies are necessary because managers, with their hierarchical authority and their power to monitor and control, can keep the opportunism of employees in check.

Unfortunately, the practical consequence of these two theories is to make managers not architects but wreckers of their own corporations. What they have in common, apart from their narrow, instrumental, and largely pessimistic view of human enterprise, is an emphasis on static rather than dynamic efficiencies. *Static efficiency* is about exploiting available economic options as efficiently as possible—making the economy more efficient by shifting existing resources to their highest valued use. *Dynamic efficiency* comes from the innovations that create new options and new resources—moving the economy to a different level. Porter's theory is static in that it focuses strategic thinking on getting the largest possible share of a fixed economic pie. In this zero-sum world, profits must indeed come at the expense of the broader society. Because of its insistence that firms are second-rate market mechanisms, Williamson's theory, too, locks firms into the market logic of static efficiency.[5]

Fit the pieces together and we can see why this unholy alliance of theory and practice should have destructive consequences. In its constant struggle for appropriating value, the company is pitted against its own employees as well as business rivals and the rest of society. The economic challenge for society is to keep human discretion in check. This is accomplished in markets through a focus on individualism and the power of sharp incentives and, within the firm, through hierarchical control. In other words, as Williamson wrote, and Geneen practiced, companies must act as if they were "a continuation of market relations, by other means." Caught as it is between the sound logic of efficiency and the harsh reality of human frailties and pathologies, it is no wonder that dominant doctrine focuses managers' attention almost exclusively on concerns of appropriation and control. The resulting pathological economic role for companies and individuals should also be no surprise. It follows naturally from the premise that "markets rule"—that any and all failures to heed the market's corrective discipline are likely to be futile for firms and individuals and inefficient for society.

When in a hole, the first thing to do is to stop digging. The outlines are beginning to take shape of a different management model, based on a better understanding of both individual and corporate motivation. If downsizing, cost-cutting, and "getting lean and mean" were the mantras of the past decade, the desire for growth and renewal will be the major concern of the next.

A NEW MANAGEMENT PHILOSOPHY

Start by turning the conventional justification for the existence of the company around: Markets begin where firms leave off. As Nobel laureate Herbert Simon has put it, modern societies are not primarily market but *organizational economies*.[6] That is, most of their value is created not by individuals transacting individually in the market, as in the economists' ideal, but by organizations involving people acting collectively, with their motives empowered and their actions coordinated by their companies' purpose. Far from destroying social welfare, the rise of the corporation over the past century has coincided with a sustained and unprecedented improvement in living standards, fueled by the ability of companies to enhance productivity and create new products and services. Indeed, the clearest evidence for Simon's contention lies in a strong positive correlation between the relative prosperity of an economy and its quotient of large, healthy companies. Growing, efficient companies help create growing, efficient economies. Not only is the premise of a fundamental conflict between corporate well-being and social welfare wrong; the reality is exactly the reverse.

In terms of static efficiency, much of what happens inside a company is inefficient. That's its point. It exists precisely to provide a haven and (temporary) respite from the laws of the market in which humans can combine to do something that markets aren't very good at: innovating. From a static viewpoint, the 15 percent of their time that 3M encourages its employees to spend on their own projects is wasted. And, indeed, a lot of it is. But the company willingly makes this sacrifice, banking that out of their efforts will come products that alter the bounds of the existing market. Sony and Intel duplicate development teams for the same purpose. Companies create fresh value for society by developing new products and services and finding better ways for providing existing ones. Markets relentlessly force the same companies eventually to "hand off" most of the newly created value to others, increasing, not diminishing, social welfare. In this symbiotic coexistence, they jointly drive the process of "creative destruction" that the Austrian economist Joseph Schumpeter identified sixty years ago as the engine of economic progress.[7]

Reversing the logic pries companies from the crushing hold of the pincer, with liberating effect for their managers and employees. The difference between old and new is not just economic but also philosophical. In an organizational economy in which the essence of the company is value creation, the corporation and society are no longer in conflict. They are interdependent, and the starting point is a new moral contract between them. In this framework, management, too, wins back its legitimacy: Not only is the "destroy it to save it" nightmare banished, but the success of the company and the economy as a whole can be seen to depend on how well management does its job. Far from being villainous or exploitative, management as a profession can be seen for what it is—the primary engine of social and economic progress. Individual inventors and entrepreneurs develop new products and, sometimes, new businesses. A vast majority of new products and new businesses, however, are created by established organizations. Managers build organizations, the embodiments of an economy's social capital—a factor that is beginning to be recognized as perhaps the key driver of economic growth.[8]

Companies as Value Creators

The contrast between these two views of a company comes sharply into focus if we compare the management approaches of Norton and 3M, or of Westinghouse and ABB. As we have described elsewhere, managers at Norton and Westinghouse lived in the zero-sum, dog-eat-dog world of traditional management theory.[9] When they found a company that had created an attractive new product or business, they bought it. When they found the market for a product to be too competitive for them to dictate terms to their buyers and suppliers, they sold those businesses. Their primary management focus was on value appropriation—not only vis-à-vis their customers and suppliers, but also vis-à-vis their own employees.

At 3M and ABB, in contrast, a very different management philosophy was at work. While Norton tried to develop increasingly sophisticated strategic resource allocation models, 3M's entire strategy was based on the value-creating logic of continuous innovation. The same power equipment business that Westinghouse abandoned as unattractive (that is, not enough opportunity for value appropriation), ABB rejuvenated, in part by its own investments in productivity and in new technologies to enhance products' functionality or their appropriateness for new markets.

The difference between these companies is not just that 3M and ABB focused on innovation and improvement while Norton and Westinghouse did not, but that this difference in focus stemmed from very different beliefs about what a company is. At Norton and Westinghouse, managers thought of their companies in market terms: They bought and sold businesses, created internal markets whenever they could, and dealt with their people with market rules. Through the power of sharp, marketlike incentives, they got what they wanted. People began to behave as they would in a market—

acting alone as independent agents with an atomistic concern only for their self-interest.

By thinking of their companies in market terms, Norton and Westinghouse became the victims of the very logic that both companies sought to live by—a market logic that left little choice but to squeeze out more efficiency in everything that was attempted. Their strategy focused entirely on productivity improvement and cost cutting. Their structures for controlling behavior rewarded autonomy, while their elaborate systems for monitoring performance were finely tuned to eliminate even the smallest pools of waste. Yet they could not create any value that was new, not because they explicitly did not want to do so, but because the logic of the market that they adopted internally is simply not very good at anything other than enhancing the efficiency of existing activities. The very sharp sense of self-interest these firms engendered, coupled with the uncertainties inherent in any innovative effort (both in terms of the size of any ultimate benefits and the distribution of those benefits), made people unable to cooperate among themselves or to pool their resources and capabilities in order to create new combinations—particularly, new combinations of knowledge and expertise—that most innovations require.

Visions like ABB's purpose "to make economic growth and improved living standards a reality for all nations throughout the world," values such as Kao Corporation's espoused belief that "we are, first of all, an educational institution," and norms like 3M's acceptance that "products belong to divisions but technologies belong to the company" all emphasize the non-marketlike nature of a company, encouraging people to work collectively toward shared goals and values rather than more restrictively within their narrow self-interests. They can share resources, including knowledge, without having to be certain of how precisely each of them will benefit personally—as long as they believe that the company overall will benefit, to their collective gain.[10] It is, ultimately, this philosophical distinction in their beliefs about what a company is that allows these organizations to create innovations through a spirit of collaboration among people that markets, and companies that think of themselves as markets, cannot engender.

The shift of emphasis is as great inside firms. In the logic of a turbulent organizational economy, competitive advantage is anchored in the company's ability to innovate its way temporarily out of relentless market pressures. As companies change focus from value appropriation to value creation, facilitating cooperation among people takes precedence over enforcing compliance, and initiative becomes more valued than obedience. The manager's primary task is redefined from institutionalizing control to embedding trust, from maintaining the status quo to leading change. As opposed to being the designers of strategy, managers take on the role of establishing a sense of *purpose* within the company. Defined in terms of how the company will create value for society, purpose allows strategy to emerge from within the organization, from the energy and alignment created by that sense of purpose. As opposed to playing with the boxes and lines that represent the company's formal structure, managers focus on building the core organizational processes that would release the entrepreneurs held hostage in the front-line units of that structure, integrate the resources and capabilities across those units to create new combinations of resources and knowledge, and create the stretch that would drive the whole organization into continuously striving for new value creation. From being the builders of systems, managers transform into the developers of people, helping each individual in the company become the best he or she can be. The three Ss of strategy, structure, and systems that were at the core of the managerial role give way to the three Ps: purpose, process, and people.

CREATING VALUE FOR PEOPLE

This kind of management also demands a qualitatively different employment relationship from that of the past. The contrast is perhaps the clearest statement of the new management philosophy in action. In a value-appropriating, cost-cutting mode, part of the firm's advantage comes from its monopoly power over people's capabilities. In return, it takes on, or was understood to take on, responsibility for the employees' careers. Counterintuitively, the offer of job security has allowed companies to extract the maximum value from their people in the past.

Unlike machines, people cannot be owned. Yet, like machines, the way people become most valuable to a company is by becoming specialized to the company's businesses and activities. The more specific the employee's knowledge and skills are to a company's unique set of customers, technologies, equipment, and so on, the more productive they become and the more efficient the company becomes in all that it does. Without employment security, employees hesitate to invest their time and energy to acquire such specialized knowledge and skills that may be very useful to the company but may have limited value outside of it. Without any assurance of a long-term association, companies, too, lack the incentive to commit resources to help employees develop such company-specific expertise. Employment security provides a viable basis for both to make such investments.[11]

While the company benefits from such specialization directly in terms of efficiency and productivity, it also benefits indirectly because the more specialized an employee is to the unique requirements of the company, the less attractive he or she becomes to other potential employers. Not only does this reduce the risk of losing valuable people, it also reduces wage demands if outsiders do not find the employee as valuable as the employing company does.

Exploitative or not, the "obedience for employment" contract was viable in a stable world in which firms like IBM, Caterpillar, and Xerox could sustain competitive advantage for long periods. But this contract has now broken down. As Jack Welch, the CEO of General Electric, points out, it produces "a paternal, feudal, fuzzy kind of loyalty" that is out of keeping with both the times and the changed needs of firms.[12] But even if they wanted to, companies can no longer meaningfully give the kind of job security that was their side of the bargain. One reason is the hypercompetition they have brought on themselves. In any case, security could hardly survive in an unstable world in which competitive advantage in one period becomes competitive disadvantage in another. To adjust to the displacement of its major markets from north and west to south and east, ABB has laid off 54,000 people in the United States and Europe and has taken on 46,000 people in the Asia-Pacific region. In the face of technological and market change of this order, guaranteeing employment is either meaningless or tantamount to committing competitive suicide.

At the same time, a free-market, hire-and-fire regime is no alternative, as many companies have come to recognize. Paradoxically, the same forces of ferocious competition and turbulent change that make job security impossible also increase the need for trust and teamwork. These can't be fostered in an affection-free environment of reciprocal opportunism and continuous spot contracting. On the contrary, firms such as Intel and 3M have intuited that value creation demands something much more inspiring than individual self-interest: a community of purpose in which individuals can share resources, including knowledge, without knowing precisely how they will benefit, but confident of collective gain. In other words, innovation depends on a company acting as a social and an economic institution, in which individuals can behave accordingly.

This requirement is embodied in a new moral contract with employees to anchor the similar contract with society. In the new contract, employees take responsibility for the competitiveness of both themselves and the part of the company to which they belong. In return, the company offers not the dependence of employment security but the independence of employability—a guarantee that they fulfill through continuous education and development. Says GE's Welch: "The new psychological contract . . . is that jobs at GE are the best in the world for people who are willing to compete. We have the best in training and development resources, and an environment committed to providing opportunities for personal and professional growth."[13] This second reversal of the conventional logic again has a pleasingly ironic twist: By enhancing employees' value to others, the company obliges itself not just to keep its development promises, but to make jobs so exciting that employees do not exercise their liberty to leave. The result: By abandoning job security, the new contract encourages the development of the durable, mutually satisfying relationship between the individual and the organization that it ruled out as its starting point.

Few companies take their commitment to employability of people more seriously than Motorola. In a context of radical decentralization of resources and decisions to the divisional level, employee education is one activity that Motorola manages at the corporate level, through the large and well-funded Motorola University that has branches all over the world. Each employee, including the chief executive, has to undertake a minimum of forty hours of formal coursework each year. Courses span a wide range of topics—from state-of-the-art coverage of new technologies to broad general management topics and issues—so as to allow Motorola employees around the world to update knowledge and skills in their chosen areas. It is this commitment to adding value to people that allowed Motorola to launch and implement its much-imitated "Six Sigma" total quality initiative. At the same time, the reputation of Motorola University increasingly has become a key source of the company's competitive advantage in recruiting and retaining the best graduates from leading schools in every country in which it operates.

More recently, Motorola has further upped the ante on its commitment to employability by launching the "Individual Dignity Entitlement" (or IDE) program. The program requires all supervisors to discuss, on a quarterly basis, six questions with everyone whose work they supervise (see box, "Motorola's Individual Dignity Entitlement"). A negative response from any employee to any one of these questions is treated as a quality failure, to be redressed in accordance with the principles of total quality management. Yet even Motorola, a company that has invested more in its people than most and that has long been an adherent of employability, was surprised to learn that some of its units reported failures in excess of

70 percent the first time that IDE was implemented. Beginning in 1995, the company began addressing the negatives systematically by identifying and then eliminating their root causes. This is the hard edge of the new moral contract on management's side—the commitment to help people become the best they can be—that counterbalances the new demands on people which the "employability for competitiveness" contract creates.

What the New Contract Is Not

While we have described at some length what a moral contract based on employability is, it is important to emphasize what it is not. *First,* it is not a catchy new slogan to free managers from a sense of responsibility to protect the jobs of their staff. At Intel, Andy Grove could make the kind of demands he did because his own past actions had established, beyond any doubt, the extent to which he was willing to go to protect the interests of his employees. During the memory-products bloodbath in the early 1980s, when every other semiconductor company in the United States immediately laid off many people, Grove adopted the 90 percent rule—with everyone, from the chairman down, accepting a 10 percent pay cut—to avoid layoffs. Then, to tide the company over the bad period without losing people he had nurtured for years, Grove sold 20 percent of the company to IBM for $250 million in cash. When cost pressures continued to mount, he implemented the 125 percent rule by asking everyone to work an extra ten hours a week with no pay increase, again to avoid cutbacks. Only after all these efforts proved insufficient did he finally close some operations, with the attending job losses. This kind of proven commitment to people makes a contract based on employability credible and its hard-edged demands on people acceptable.

Second, the new contract is not an act of altruism, aimed at helping educate and develop people at company cost so they then can find better jobs elsewhere. In fact, this new relationship actually enhances a company's chances of retaining its best people. Under the old contract based on employment security, those who

▼

Motorola's Individual Dignity Entitlement

1. Do you have a substantive, meaningful job that contributes to the success of Motorola?
2. Do you know the on-the-job behaviors and have the knowledge base to be successful?
3. Has the training been identified and been made available to continuously upgrade your skills?
4. Do you have a personal career plan, and is it exciting, achievable, and being acted on?
5. Do you receive candid, positive or negative, feedback at least every thirty days that is helpful in improving or achieving your personal career plan?
6. Is there appropriate sensitivity to your personal circumstances, gender, and cultural heritage so that such issues do not detract from your personal career plan?

lost their mobility through overspecialization or skill obsolescence stayed with the company, because they, at least in part, had no alternative. But those who could, typically the very best people, often left, frustrated by the constraints and controls that were the other side of the coin. In contrast, the promise of employability itself is a great motivator for people to remain with a company, because they know that even if they can cash in their current employability at a premium, they run the risk of falling victim to the next round of skill obsolescence in a company that does not have the same commitment to adding value to people. Besides, the same broad and advanced skills that make people employable outside the company also make them more adaptable to different jobs and needs within the company, thereby making it easier for the company to use their expertise more flexibly and in higher-value jobs.

Third, the contract based on employability is not some program that can be installed by a company's HR department. Rather, it must be inculcated as a very different philosophy—one that requires management at every level to work hard, on an ongoing basis, to create an exciting and invigorating work environment, a place of enormous pride and satisfaction that bonds people to the company even more tightly than any bond of dependency that employment security could create. The combination of a moral contract based on employability and a management commitment to empowerment leads, as a consequence, to the durable long-term and mutually satisfying relationship between the individual and the organization that the traditional employment contract abandoned. But by building the new company-employee relationship on a platform of mutual value-adding and continuous choice, rather than on a self-degrading acceptance of one-way dependence, the new contract is not just functional. It is also moral.

BUILDING SHARED DESTINY RELATIONSHIPS

Is this notion of the modern corporation focused on creating value externally and internally what the British call "cloud-cuckoo land"? Is it all wishful thinking of wet-behind-the-ears softies who do not know how hard and unforgiving the world of business really is, or worse, of ivory tower academics who preach what they cannot do?

The business world is full of examples of companies that earn healthy profits year after year by focusing continuously on the task of creating value for themselves and others, rather than on expropriating as much value as they can. Canon made its own highly successful laser-printer technology obsolete by inventing and then promoting aggressively the bubble-jet printer on the ground that its functionality-to-cost ratio yielded higher value to customers. Intel fueled the information revolution by relentlessly following "Moore's law," creating the next generation of chips that allowed its customers to do new things, while at the same time wiping out its earlier generation of products. Kao decided to enter the cosmetics industry and use its advanced technology to create the high-functionality Sofina range to compete with overpriced mediocre products in expensive jars. In each company, value creation was both the stated objective and the proven outcome.

Without a moral contract based on adding value to people, McKinsey & Company and Andersen Consulting could not be in business. Recruiting the very best talent is the number one success factor in the consulting industry. Yet these companies can make partners of only one in seven of all the people they hire. The rest must leave the company. The promise of employability is a big reason fresh graduates worldwide seek to join these companies. And to the extent that companies deliver on that promise, the larger and more valued will be their alumni networks.

But these are examples of companies that have practiced the philosophy of value creation for a long time, often from inception. Can others, steeped in the more traditional approach, adopt this new philosophy? Yes, they can.

Unipart, a struggling auto parts manufacturer, is a good example of a company that transformed itself under this powerful management philosophy. At its birth out of the 1987 dismemberment of the chronically sick, government-owned British Leyland, Unipart suffered a two-to-one handicap vis-à-vis Japanese auto parts companies in terms of its costs and an astonishing hundred-to-one gap in quality, according to a U.K. Department of Trade and Industry study. The new company inherited an extremely confrontational work climate, the product of a heavily unionized workforce crossed with a traditional and autocratic management. Furthermore, the company inherited adversarial relationships that extended to its suppliers and its customers, principal among them Rover, the U.K. car company that earlier was a unit within British Leyland.

A decade later, the story had utterly changed. Annual revenues had shot up to more than £1 billion ($1.6 billion), and profits had quadrupled to £32 million. A Department of Trade and Industry study had announced that Unipart was the only United Kingdom–based company in its business to meet world-class standards on quality.

Behind the company's transformation was Unipart CEO John Neill and his absolute commitment to what he called "shared destiny relationships." The philosophy was not an ex post rationalization of success but was stated clearly and firmly by Neill in 1987 as the fundamental principle on which the company would function: "We have made a mess of our industry. The short-term power-based relationships have failed us. Many Western companies still believe that it is a superior way to secure competitive advantage. I think they are absolutely wrong. . . . We must create shared destiny relationships with all our stakeholders: customers, employees, suppliers, governments, and the communities in which we operate. It is not altruism; it is commercial self-interest."[14]

While acknowledging the interdependence between a company and all its key stakeholders, Neill's notion of shared destiny relationships is very different from "being and doing good to all," as the stakeholder concept is often portrayed. With suppliers, his program emphasized the need to work together to radically improve performance across ten criteria ranging from transaction costs and lead times to defect rates and delivery errors—and to ultimately reduce each to as close to zero as possible. These efforts created value, not just for Unipart and its suppliers, but also for the industry, as suppliers worked to transfer what they had learned from working closely with Unipart to their relationships with other buyers. This, in turn, increased the pressure on Unipart to continue striving for new sources of value, this time without their traditional recourse to appropriation from others. Similarly, within the organization, programs like "our contribution counts" emphasized the hard two-way dependence between the company and its employees inherent in the concept of shared destiny, and the need for continuous performance improvement to make that destiny mutually attractive.

Neill's vision for Unipart came not from some narrowly defined model for achieving profitability through the zero-sum game of extracting value from others. Rather, it was based on an expansive positive-sum value-creation perspective that we found much more typical of successful managers in the companies we have studied. Like Neill, these executives have enormous faith in what they can create by engaging, energizing, and empowering their constituencies to work together for mutual benefit. The result of the collective actions of these executives is generally greater than was originally anticipated. The emergence of a more realistic and assertive philosophy of the corporation's role as an important social institution, as well as a powerful economic entity, enabled these companies to use their economic resources to add value to society generally and to peoples' lives individually. These executives are the standard bearers for a new manifesto of companies and managers as value creators.

A Manifesto for Reclaiming Managerial Legitimacy

Institutions decline when they lose their source of legitimacy. This happened to the monarchy, to organized religions, and to the state. This will happen to companies unless managers accord the same priority to the collective task of rebuilding the credibility and legitimacy of their institutions as they do to the individual task of enhancing their company's economic performance.

Far from thinking of their companies as agents for destroying social welfare, most managers we have met believe that their primary role should be to create value. Their guilt lies in their unwillingness to confront explicitly the role their companies play in society or to articulate a moral philosophy for their own professions. Through this act of omission, they have left others—economists, political scientists, journalists, and so on—to define the normative order that shapes the public's perception about them and about their institutions. Those perceptions, in turn, have seduced many managers into thinking about their companies in very narrow terms, and, in the process, have made them unwitting victims of the value-appropriation logic and have weakened their ability to create new value for society.

We believe that individuals like Chairman of ABB Percy Barnevik, CEO of GE Jack Welch, and Chairman of Kao Yoshio Maruta will each earn a place in history—not because of their firms' economic performance while they were in the saddle—but because they have regained the initiative to define a new corporate philosophy that explicitly sees companies as value-creating institutions of society. They have not reinvented the old, tired debate of the social responsibility of business; instead they have made *value creation for all constituencies* their fundamental business. Then they have reshaped their organizational and management processes around this new philosophy to give birth to a new corporate form that we have labeled elsewhere the individualized corporation.[15]

This new moral contract of creating value for society is not only more satisfying for managers, it is also a more effective basis for protecting and growing their companies. The problem of a strategy of value appropriation is that, ultimately, it is self-defeating. It is like a strategy of holding back the tide, and like the tide, the ability of others to overcome a company's defenses cannot be held back forever. With such a strategy, the company gets squeezed more and more into a corner, with every round of value appropriation consuming ever more effort, until finally, there is no value left to appropriate. By thinking of themselves as a market, such companies ultimately succumb to the market, as happened in Norton's acquisition by St. Gobain and by Westinghouse's dismemberment under Michael Jordan. Hanson Trust followed a classic value appropriation strategy, as did ITT under Harold Geneen. Ultimately, each company fell victim to the same market logic that it had embraced so enthusiastically. In the process, value was destroyed for all constituents, including customers, shareholders, and employees.

In contrast, 3M and Kao continue to grow profitably, spawning new products and businesses and creating customer satisfaction, employee enthusiasm, and shareholder wealth, and ABB continues to expand and strengthen its leadership position in its businesses, at times by acquiring the spent parts of companies like Westinghouse and rejuvenating them with the power of its very different philosophy. They are role models demonstrating the spirit, passion, and moral commitment of which management is capable, and which the dominant doctrine has all but destroyed.

Ideas matter. In a practical discipline like management, the normative influence of ideas can be powerful, as they can manifest themselves as uniquely beneficial or uniquely dangerous. Bad theory and a philosophical vacuum have caused managers to subvert their own practice, trapping them in a vicious circle. But there is a choice. Management can continue down the well-worn path to illegitimacy or begin to chart a new course by laying claim to a higher purpose. When the solution to a recurring problem is always "try harder," there is usually something wrong with the terms, not the execution. Get out of the pincer's grip. Throw out the old paradigm while you still can, before the growing gap between companies' economic power and their social legitimacy proves it right. Take responsibility before management is held to blame for stunting the growth potential of individuals, companies, and society.

NOTES

1. M. E. Porter, "What Is Strategy?" *Harvard Business Review,* November-December 1996, 74, 61–78.
2. S. S. Roach, "The Hollow Ring of the Productivity Revival," *Harvard Business Review,* November-December 1996, 74, 81–89.
3. M. E. Porter, *Competitive Strategy: Techniques for Analyzing Industries and Competitors* (New York: Free Press, 1980).
4. O. E. Williamson, "Comparative Economic Organization: The Analysis of Discrete Structural Alternatives," *Administrative Science Quarterly,* June 1991, 36, 269–296. See also O. E. Williamson, *Economic Institutions of Capitalism* (New York: Free Press, 1985).
5. Elsewhere, we have used the terms "allocative" and "adaptive" in place of "static" and "dynamic," respectively, to better distinguish the type of efficiency that results from two types of resource deployments. Allocatively efficient deployments are those that tend to allocate resources to their best-known use (i.e., "best" as defined by the combination of resources and forces that exist at any time). As Schumpeter cautions, however, these allocatively efficient deployments may prove in the

long run to be mistakes. Adaptively efficient deployments are those (often allocatively inefficient) deployments that facilitate the pursuit of new and possibly better uses (thus permitting the resources and forces that define what is allocatively efficient to more efficiently adapt to possibilities that arise. See J. A. Schumpeter, *Capitalism, Socialism, and Democracy* (London: Unwin University Books, 1942), p. 83; D. C. North, "Institutions," *Journal of Economic Perspectives,* Winter 1991, 5, 80, 97–112; and P. Moran and S. Ghoshal, "Markets, Firms, and the Process of Economic Development," *Academy of Management Review,* forthcoming.

6. H. A. Simon, "Organizations and Markets," *Journal of Economic Perspectives,* Spring 1991, 5, 25–44.

7. Schumpeter (1942).

8. J. Nahapiet and S. Ghoshal, "Social Capital, Intellectual Capital, and the Organizational Advantage," *Academy of Management Review,* April 1998, 23, 242–266.

9. C. A. Bartlett and S. Ghoshal, "Rebuilding Behavioral Context: Turn Process Reengineering into People Rejuvenation," *Sloan Management Review,* Fall 1995, 37, 11–23.

10. This is what Coleman describes as "independent viability" and "global viability" that, according to Moran and Ghoshal, characterize organizations. See J. S. Coleman, *The Foundations of Social Theory* (Cambridge: Harvard University Press, 1990) and P. Moran and S. Ghoshal, "Value Creation by Firms," in J. B. Keys and L. N. Dosier, eds., *Academy of Management Best Paper Proceedings,* 1996.

11. This is a core argument of the theory of internal labor markets. See P. B. Doeringer and M. J. Poire, *Internal Labor Markets and Manpower Analysis* (Lexington, Massachusetts: D.C. Heath, 1971).

12. N. Tichy and R. Charan, "Speed, Simplicity, Self-Confidence: An Interview with Jack Welch," *Harvard Business Review,* September-October 1989, 67, 112–120.

13. Ibid.

14. A. Duncan, *Unipart Group of Companies: Uniting Stakeholders to Build a World-Class Enterprise* (London: London Business School Case, 1996), pp. 4–5.

15. S. Ghoshal and C. A. Bartlett, *The Individualized Corporation* (New York: HarperCollins, 1997).

CHAPTER TWO

Reflecting on the Strategy Process

HENRY MINTZBERG
JOSEPH LAMPEL

We are the blind people and strategy formation is our elephant. Each of us, in trying to cope with the mysteries of the beast, grabs hold of some part or other, and in the words of John Godfrey Saxe's poem of the last century,

> *Rail on in utter ignorance*
> *of what each other mean,*
> *And prate about an Elephant*
> *Not one of [us] has seen!*

Consultants have been like big game hunters embarking on their safaris for tusks and trophies, while academics have preferred photo safaris—keeping a safe distance from the animals they pretend to observe.

Managers are encouraged to take one narrow perspective or another—the glories of planning or the wonders of learning, the demands of external competitive analyses or the imperatives of an internal "resource-based" view. Much of this writing and advising has been decidedly dysfunctional, simply because managers have no choice but to cope with the entire beast.

In the first part of this article, we review briefly the evolution of the field in terms of ten "schools."[1] We ask whether these perspectives represent fundamentally different processes of strategy making or different *parts* of the same process. In both cases, our answer is yes. We seek to show how some recent work tends to cut across these historical perspectives—in a sense, how cross-fertilization has occurred. To many academics, this cross-fertilization represents confusion and disorder, whereas to others—including ourselves—it expresses a certain welcome eclecticism, a broadening of perspectives. We discuss this in terms of another metaphor that is also popular in strategic management: the tree with its roots and branches.

TEN SCHOOLS OF STRATEGY FORMATION

In his article "The Magic Number Seven, Plus or Minus Two: Some Limits on Our Capacity for Processing Information," psychologist George Miller suggested in 1956 that the popularity of typologies using the number seven implies the number of "chunks" of information people can comfortably retain in their short-term memory.[2]

We hope that people interested in strategy can function at the upper limit of this range and, indeed, a bit beyond, because our historical survey of strategy literature suggests that it has been characterized by ten major schools since its inception in the 1960s—three *prescriptive* (or "ought") and seven *descriptive* (or "is").

We assume that the reader is familiar with the literature and practice of strategic management, if not necessarily with this particular characterization of them. Accordingly, we briefly summarize the schools (see also Table 2.1).

Design School: A Process of Conception
The original perspective—dating back to Selznick, followed by Chandler, and given sharper definition by Andrews—sees strategy

formation as achieving the essential fit between internal strengths and weaknesses and external threats and opportunities.[3] Senior management formulates clear, simple, and unique strategies in a deliberate process of conscious thought—which is neither formally analytical nor informally intuitive—so that everyone can implement the strategies. This was the dominant view of the strategy process, at least into the 1970s and, some might argue, to the present day, given its implicit influence on most teaching and practice. The design school did not develop, however, in the sense of giving rise to variants within its own context. Rather, it combined with other views in rather different contexts.

Planning School: A Formal Process

The planning school grew in parallel with the design school—indeed H. Igor Ansoff's book appeared in 1965, as did the initial Andrews text.[4] But in sheer volume of publication, the planning school predominated by the mid-1970s, faltered in the 1980s, yet continues to be an important branch of the literature today. Ansoff's book reflects most of the design school's assumptions except a rather significant one: that the process is not just cerebral but formal, decomposable into distinct steps, delineated by checklists, and supported by techniques (especially with regard to objectives, budgets, programs, and operating plans). This means that staff planners replaced senior managers, de facto, as the key players in the process.

Positioning School: An Analytical Process

The third of the prescriptive schools, commonly labeled positioning, was the dominant view of strategy formation in the 1980s. It was given impetus especially by Michael Porter in 1980, following earlier work on strategic positioning in academe (notably by Hatten and Schendel) and in consulting by the Boston Consulting Group and the PIMS project—all preceded by a long literature on military strategy, dating back to Sun Tzu in 400 B.C.[5] In this view, strategy reduces to generic positions selected through formalized analyses of industry situations. Hence, the planners become analysts. This

Table 2.1. Dimensions of the Ten Schools.

	Design	Planning	Positioning	Entrepreneurial	Cognitive
Sources	P. Selznick (and perhaps earlier work, for example, by W.H. Newman), then K.R. Andrews.[a]	H.I. Ansoff.[b]	Purdue University work (D.E. Schendel, K.J. Hatten), then notably M.E. Porter.[c]	J.A. Schumpeter, A.H. Cole, and others in economics.[d]	H.A. Simon and J.G. March.[e]
Base Discipline	None (architecture as metaphor).	Some links to urban planning, systems theory, and cybernetics.	Economics (industrial organization) and military history.	None (although early writings come from economists).	Psychology (cognitive).
Champions	Case study teachers (especially at or from Harvard University), leadership aficionados—especially in the United States.	"Professional" managers, MBAs, staff experts (especially in finance), consultants, and government controllers—especially in France and the United States.	As in planning school, particularly analytical staff types, consulting "boutiques," and military writers—especially in the United States.	Popular business press, individualists, small business people everywhere, but most decidedly in Latin America and among overseas Chinese.	Those with a psychological bent—pessimists in one wing, optimists in the other.
Intended Message	Fit.	Formalize.	Analyze.	Envision.	Cope or create.
Realized Message	Think (strategy making as case study).	Program (rather than formulate).	Calculate (rather than create or commit).	Centralize (then hope).	Worry (being unable to cope in either case).

School Category	Prescriptive.	Prescriptive.	Prescriptive.	Descriptive (some prescriptive).	Descriptive.
Associated Homily	"Look before you leap."	"A stitch in time saves nine."	"Nothin' but the facts, ma'am."	"Take us to your leader."	"I'll see it when I believe it."

[a] P. Selznick, *Leadership in Administration: A Sociological Interpretation* (Evanston, Illinois: Row, Peterson, 1957); W. H. Newman, *Administrative Action: The Techniques of Organization and Management* (Englewood Cliffs, New Jersey: Prentice Hall, 1951); and E. P. Learned, C. R. Christensen, K. R. Andrews, and W. D. Guth, *Business Policy: Text and Cases* (Homewood, Illinois: Irwin, 1965).

[b] H. I. Ansoff, *Corporate Strategy* (New York: McGraw-Hill, 1965).

[c] K. J. Hatten and D. E. Schendel, "Heterogeneity within an Industry: Firm Conduct in the U.S. Brewing Industry, 1952–1971," *Journal of Industrial Economics, 26*, December 1977, 97–113; M. E. Porter, *Competitive Strategy* (New York: Free Press, 1980); and M. E. Porter, *Competitive Advantage: Creating and Sustaining Superior Performance* (New York: Free Press, 1985).

[d] J. A. Schumpeter, *The Theory of Economic Development* (Cambridge, Massachusetts: Harvard University Press, 1934); and A. H. Cole, *Business Enterprise in Its Social Setting* (Cambridge, Massachusetts: Harvard University Press, 1959).

[e] H. A. Simon, *Administrative Behavior* (New York: Macmillan, 1947); and J. G. March and H. A. Simon, *Organizations* (New York: Wiley, 1958).

Table 2.1. Continued.

	Learning	Power	Cultural	Environmental	Configuration
Sources	C. E. Lindblom, R. M. Cyert and J.G. March, K. E. Weick, J.B. Quinn, and C. K. Prahalad and G. Hamel.[f]	G. T. Allison (micro), J. Pfeffer and G. R. Salancik, and W. G. Astley (macro).[g]	E. Rhenman and R. Normann in Sweden. No obvious source elsewhere.[h]	M. T. Hannan and J. Freeman. Contingency theorists (e.g., D. S. Pugh et al.).[i]	A. D. Chandler, McGill University group (H. Mintzberg, D. Miller, and others), R. E. Miles and C. C. Snow.[j]
Base Discipline	None (perhaps some peripheral links to learning theory in psychology and education). Chaos theory in mathematics.	Political science.	Anthropology.	Biology.	History.
Champions	People inclined to experimentation, ambiguity, adaptability—especially in Japan and Scandinavia.	People who like power, politics, and conspiracy—especially in France.	People who like the social, the spiritual, the collective—especially in Scandinavia and Japan.	Population ecologists, some organization theorists, splitters, and positivists in general—especially in the Anglo-Saxon countries.	Lumpers and integrators in general, as well as change agents. Configuration perhaps most popular in the Netherlands. Transformation most popular in the United States.
Intended Message	Learn.	Promote.	Coalesce.	React.	Integrate, transform.
Realized Message	Play (rather than pursue).	Hoard (rather than share).	Perpetuate (rather than change).	Capitulate (rather than confront).	Lump (rather than split, adapt).

School Category	Descriptive.	Descriptive.	Descriptive.	Descriptive.	Descriptive and prescriptive.
Associated Homily	"If at first you don't succeed, try, try again."	"Look out for number one."	"An apple never falls far from the tree."	"It all depends."	"To everything there is a season. . . ."

[g] D. Braybrooke and C. E. Lindblom, *A Strategy of Decision* (New York: Free Press, 1963); R. M. Cyert and J. G. March, *A Behavioral Theory of the Firm* (Englewood Cliffs, New Jersey: Prentice Hall, 1963); K. E. Weick, *The Social Psychology of Organizing* (Reading, Massachusetts: Addison-Wesley, first edition 1969, second edition 1979); J. B. Quinn, *Strategies for Change: Logical Incrementalism* (Homewood, Illinois: Irwin, 1980); and G. Hamel and C. K. Prahalad, *Competing for the Future* (Boston: Harvard Business School Press, 1994).

[g] G. T. Allison, *Essence of Decision: Explaining the Cuban Missile Crisis* (Boston: Little, Brown, 1971); J. Pfeffer and G. R. Salancik, *The External Control of Organizations: A Resource Dependence Perspective* (New York: Harper & Row, 1978); and W. G. Astley, "Toward an Appreciation of Collective Strategy," *Academy of Management Review*, volume 9, July 1984, pp. 526-533.

[h] E. Rhenman, *Organization Theory for Long-Range Planning* (London: Wiley, 1973); and R. Normann, *Management for Growth* (New York: Wiley, 1977).

[i] M. T. Hannan and J. Freeman, "The Population Ecology of Organizations," *American Journal of Sociology*, volume 82, March 1977, pp. 929-964; and D. S. Pugh, D. J. Hickson, C. R. Hinings, and C. Turner, "Dimensions of Organizational Structure," *Administrative Science Quarterly*, volume 13, June 1968, pp. 65-105.

[j] A. D. Chandler, *Strategy and Structure: Chapters in the History of the Industrial Enterprise* (Cambridge, Massachusetts: MIT Press, 1962); H. Mintzberg, *The Structuring of Organizations* (Englewood Cliffs, New Jersey: Prentice Hall, 1979); D. Miller and P. H. Friesen, *Organizations: A Quantum View* (Englewood Cliffs, New Jersey: Prentice Hall, 1984); and R. E. Miles and C. C. Snow, *Organizational Strategy, Structure, and Process* (New York: McGraw-Hill, 1978).

proved especially lucrative to consultants and academics alike, who could sink their teeth into hard data and promote their "scientific truths" to journals and companies. This literature grew in all directions to include strategic groups, value chains, game theories, and other ideas—but always with this analytical bent.

Entrepreneurial School: A Visionary Process

Meanwhile, on other fronts, mostly in trickles and streams rather than waves, wholly different approaches to strategy formation arose. Much like the design school, the entrepreneurial school centered the process on the chief executive; but unlike the design school and opposite from the planning school, it rooted that process in the mysteries of intuition. That shifted strategies from precise designs, plans, or positions to vague *visions* or broad perspectives, to be seen, in a sense, often through metaphor. This focused the process on particular contexts—start-up, niche, or private ownership, as well as "turnaround" by the forceful leader—although the case was certainly put forth that every organization needs the vision of a creative leader. In this view, however, the leader maintains such close control over *implementing* his or her *formulated* vision that the distinction central to the three prescriptive schools begins to break down.

Cognitive School: A Mental Process

On the academic front, the origin of strategies generated considerable interest. If strategies developed in people's minds as frames, models, maps, concepts, or schemas, what could be understood about those mental processes? Particularly in the 1980s and continuing today, research has grown steadily on cognitive biases in strategy making and on cognition as information processing, knowledge structure mapping, and concept attainment—the latter important for strategy formation, yet on which progress has been minimal. Meanwhile, another, newer branch of this school adopted a more subjective *interpretative* or *constructivist* view of the strategy process: that cognition is used to construct strategies as creative interpretations, rather than simply to map reality in some more or less objective way, however distorted.

Learning School: An Emergent Process

Of all the *descriptive* schools, the learning school grew into a veritable wave and challenged the always dominant prescriptive schools. Dating back to Lindblom's early work on disjointed incrementalism and running through Quinn's logical incrementalism, Bower's and Burgelman's notions of venturing, Mintzberg et al.'s ideas about emergent strategy, and Weick's notion of retrospective sense making, a model of strategy making as learning developed that differed from the earlier schools.[6] In this view, strategies are emergent, strategists can be found throughout the organization, and so-called formulation and implementation intertwine.

Power School: A Process of Negotiation

A thin, but quite different stream in the literature has focused on strategy making rooted in power. Two separate orientations seem to exist. *Micro* power sees the development of strategies *within* the organization as essentially political—a process involving bargaining, persuasion, and confrontation among actors who divide the power. *Macro* power views the organization as an entity that uses its power over others and among its partners in alliances, joint ventures, and other network relationships to negotiate "collective" strategies in its interest.

Cultural School: A Social Process

Hold power up to a mirror and its reverse image is culture. Whereas the former focuses on self-interest and fragmentation, the latter focuses on common interest and integration—strategy formation as a social process rooted in culture. Again, we find a thin stream of literature, focused particularly on the influence of culture in discouraging significant strategic change. Culture became a big issue in the U.S. literature after the impact of Japanese management was fully realized in the 1980s; later, some attention to the implications for strategy formation followed. However, interesting research developed in Sweden in the 1970s with culture as a central, although hardly exclusive, theme, stimulated by the early work of Rhenman and Normann, and carried out by people such as Hedberg and Jonsson and others.[7]

Environmental School: A Reactive Process

Perhaps not strictly strategic management, if one defines the term as being concerned with how organizations use degrees of freedom to maneuver through their environments, the environmental school nevertheless deserves some attention for illuminating the demands of environment. In this category, we include so-called *"contingency theory"* that considers which responses are expected of organizations facing particular environmental conditions and *"population ecology"* writings that claim severe limits to strategic choice. *"Institutional theory,"* which is concerned with the institutional pressures faced by organizations, is perhaps a hybrid of the power and cognitive schools.

Configuration School: A Process of Transformation

Finally, we come to a more extensive and integrative literature and practice. One side of this school, more academic and descriptive, sees organization as configuration—coherent clusters of characteristics and behaviors—and integrates the claims of the other schools—each configuration, in effect, in its own place. Planning, for example, prevails in machine-type organizations under conditions of relative stability, while entrepreneurship can be found under more dynamic configurations of start-up and turnaround. But if organizations can be described by such *states,* change must be described as rather dramatic *transformation*—the leap from one state to another. And so, a literature and practice of transformation—more prescriptive and practitioner oriented (and consultant promoted)—developed. These two different literatures and practices nevertheless complement one another and so, in our opinion, belong to the same school.

PRATING ABOUT STRATEGIC MANAGEMENT

During the nineteenth century, numerous explorers went in search of the source of the Nile. In time, it became increasingly evident that the source was not definitive. This was not something the expedition backers or the public wanted to hear. After some debate, the explorers announced their discovery: The source of the Nile was Lake Victoria! This is a verdict generally rejected by contemporary geographers, who believe the headstreams of the Kagera River in the highland of Burundi is a better answer. Different views may prevail in the future: The source of a river, after all, is a matter of interpretation, not a fact waiting to be discovered.

Strategic management has suffered from the problem that bedeviled the Victorian explorers. We, too, are a community of explorers, competing for discoveries, with backers eager for results and a public that demands answers.

Some explorers searching for the source of strategy have found "first principles" that explain the nature of the process. These have usually been rooted in basic disciplines, such as economics, sociology, or biology. Others have invoked a central concept, such as organization culture, to explain why some strategies succeed and others do not. The consequence has been to grasp one part of the strategic management elephant and prate about it as though none other exists. Or to acknowledge that other parts exist, but dismiss them as irrelevant. Consider Michael Porter's article "What Is Strategy?" which depicts the strategy process as deliberate and deductive.[8] Porter does not dismiss strategic learning so much as deny its very existence: "If strategy is stretched to include employees and organizational arrangements, it becomes virtually everything a company does or consists of. Not only does this complicate matters, but it obscures the chain of causality that runs from competitive environment to position to activities to employee skills and organization."[9]

But why can't strategy be "everything a company does or consists of"? Is that not strategy as perspective—in contrast to position?

And why must there be such a chain of causality, let alone one that runs in a single direction?

Porter's view of the strategy process leads him to the surprising conclusion that Japanese companies "rarely have strategies" and that they "will have to learn strategy."[10] Were this true, and given the performance of so many Japanese companies, strategy would hardly seem to be a necessary condition for corporate success. In our opinion, however, this is not the case. (Bear in mind that current problems in the Japanese economy or in its banking systems have not rendered many Japanese companies any less effective in their managerial practices.) Rather than having to learn about strategy, the Japanese might better teach Michael Porter about strategic learning.

Of course, in the affairs of writing and consulting, to succeed and to sell, champions must defend their positions, erecting borders around their views while dismissing or denying others. Or, to return to our metaphor, like butchers (we include ourselves in this group), they chop up reality for their own convenience, just as poachers grab the tusks of the elephant and leave the carcass to rot.

To repeat a key issue, such behavior ultimately does not serve the practicing manager. These people, as noted, have to deal with the entire beast of strategy formation, not only to keep it alive but to help sustain some real life energy. True, they can use it in various ways—just as an elephant can be a beast of burden or a symbol of ceremony—but only if it remains intact as a living being. The greatest failings of strategic management have occurred when managers took one point of view too seriously. This field had its obsession with planning, then generic positions based on careful calculations, and now learning.

OPENING UP THE SCHOOLS

Hence, we take pleasure in noting that some of the more recent approaches to strategy formation cut across these ten schools in eclectic and interesting ways. This suggests a broadening of the literature. (See Table 2.2 for a list of these across-school approaches.) For example, research on stakeholder analysis links the planning and positioning schools, whereas the work of Porter and others on what can be called strategic maneuvering (first-mover advantage, use of feints, and so on) connects the positioning to the power school.

Particularly popular are recent variants that blend the learning school with insights from other schools. Chaos theory, as applied to strategic management, might be seen as a hybrid of the learning and environmental schools. Perhaps best known is the *"dynamic capabilities"* approach of Prahalad and Hamel. We see their notions of core competence, strategic intent, and stretch—reminiscent of Itami's earlier work—as a hybrid of the learning and design schools: strong leadership to encourage continuous strategic learning.[11] *"Resource-based theory,"* which seems similar, in fact appears more like a hybrid of the learning and cultural schools. These two new views differ in orientation, if not content—the former more prescriptive and practitioner-focused, the latter more descriptive and research-focused. Leadership (as favored in the design school) is not a central concern to resource-based theorists. Instead they focus on competencies rooted in the essence of an organization (namely, its culture).[12]

Table 2.2. Blending of the Strategy Formation Schools.

Approach	Schools
Dynamic capabilities	Design, learning
Resource-based theory	Cultural, learning
Soft techniques (e.g., scenario analysis and stakeholder analysis)	Planning, learning, or power
Constructionism	Cognitive, cultural
Chaos and evolutionary theory	Learning, environmental
Institutional theory	Environmental, power, or cognitive
Intrapreneurship (venturing)	Environmental, entrepreneurial
Revolutionary change	Configuration, entrepreneurial
Negotiated strategy	Power, positioning
Strategic maneuvering	Positioning, power

ONE PROCESS OR DIFFERENT APPROACHES

As distinct as the schools may be, one issue about them is not clear. Do they represent different processes, that is, different approaches to strategy formation, or different parts of the same process? We have been ambiguous on this point, and we prefer to remain so, because we find either answer too constraining.

Some of the schools clearly are stages or aspects of the strategy formation process (see Figure 2.1):

▼ The cognitive school resides in the mind of the strategist located at the *center.*

▼ The positioning school looks *behind* at established data that are analyzed and fed into the black box of strategy making.

▼ The planning school looks slightly *ahead* to program the strategies created in other ways.

▼ The design school looks farther *ahead* to a strategic perspective.

▼ The entrepreneurial school looks *beyond* to a unique vision of the future.

▼ The learning and power schools look *below,* enmeshed in details. Learning looks into the grass roots, whereas power looks under the rocks to places that organizations may not want to expose.

▼ The cultural school looks *down,* enshrouded in clouds of beliefs.

▼ Above the cultural school, the environmental school looks *on,* so to speak.

▼ The configuration school looks *at* the process or, we might say, *all around* it, in contrast to the cognitive school, which tries to look *inside* the process.

Dealing with all this complexity in one process may seem overwhelming. But that is the nature of the beast, for the fault lies neither in the stars nor in ourselves, but in the process itself. Strategy formation *is* judgmental designing, intuitive visioning, and emergent learning; it is

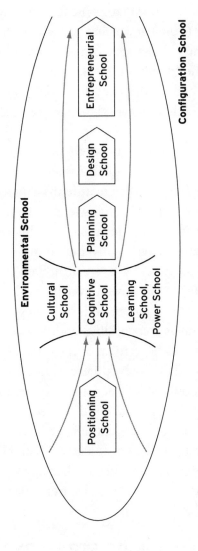

Figure 2.1. Strategy Formation as a Single Process.

about transformation as well as perpetuation; it must involve individual cognition and social interaction, cooperative as well as conflictive; it has to include analyzing before and programming after as well as negotiating during; and all this must be in response to what may be a demanding environment. Try to omit any of this, and watch what happens!

Yet, just as clearly, the process can tilt toward the attributes of one school or another: toward the entrepreneurial school during start-up or when there is the need for a dramatic turnaround, toward the learning school under dynamic conditions when prediction is well nigh impossible, and so on. Sometimes the process has to be more individually cognitive than socially interactive (in small business, for example). Some strategies seem to be more rationally deliberate (especially in mature mass-production industries and government), whereas others tend to be more adaptively emergent (as in dynamic, high-technology industries). The environment can sometimes be highly demanding (during social upheaval), yet at other times (or even at the same time) entrepreneurial leaders are able to maneuver through it with ease. There are, after all, identifiable stages and periods in strategy making, not in any absolute sense but as recognizable tendencies.

The inclination has been to favor the interpretation that the schools represent fundamentally different processes. (Figure 2.2 plots the schools along two dimensions: states of the internal process and states of the external world. The schools scatter across the plot, implying that they represent different processes.) This may not be so bad if practitioners can at least pick and choose among the various processes (or combine them when appropriate)—as long as any one is not pushed to its illogical extreme (see Table 2.3).

EVOLUTION OF STRATEGY?

Safari may be a single idea, but it is many experiences. As noted at the outset, there are safaris at ground level, whether of big game hunters or of tourists snapping pictures. There are also safaris from

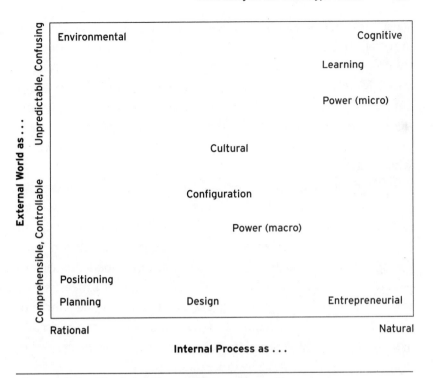

Figure 2.2. Strategy Formation as Many Processes.

Table 2.3. Going Over the Edge in Strategy Formation.

School	Illogical Extreme
Design	Fixation
Planning	Ritual
Positioning	Fortification
Entrepreneurial	Idolatry
Cognitive	Fantasy
Learning	Drift
Power	Intrigue
Cultural	Eccentricity
Environmental	Conformity
Configuration	Degeneration

the air, which take a bird's eye view of different species as they hunt and rest. All reveal important truths. The problem for the thoughtful observer is to balance and combine these short- and long-term views. One way is to take an evolutionary perspective: strategy evolves, not passively but creatively, and so unpredictably, simply because organizations seek to be unique. The ingenuity of those who practice strategy should, therefore, constantly surprise those who study it.

Chandler and others observed that there is a cycle of innovation in strategy: spurts of innovation followed by imitation and consolidation.[13] Yet researchers often fail to look beyond their current contexts. Some studied periods characterized by consolidation, such as the 1970s and early 1980s, and then developed theories of generic strategies. Others observe today's ferment unleashed by information technologies and declare chaos theory the source of truth. For researchers to observe what some organizations do and systematically make sense of it is one thing, but to turn a generality into an object of reverence is quite another.

Hence, the field of strategy management should seek an understanding of its own evolution. But it must do so without adopting a pseudoscientific theory of change. It may be that the development of strategic management is at odds with the assumed development in evolutionary biology. This presumes a succession of species, with one often replacing another—the zebra and the horse, for example, descending from some extinct animal. The schools of strategy represent a line of descent through the history of the field, but this may not be a descent by replacement.

The design school may be an ancestor of the positioning school, but it is not extinct. Older schools contribute to newer ones in complicated and often subterranean ways. They continue to live in practice, infiltrating newer frameworks under various guises.

The evolution of strategic management obeys different principles because it is driven by ideas and practices that originate from qualitatively different sources. We note four:

▼ New kinds of strategies emerge from *collaborative contacts* between organizations. Firms cannot avoid learning and borrowing when they trade and work together.

▼ The evolution of strategy is also pushed along by *competition and confrontation*. In strategy, as in other areas, necessity is the mother of invention, and, as elsewhere, new ideas and practices arise when managers try to outwit or beat back powerful rivals.

▼ New strategies are often a *recasting of the old*. In a sense, old strategic ideas never disappear entirely. They go underground and infiltrate new practices covertly. They are not so much like old wines in new bottles, but more like the blending of old and new malt whiskies.

▼ Finally, strategy is pushed along by the *sheer creativity* of managers, because they explore new ways of doing things.

Biologists often use the tree as a device for illustrating the relationship between species. Here, for us, the roots are the basic disciplines—economics, psychology, sociology, anthropology, political science, biology, and so on—that nourish and so exert a powerful influence over growth. The branches are our two types of schools. On the right side are the prescriptive schools: design, planning, positioning, and (partly perhaps) entrepreneurial. These are relatively well defined—carefully trimmed, if you like. On the left are the more descriptive schools, especially cultural, learning, cognitive, power, and environmental. These schools may have grown as relatively distinct and coherent, but they have become intertwined. In fact, as noted earlier, we find a general blurring of the boundaries here—or, if you like, tangling of the branches. The descriptive schools stray into each other's space, over time increasingly borrowing from each other.

The contrast between the prescriptive and descriptive schools is to some extent due to a fundamentally different attitude toward how research and knowledge should be developed. The proponents of the prescriptive schools tend to adopt a "managed growth" approach to knowledge: they fertilize and trim carefully to curb disruptive influence. In contrast, the descriptive schools prefer a more "natural growth," although they do graft to see what results.

There are obvious advantages and dangers to both approaches. The prescriptive schools are clear and consistent. This makes discussion and transmission of ideas easier, but it can also foster sterility in thinking and application. The descriptive schools tend to be fuller and richer, allowing for more experimentation and innovation. At the same time, they can end up in tangled confusion, generating many contingencies and multiple perspectives that stymie application.

In the end, the tree may be a more suitable image for the growth and development of strategy formation than Darwinian evolution because it does not favor a progression of what is newer and more elaborate. In a tree, the branches are no more or less important than the roots, and the branches on either side cannot be cut off without putting the tree out of balance. The structure seems untidy, but it is actually quite attractive. And it has and will continue to bear fruit!

IN SEARCH OF STRATEGIC MANAGEMENT

Scholars and consultants should certainly continue to probe the important elements of each school. But more importantly, we have to get beyond the narrowness of each school: We need to know how strategy formation, which combines all these schools and more, really works.

We need to ask better questions and generate fewer hypotheses—to allow ourselves to be pulled by real-life concerns rather than being pushed by reified concepts. We need better practice, not neater theory. So we must concern ourselves with process and content, statics and dynamics, constraint and inspiration, the cognitive and the collective, the planned and the learned, the economic and the political. In other words, we must give more attention to the entire elephant—to strategy formation as a whole. We may never see it fully, but we can certainly see it better.

NOTES

1. H. Mintzberg, B. Ahlstrand, and J. Lampel, *Strategy Safari: A Guided Tour through the Wilds of Strategic Management* (New York: Free Press, 1998). See also H. Mintzberg, "Strategy Formation: School of Thought," in J. Frederickson, ed., *Perspectives on Strategic Management* (New York: HarperCollins, 1990); and H. Mintzberg, *The Rise and Fall of Strategic Planning* (New York: Free Press, 1994).
2. G. A. Miller, "The Magic Number Seven Plus or Minus Two: Some Limits on Our Capacity for Processing Information," *Psychology Review,* March 1956, *63,* 81–97.
3. P. Selznick, *Leadership in Administration: A Sociological Interpretation* (Evanston, Illinois: Row, Peterson, 1957); A. D. Chandler, *Strategy and Structure: Chapters in the History of the Industrial Enterprise* (Cambridge, Massachusetts: MIT Press, 1962); and E. P. Learned, C. R. Christensen, K. R. Andrews, and W. D. Guth, *Business Policy: Text and Cases* (Homewood, Illinois: Irwin, 1965).
4. H. I. Ansoff, *Corporate Strategy* (New York: McGraw-Hill, 1965).
5. M. E. Porter, *Competitive Strategy: Techniques for Analyzing Industries and Competitors* (New York: Free Press, 1980); K. J. Hatten and D. E. Schendel, "Heterogeneity within an Industry: Firm Conduct in the U.S. Brewing Industry, 1952–1971," *Journal of Industrial Economics,* December 1977, *26,* 97–113; B. D. Henderson, *Henderson on Corporate Strategy* (Cambridge, Massachusetts: Abt Books, 1979); S. Schoeffler, R. D. Buzzell, and D. F. Heany, "Impact of Strategic Planning on Profit Performance," *Harvard Business Review,* March-April 1974, *54,* 137–145; and Sun Tzu, *The Art of War* (New York: Oxford University Press, 1971).
6. D. Braybrooke and C. E. Lindblom, *A Strategy of Decision* (New York: Free Press, 1963); J. B. Quinn, *Strategies for Change: Logical Incrementalism* (Homewood, Illinois: Irwin, 1980); J. L. Bower, *Managing the Resource Allocation Process: A Study of Planning and Investment* (Boston: Harvard University Business School, 1970); R. A. Burgelman,

"A Process Model of Internal Corporate Venturing in the Diversified Major Firm," *Administrative Science Quarterly,* June 1983, *28,* 223–244; H. Mintzberg, "Patterns in Strategy Formation," *Management Science,* May 1978, 24(9), 934–948; H. Mintzberg and A. McHugh, "Strategy Formation in an Adhocracy," *Administrative Science Quarterly,* June 1985, *30,* 160–197; H. Mintzberg and J. A. Waters, "Of Strategies, Deliberate and Emergent," *Strategic Management Journal,* July-September 1985, *6,* 257–272; and K. E. Weick, *The Social Psychology of Organizing* (Reading, Massachusetts: Addison Wesley, 1979).

7. E. Rhenman, *Organization Theory for Long-Range Planning* (London: Wiley, 1973); R. Normann, *Management for Growth* (New York: Wiley, 1977); and B. Hedberg and S. A. Jonsson, "Strategy Formulation as a Discontinuous Process," *International Studies of Management and Organization,* Summer 1977, *7,* 88–109.

8. M. E. Porter, "What Is Strategy?" *Harvard Business Review,* November-December 1996, *74,* 61–78.

9. "What Is Strategy?" *Harvard Business Review,* March-April 1997, *75,* 162 (letter to the editor).

10. Ibid., p. 163.

11. C. K. Prahalad and G. Hamel, "The Core Competence of the Corporation," *Harvard Business Review,* May-June 1990, *68,* 79–91; and H. Itami and T. W. Roehl, *Mobilizing Invisible Assets* (Cambridge, Massachusetts: Harvard University Press, 1987).

12. See especially J. B. Barney, "Organizational Culture: Can It Be a Source of Sustained Competitive Advantage?" *Academy of Management Review,* July 1986, *11,* 656–665.

13. Chandler (1962).

PART TWO

Flexibility

CHAPTER THREE

The Delta Model: Adaptive Management for a Changing World

ARNOLDO C. HAX
DEAN L. WILDE II

The most influential contemporary strategic framework, espoused by Michael Porter, is based on two exclusive ways to compete: low cost or differentiation.[1] Although low cost and differentiation call for fairly distinct strategies, both center on product economics or on delivering the "best product." Customers are attracted by a low price or by the differentiating product characteristics that go beyond price.

Although the best-product strategy continues to be relevant, our research shows that it does not describe all the ways companies compete in the current environment. Two companies illustrate this point:

▼ Microsoft has been a phenomenal success, perhaps the model for a modern business in a complex environment. By 1998, Microsoft had created $270 billion of market value in excess of debt and equity. Did it do this by having the best product? Microsoft does not have a 90 percent share of the market for personal computer operating systems because of low price. While it may have an effective cost infrastructure, its position is not based on being the low-cost provider. However, its operating system and, most certainly, the MS-DOS product that fueled its dominance, has never had the best features or been the easiest to use. In fact, many would argue that Apple had the best set of differentiated features. Nonetheless, Microsoft is unambiguously the market leader. The source of its success is a distinctive competitive position that is not best product, but rather one supported by the economics of the system as a whole, which we label system *"lock-in."*

▼ During a ten-year period, MCI WorldCom has grown to $100 billion in market value, with about $30 billion in annual revenue and a price-to-earnings ratio of more than 100. MCI WorldCom has generated the third highest shareholder return over the past ten years with a 53 percent annual growth from 1986 to 1996. How did MCI WorldCom do this? The predominant activity in Jackson, Mississippi, its headquarters, is acquisitions; MCI WorldCom has acquired more than thirty companies since its inception in 1985. The focus of the acquisitions is not to create the lowest cost product. On the contrary, acquisitions have expanded the breadth of its products from long distance to local through the acquisition of MFS and Brooks Fiber, to the Internet through the acquisition of UUNet and ANS, and to data services through the acquisition of WilTel. It now has a small product market share across many products. The focus of the acquisitions is not on product differentiation. In fact, each product could be considered almost a commodity when weighed against respective competitors. Notwithstanding this, MCI WorldCom created enormous market value by pursuing a distinctive competitive position in the industry, one focused on the customer, which we label *"customer solutions."*

Clearly, existing management frameworks do not address the challenges managers face today. Based on our research on more than a hundred companies, we have developed the Delta model, which makes four major contributions. First, the *Triangle:* to capture three different strategic positions that reflect fundamental new sources of profitability. Second, the *Adaptive Processes:* to align the key tasks of execution with the desired strategic option. Third, *Aggregate Metrics:* to establish the overall scorecard for business performance. And fourth, *Granular Metrics:* to provide a deep understanding of the business drivers that allow us to learn, innovate, and change using appropriate feedback mechanisms.

THE TRIANGLE: THREE STRATEGIC OPTIONS

Our research gave rise to a new business model, the *"triangle,"* that better reflects the many ways to compete in the current economy (see Figure 3.1). The new model fills a significant void in the development of strategic thinking by offering *three* potential options: best product, customer solutions, and system lock-in.

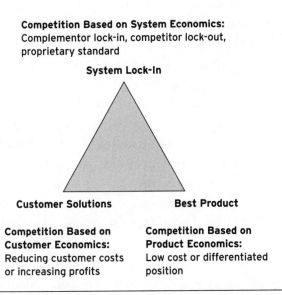

Competition Based on System Economics:
Complementor lock-in, competitor lock-out,
proprietary standard

System Lock-In

Customer Solutions   Best Product

Competition Based on   Competition Based on
Customer Economics: Product Economics:
Reducing customer costs   Low cost or differentiated
or increasing profits   position

Figure 3.1. The Triangle: Three Distinct Strategic Options.

The *best-product* strategic option is built on the classic forms of competition through low cost or differentiation. Its relevant economic drivers are centered on a product or service. A company can achieve cost leadership by aggressively pursuing economies of scale, product and process simplification, and significant product market share that allow it to exploit experience and learning effects. A company can differentiate by enhancing product attributes in a way that adds value for the customer. It can achieve this differentiation through technology, brand image, additional features, or special services. Every strategic option searches for a way to bond with the customer, which is reflected in a significant switching cost. Through the best-product option, companies bond with customers through the intrinsic superiority of their product or service. Important aids for this purpose are introducing products rapidly, being first to market, and establishing a so-called dominant design.[2]

The *customer solutions* strategic option is based on a wider offering of products and services that satisfies most if not all the customer's needs. The focus here is on the customer's economics, rather than the product's economics. A company might offer a broad bundle of products and services that is targeted and customized to a specific customer's needs. In that respect, the most relevant performance measurement of this option is customer market share. Customer bonding, obtained through close proximity to the client, allows a company to anticipate needs and work jointly to develop new products. Bonding is enhanced by learning and customization. Learning has a dual effect: The investment the customer makes in learning how to use a product or service can constitute a significant switching cost; learning about customer needs will increase the company's ability to satisfy customer requirements. Both have a positive impact in the final bonding relationship. Often this strategic option calls for the development of partnerships and alliances, which could include other suppliers, competitors, and customers linked by their ability to complement a customer offering.

The *system lock-in* strategic option has the widest possible scope. Instead of narrowly focusing on the product or the customer, the company considers all the meaningful players in the system that contribute to the creation of economic value. In this strategic position, bonding plays its most influential role. The company is particularly concerned with nurturing, attracting, and retaining so-called "complementors,"[3] along with the normal industry participants. A complementor is not a competitor but a provider of products and services that enhance a company's offering. Typical examples include computer hardware and software producers; high-fidelity equipment manufacturers and CD disk providers; TV set, video recorder, and videocassette makers; and producers of telephone handsets and telecom networks. The critical issue here is looking at the overall architecture of the system: How can a company gain complementors' share in order to lock out competitors and lock in customers? The epitome of this position is achieving the de facto proprietary standard.

Throughout Nucor, there is a strong alignment between the objectives and metrics critical to the strategy, namely, to be low cost, and to the measurements and incentives for teams and individuals.

UNDERSTANDING THE STRATEGIC POSITIONS

We can see the distinct nature of the three strategic positions by examining some companies that share the same outstanding business success but have achieved their high performance through strikingly different strategies and draw on fundamentally different sources of profitability (see Figure 3.2).

Best-Product Position
Nucor Corporation is the fourth largest steel producer in the United States and the largest minimill producer. The objective of its classic best-product strategy is to be the lowest cost producer in the steel industry. Its costs are $40 to $50 per ton less than those in the modern, fully integrated mills. Its sales per employee are $560,000 per year, compared to an average $240,000 for the industry. It has

achieved this performance through a single-minded focus on product economics. Nucor's former CEO John Correnti attributes 80 percent of its low-cost performance to a low-cost culture and only 20 percent to technology. In fact, during Nucor's boom years, between 1975 and 1986, twenty-five of its minimill competitors were closed or sold. Metrics reinforce this low-cost culture. Throughout the corporation, there is a strong alignment between the objectives and metrics critical to the strategy, namely, to be low cost, and to the measurements and incentives for teams and individuals.

Nucor's financial performance resulting from this strategy is extraordinary. Before new management took over Nucor in 1966, the company was worth $13 million in market value. Thirty-two years later, the management and the processes it employed took Nucor to $5 billion in market value or 35 percent compounded growth—a spectacular result in the steel industry.

Southwest Airlines is another example of phenomenal performance through a best-product strategy. It relentlessly focuses on product economics and drives to cut product costs, sometimes reducing the scope and eliminating features from its service in the process. For example, it does not offer baggage handling, passenger ticketing, advance reservations, or hot food.

Southwest does the activities that Southwest continues to perform differently. It emphasizes shuttle flights that efficiently use an

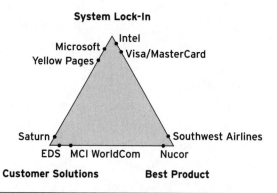

Figure 3.2. Options for Strategic Positioning.

aircraft on repeated trips between two airports, rather than using the hubs and spokes of the full-service carriers. It exclusively uses the Boeing 737, rather than the diverse fleets of the established carriers, thus reducing the costs of maintenance and training.

New companies may have an advantage over existing firms in originating radically new strategic positions founded on low cost because they may find it easier to redefine activities. Existing firms have embedded systems, processes, and procedures that are often obstacles to change and normally carry a heavy cost infrastructure. Many successful small companies have penetrated well-established industries and promptly reached a position of cost leadership in a more narrowly defined product segment, as in the cases of Nucor and Southwest, Dell and Gateway in personal computers, and WilTel in telecommunications. All these companies have had the same pattern: They narrowed the scope of their offering relative to the incumbents, they eliminated some features of the product, and they collapsed the activities of the value chain by eliminating some and outsourcing others. They perform the remaining activities differently, for either cost or product differentiation.

Customer Solutions Position

This competitive position reflects a shift in strategic attention from product to customer—from product economics to customer economics and the customer's experience.

Electronic Data Systems (EDS) is a clear example of a customer solutions provider. EDS has achieved prominence in the data processing industry by singularly positioning itself as a firm that has no interest in individual hardware or software companies. Its role is to provide the best solutions to cover total information needs, regardless of the components' origins. In the process, it has built a highly respected record by delivering cost-effective and tailor-made solutions to each customer. EDS has completely changed the perception of how to manage IT resources. While once IT was regarded as the brain of the company and every firm developed its own strong, internal IT group, now IT outsourcing is commonplace and even expected. As a customer solutions provider, EDS measures its success by how much it improves the customer's bottom line or how it enhances the customer's economics. Typically, it goes into an organization that is currently spending hundreds of millions of dollars annually and delivers significant savings while at the same time enhancing the firm's current information technology (IT) capabilities. This achievement is important in an industry that is cost-sensitive, rapidly changing, and extremely complex and sophisticated. EDS achieves these gains by extending the scope of its services to include activities previously performed by the customer. By focusing on IT, operations scale, and experience relative to the customer, it can offer services at a lower cost or higher quality (or both) than the customers themselves can.

MCI WorldCom provides a contrasting example of a customer solutions position. Where EDS has built value by *"vertically"* expanding its service scope into activities previously performed by the customer, MCI WorldCom is an almost pure example of expanding *"horizontally"* across a range of related services for the targeted customer segment, or *bundling*. It bundles the services together to reduce complexity for the customer. The customer benefits from a single bill, one contact point for customer service and sales, and potentially a more integrated, highly utilized network, but the products are the same. MCI WorldCom benefits through higher revenue per customer and longer customer retention, because it is harder to change vendors, and through lower cost customer service and sales. Clearly, MCI WorldCom is following a strategy that is changing the rules of competition in the telecom industry and drawing on new sources of profitability. It is shifting the dimension of competitive advantage from product share to customer share.

Saturn, another example of the customer solutions position, is one of the most creative managerial initiatives in the past ten years. It abandoned a focus on products and turned its attention to changing the customer's full life-cycle experience. Saturn deliberately decided to design a car that would produce a driving experience close to the Toyota Corolla or the Honda Civic. It satisfied owners of these Japanese cars and therefore wanted to make the transition as easy as possible. Inherently, Saturn abandoned the best-product strategy and decided to create a product that was no different from the leading competition.

Instead, Saturn redefined the terms of engagement with the customer at the dealership. As any American buyer knows, purchasing a car can be unpleasant, subject to all kinds of uncomfortable pressures. Saturn targeted its dealers from a list of the top 5 percent of dealers in the United States, regardless of the brands they represented. Saturn offered extraordinary terms, which required a major commitment from the dealers to learn the Saturn culture and to make multimillion-dollar investments in the dealership.

First, and not just symbolically, Saturn changed the name *"dealer,"* with the implicit connotation of negotiation and haggling, to *"retailer,"* which connotes loyalty and fairness. Next, it instituted a no-haggling policy. Every car, and every accessory in the car, had a fixed price throughout the United States. In fact, the dealers educated customers on the features and price of the car and how they compared to competitors. Saturn also established a complete rezoning and expansion of retailer areas, thus limiting competition and allowing for more effective use of a central warehouse that a circle of Saturn dealers could share to lower inventory and costs. It also broke with tradition in the auto industry by offering a remarkable deal: "Satisfaction guaranteed, or your money back, with no questions asked." Saturn also implemented, for the first time, a "full car" recall. It replaced the complete car, not simply a component, and issued the recall within two weeks of finding symptoms of the problem.

Not surprisingly, customer response was overwhelming, creating what has become a cult among Saturn owners and thus giving Saturn the highest customer satisfaction rating in the industry—a phenomenal accomplishment for a car that retails for about one-fourth the price of luxury cars. Saturn's most powerful advertising campaign became the "word of mouth" from pleased customers, proving that focusing on the customer can be as strong a force in achieving competitive advantage as focusing on the product.

System Lock-In Position

In the system lock-in position are companies that can claim to own de facto standards in their industry. These companies are the beneficiaries of the massive investments that other industry participants make to complement their product or service. Microsoft and Intel are prime examples. Eighty to 90 percent of the PC software applications are designed to work with Microsoft's personal computer operating system (for example, Windows 98) and with Intel's microprocessor design (for example, Pentium), the combination often referred to as Wintel. As a customer, if you want access to the majority of the applications, you have to buy a Microsoft Windows operating system; 90 percent do. As an applications software provider, if you want access to 90 percent of the market, you have to write your software to work with Microsoft Windows; most do.

This is a *virtuous feedback loop* that accelerates independent of the product around which it is spinning. The same relationship supports the demand for Intel's microprocessors. Microsoft and Intel do not win on the basis of product cost, product differentiation, or a customer solution; they have system lock-in. Apple Computer has long had the reputation of having a better operating system or a better product. Motorola has frequently designed a faster microprocessor. Microsoft and Intel, nonetheless, have long held the lock on the industry.

Not every product or service can be a proprietary standard; there are opportunities only in certain parts of the industry architecture and only at certain times. Microsoft, Intel, and Cisco have shrewd ability to spot this potential in their respective fields and then relentlessly pursue the attainment, consolidation, and extension of system lock-in. Some of the most spectacular value creation in recent history has resulted. By 1998, Microsoft had created $270 billion of market value in excess of the debt and equity investment in the company, Intel had created $160 billion, and Cisco had created $100 billion.

In a nontechnology area, the Yellow Pages is one of the most widely recognized directories and most strongly held proprietary standards in the United States. The business, which has massive 50 percent net margins, is a fundamentally simple business. The Regional Bell Operating Companies, including Bell Atlantic, Ameritech, Bell South, and so on, owned the business and outsourced many of its activities, such as sales and book production. In 1984, when the Yellow Pages market opened for competition, there were many new entrants, including the companies that had provided the outsourcing services. Experts predicted rapid loss of market share and declining margins. Afterward, the incumbent providers retained 85 percent of the market, and their margins were unchanged. How did this happen?

The Yellow Pages has tremendous system lock-in. Businesses want to place their ads in a book with the most readership, and consumers want to use the book that has the most ads. When new companies entered the market, they could distribute books to every household but could not guarantee usage. Even with the steep 50 to 70 percent discounts the new books offered, businesses could not afford to discontinue their ads in the incumbent book with proven usage. Despite enhancements like color maps and coupons, consumers found the new books with fewer and smaller ads to have more size advantage than utility and threw them out. The virtuous circle could not be broken, and the existing books sustained their market position.

Financial services are another industry in which standards have emerged and are a force in determining competitive success. The key players in the credit card system are merchants, cards, consumers, and banks. American Express was the dominant competitor early on, albeit with a charge card rather than a credit card. Its strategy was to serve high-end business people, particularly those traveling abroad. The well-known slogan, "Don't leave home without it," and a worldwide array of American Express offices helped Amex achieve something close to a customer solutions position. Securing a lot of merchants was not part of Amex's strategy.

In contrast, Visa and MasterCard designed an open system, available to all banks, and aggressively pursued all merchants, in part through lower merchant fees. They created a virtuous loop—consumers prefer the cards accepted by the majority of the merchants, and merchants prefer the card held by the majority of the customers. This strategy culminated in strong system lock-in and MasterCard and Visa's achievement of a proprietary standard. Visa and MasterCard now represent more than 80 percent of the cards in circulation. It is interesting that at this time, Microsoft, Intel, Visa, and MasterCard are all under threats of suits by the U.S. Department of Justice. Excessive power can lead to alleged abuses that call the attention of regulatory agencies.

One should not necessarily conclude that the pursuit of one strategic position is always more attractive than the other. There are big winners and losers in every option. Apple failed at owning the dominant operating standard. Banyan failed at achieving a de facto standard in the local area network operating system market, relative to Novell. The right option for a firm depends on its particular circumstances.

THE BONDING CONTINUUM

Bonding is a primary element in each distinct strategic position and deserves closer examination. Bonding is a continuum that extends from the customer's first loyalty to a product to full system lock-in with proprietary standards. We have identified four stages in bonding (see Figure 3.3).

Establishing Dominant Design
In the first stage, dominant design, customers are attracted to a product because it uniquely excels in the dimensions they deeply

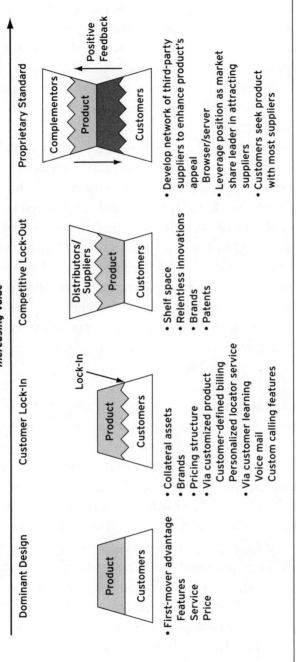

Figure 3.3. Bonding Continuum.

care about. If the product positioning is one of low cost, then low price leads to loyalty. If the strategic positioning is differentiated, the features or services that accompany the product could attract and retain the customer. In an embryonic industry that does not yet have a defined product design, various competitors do enormous experimentation. Product variety eventually consolidates to a common design that has the features and characteristics that customers expect from the product type.

This emerging dominant design fills the requirements of many users for a particular product, although it may not exactly meet the requirements of any particular segment of the customer base. In that regard, the dominant design is generic and standardized as opposed to customized. The competitor generating this design captures the first element of loyalty from customers and has first-mover advantage. For example, IBM benefited from a dominant design—the IBM PC. Its format included a monitor, a standard disk drive, the QWERTY keyboard, the Intel chip, open architecture, and the MS-DOS operating system. They came together to define the ideal PC for the market, which every other PC-compatible manufacturer would later have to emulate.

Locking In Customers

Beyond the stage of dominant design, there are clear opportunities to achieve higher, more tangible switching costs on the part of the customer. One such move is to enhance the product's inherent characteristics by offering additional support that makes it more accessible and attractive and thus harder to switch from, thereby locking in the customer. Collateral assets, which the firm owns and which complement the core product, can be effective in achieving this goal. Ownership of distribution channels, specialized sales forces, technical support staff, and a brand-supporting image can significantly increase product function, make it more appealing to the customer, and make the whole package more difficult to imitate. Brands as a collateral asset can reinforce lock-in when the product is unfamiliar and the functionality unknown, so the assurance of support can dissipate doubts about product performance and encourage repeat purchase.

National Starch, a customer solutions company, provides an excellent example of customer lock-in. National Starch appears deeply rooted in rather mundane and pedestrian products, glue and starch. However, it has an unsurpassed history of long-term superior performance, not only in its industry, but also compared to most U.S. corporations. The source of its success is its extraordinary technological capabilities coupled with an intimate knowledge of all its key customers. R&D personnel, technical service staff, and marketing and sales managers have accumulated enormous knowledge on customer needs, the state of new product development, and ways to aid customers in revenue expansion and cost containment. The essence of National Starch's business is a joint working relationship with the customer.

One spectacular product that emerged from this relationship was a sophisticated adhesive that eliminated welding airplane wings to an aircraft body. First, this product contributes to the total quality of the final product, the airplane. Second, despite its criticality, the product accounts for a negligible portion of the total cost of the airplane. These two conditions give National Starch high-profit potential. The moral here is that by creatively constructing a tight working relationship with the customer, a company can "decommoditize" a product. The bonds are strong because the company is not only providing a product but embracing its economics.

Price structure can influence bonding with customers as well. Two of the most innovative marketing programs in the 1980s were American Airlines' Frequent Flyer program and MCI's "Friends and Family" promotion. Both programs were widely acclaimed because they created some lock-in for traditional commodity businesses.

Customized products and services can also lock in customers through personalized services, customer care, and even billing. In the consumer market for the financial services industry, Merrill Lynch first introduced customer management accounts, but Fidelity, Schwab, and other institutions followed. The accounts are tailored to the user's circumstances; characteristics of bill payment, broker-age, mutual fund investments, IRA accounts, credit cards, and checking accounts are specific to and chosen by the customer. The effort to move this information to a new account creates a switch-ing cost for the customer.

Another benefit of customer proximity is that the customer and the supplier bond over time. A newcomer finds it hard to break into a relationship that has developed mutual investments and ben-efits. In addition, a product can create its own learning experience. For example, once you learn the intricacies of the Microsoft Excel spreadsheet application, there is a significant additional effort to switch to Lotus 1-2-3 or another spreadsheet product.

Locking Out Competitors

There is a thin line between locking in customers and locking out competitors. First, once a company acquires a customer, it is hard for that customer to switch to an alternative. Second, significant barriers make it difficult for a competitor to imitate or to enter the business.

Four forces contribute to competitor lock-out. The first is based on the restrictions of distribution channels. Physical distri-bution channels, in particular, are limited in their ability to handle multiple product lines. At the extreme end of the spectrum are channels that carry only one product, such as soda fountains that serve only one brand of soda. Coca-Cola captures the channel; Pepsi is preempted from that specific market and vice versa.

In this environment, brands can also generate competitor lock-out. They create customer demand that causes retailers to stock the branded product, at the expense of competitive products, given the physical constraints. In turn, shelf presence further enhances demand and the brand because people can buy only the products available. This reinforcing loop causes branding to be particularly effective for consolidating share and creating system lock-in when the industry structure includes physical distribution channels; this is in contrast to an industry that uses expandable channels such as telemarketing or direct mail.

Another way to lock out competitors is to establish a continuous stream of new products that can result in self-obsolescence and create enormous barriers to imitation or entry. Digital Equipment Corporation's origins in the 1950s provide a good example of competitor lock-out in an embryonic industry. DEC engineers had great freedom to both propose and follow through on their innovations. There was an unprecedented stream of new computers, with one breakthrough after another. DEC produced more than fifteen new versions in less than six years. As a result, competitors had difficulty passing a moving target. Furthermore, DEC users had to develop tailor-made software applications. Most importantly, all DEC computers were compatible with each other, so legacy software could run on the new equipment. The DEC architecture was not open; competitors therefore not only had to match the technical features, but they also had to be compatible with the existing software base. In ten years, DEC became the second largest computer company in the world.

Patents can lock out competitors but also offer some challenges. In the pharmaceutical industry, a significant portion of a patent's length is often consumed before the product is released because of the time required for trials and FDA approval. Sometimes, half a patent's life expires before the product is introduced. This is compounded when patents are required in other countries, each with different requirements for documentation, languages, testing, legal compliance, and so on. In this situation, speed is key to competitive lock-out.

Sustaining Proprietary Standards

If a firm is able to reach and sustain proprietary standards, the rewards are immense. There are two requirements for this position. First, customer switching costs need to be high. Second, it has to be difficult or expensive for a competitor to copy the product. There are a number of ways to achieve system lock-in and to secure a proprietary standard. While one might presume that this would be the dominant of the three positions in our business model, it is not always possible to develop a standard in every market segment. Even if a standard can be developed, a single firm might not be able to appropriate it. And not all firms have the capabilities to achieve a proprietary standard.

Managers can ask several questions to assess whether their company can achieve a proprietary standard:

▼ Do we have an open architecture, or can we create one? An open architecture allows the attraction, development, and innovation of many complementors.

▼ Is there a potential for a large variety and number of complementors that can be enabled through a standard?

▼ Is the standard hard to copy? A complex interface that is rapidly evolving makes it difficult for competitors to imitate.

▼ Is the industry architecture being redefined?

ADAPTIVE PROCESSES TO LINK STRATEGY WITH EXECUTION

By describing the three fundamental strategic positions, we have provided the mechanism to define the vision of a business—that elusive but indispensable requirement in successful management. The first challenge is to construct distinct business options that respond to the new realities of the current environment.

The next challenge is to link strategy with execution. More strategies fail because of ineffective execution than poor design. More often than not a company's basic business processes are not aligned with the strategy. During the past few years, a proliferation of the so-called best business practices, including total quality management, business reengineering, continuous improvement, benchmarking, time-based competition, and lean production, have been primarily directed at improving a firm's operational effectiveness. In theory and in application, these practices are decoupled from strategy. As a result, they contribute to creating a pattern of commoditization as companies imitate each other, thus preventing a truly differentiated strategic position.

The Delta model starts with the selection of a distinctive strategic position and then calls for the integration of the collective processes, not of one individual business process such as operational effectiveness. It is the *balance* of the fundamental processes that creates a unique and sustainable competitive position.

Complexity and uncertainty in the market create a problem in implementing any plan. The only assumption that remains valid over time is that all other assumptions will change. Strategy needs to adapt continuously, and therefore implementation needs to respond to market changes and to an improved understanding of the market. That understanding becomes apparent only during implementation.

In the Delta model, adaptive processes link strategy with execution by (1) defining the key business processes that are the repository of the primary operational tasks, (2) aligning their role with the desired strategic position, (3) seeking a coherent integration across these processes to produce unifying action, and (4) incorporating responsive mechanisms as a core part of each process to ensure flexibility and change in an uncertain market.

THREE ADAPTIVE PROCESSES

In the early 1990s, a powerfully simple idea developed: Businesses should be viewed not just in terms of functions, divisions, or products, but also as processes.[4] Processes should be the central focus when companies want to link strategy and execution. We have identified three fundamental processes that are always present and are the repository of key strategic tasks:

1. *Operational effectiveness*—the delivery of products and services to the customer. Conceived in its broadest sense, this process includes all the supply chain elements. Its primary focus is to produce the most effective cost and asset infrastructure to support the business's desired strategic position. It is the heart of the productive engine and the source of capacity and efficiency. Although it is relevant for all businesses, it becomes most important when a company chooses a strategic position of best product.

2. *Customer targeting*—the activities that attract, satisfy, and retain the customer. This process ensures that customer relationships are managed most effectively. It identifies and selects attractive customers and enhances customer performance, either by reducing the customer's cost base or by increasing its revenue stream. At its heart, this process establishes the best revenue infrastructure for the business. While customer targeting is critical to all businesses, it is most important when the strategic position is that of total customer solutions.

3. *Innovation*—a continuous stream of new products and services to maintain the business's future viability. This process mobilizes all the firm's creative resources, including technical, production, and marketing capabilities to develop an innovative infrastructure. The center of this process is the renewal of the business in order to sustain its competitive advantage and its superior financial performance. While preserving the innovative capabilities is critical to all businesses, it becomes central when the strategic position is that of system lock-in.

ALIGNMENT OF ADAPTIVE PROCESSES WITH STRATEGY

The triangle we discussed earlier is the motor that drives the selection of strategic positioning, which, in turn, defines the role of each adaptive process. A firm's actions must be aligned with its strategic position, and the results must give feedback for adapting the strategy. This is the essence of adaptive management. Consistency, congruency, and feedback are the guiding principles. Not only does the role of each process need to adapt to each strategic option, but also the priorities with regard to each are affected. Next we examine the role of each adaptive process in supporting each strategic position of the business (see Figure 3.4).

Operational Effectiveness

When operational effectiveness supports a best-product strategy, it is imperative to reduce the product costs by paying careful attention to the drivers of that cost. However, in the case of customer solutions, operational effectiveness is also concerned with the horizontal linkages between products in the bundled offer. The ultimate goal is to improve the customer's economics, even if that sometimes raises the product's costs. The relevant cost focus is the combined impact on the customer's business and the company's. In the system lock-in strategy, the product cost is perhaps the least relevant among all the positions. What is important is the value of the system through the creation of standards, the investments by the complementors, and their integration to improve overall performance.

For example, a data communications provider of private lines seeking a best-product position would focus on reducing maintenance costs to a minimum, given certain quality guidelines. A customer solutions provider would look closely at the customer's activities. It would reduce the customer's costs by adding equipment to diagnose a problem or perhaps by adding large-scale alternate back-up systems. In intranet services, in which a customer buys a highly secure private-line network using Internet protocols, a company might attempt a system lock-in position. Customers may find it increasingly expensive to switch or split vendors as they add applications and geographic locations to the same secure intranet. Establishing a low-cost infrastructure is less important than encouraging the customer to install more sites and to use more applications that run on an intranet platform.

Strategic Positioning

	Best Product	Customer Solutions	System Lock-in
Operational Effectiveness	**Best Product Cost** • Identify product cost drivers • Improve stand-alone product cost	**Best Customer Value** • Improve customer's economics • Improve horizontal linkages across components of the total solutions	**Best System Performance** • Improve system performance • Integrate complementors
Customer Targeting	**Target Distribution Channels** • Maximize coverage through multiple channels • Obtain low cost distribution • Optimize channel mix and channel profitability	**Target Customer Bundles** • Enhance customer interfaces • Explore alliances to bundle solutions • Select key vertical markets • Examine channel ownership options	**Target System Architecture** • Identify leading complementors in the system • Enhance complementor interfaces • Harmonize system architecture • Expand number and variety of complementors

Innovation	**Product Innovation**
	• Develop family of products based on common platform
	• First to market, or follow rapidly – stream of products
		Customer Sourced Innovation
		• Identify and exploit joint development linked to the customer value chain
		• Expand your offer into the customer value chain to improve customer economics
		• Integrate and innovate customer care functions
		• Increase customer lock-in through customization and learning
			System Innovation
			• Emphasize features supporting lock-in
			• Proliferate complementors
			• Design proprietary standards within open architecture
			  Complex interfaces
			  Rapid evolution
			  Backward compatibility

Adaptive Process

Figure 3.4. Role of Adaptive Processes in Supporting Strategy.

Customer Targeting

When supporting a customer solutions position, companies seek to target key customers by offering a bundled solution, either alone or through alliances. This often requires targeting vertical markets and resorting to customized products as appropriate.

Channel ownership itself becomes an issue in order to gain greater knowledge and access to the customer. For instance, in 1993, Merck, a leading research-based pharmaceutical company, acquired Medco, a premier distributor of generic drugs. This allowed Merck to obtain the leading mail-order catalog, have access to unique distribution, and gain ownership of a customer database covering patients, physicians, and proprietary formulary.

When locking in a system, the key "customer" targets are the complementors, so the company can consolidate the lock-in position and neutralize the competitor's actions. In short, the targeted customer is fundamentally different in these three options. At times, the final consumer or product user, although important, is not the critical strategic target. For example, we all know that its customers do not universally love Microsoft. The power of the owner of the systems standards gives the end user few choices.

In the software industry, software game providers typically adhere to a best-product strategic position and target customers as a way to get access to as many customers as possible. American Management Systems, which has a customer solutions position, implements customized software and thus targets vertical markets. Novell, which has a system lock-in position, has the proprietary standard for LAN operating systems and needs to put its premium effort into attracting and serving application developers and the 30,000 value-added resellers that distribute and customize NetWare.

Innovation

When it comes to supporting a best-product strategy, renewal of the business is seen in terms of securing a continuous stream of products, often by sharing a common platform. If truly successful, that innovation will lead to establishment of a dominant design that represents the strongest base for competitive advantage with a best-product strategy. In the case of the customer solutions strategy, innovation plays an important role through the successful development of joint products with key customers. In this respect, this adaptive process is central not only for developing future customers, but for maintaining current ones. Furthermore, the customer is the primary source of innovation, not the conventional R&D labs.

The role of innovation in system lock-in is perhaps more critical than in any other strategic option. Often the technology is responsible for designing the architecture that will generate the system standard, that will allow the ownership of that standard, and that will preclude the standard from being copied or becoming obsolete. As we have indicated, it is more likely that a standard will be achieved if the architecture is based on open interfaces and characterized by rapid evolution with backward compatibility. In this instance, it is the innovation of the complementors that sustains the standard.

In the semiconductor industry, Hitachi and NEC are among the leading producers in dynamic random access memory (DRAM) semiconductors. This segment has been characterized by short product life cycles and declining prices. To succeed, every one to two years these companies develop new chips, which employ technology four times better than the previous generation, in facilities that cost more than $1 billion to construct. These two companies have chosen the best-product position and pursue innovation to support their competitive advantage.

Motorola's semiconductor business follows a customer solutions strategy that focuses on the automobile industry, among others. The BMW 740 has fifty microprocessors that control many aspects of its functionality and are critical to its differentiation. Motorola works with the manufacturers to develop these customized chips; the innovations are joint.

As a system lock-in provider, Intel depends on the rapid development of a complex standard. It developed five microprocessors, from the 8086 to the Pentium, from 1978 to 1996. This innovation is unique in at least two respects. First, it requires backward compatibility, which allows old complementors to work with the new product and ensures the continuation of the standard. Second, having secured the standard, it has the luxury of occasionally incorporating a larger part of the system into its standard to enhance its features and to further extend the interfaces with applications. There is a balancing act in grabbing additional functions from one complementor and in preserving the relationships and open architecture with other complementors, but a proven standard allows Intel the freedom to do this.

AGGREGATE METRICS, GRANULAR METRICS, AND FEEDBACK

Just as activities need to vary by strategy, so do the measures of success. The Delta model highlights three additional factors essential to execution: *aggregate metrics, granular metrics,* and *feedback.* These, however, are a story in their own right. For the purpose of providing some perspective on the overall integrated Delta Model framework, we will mention a few words on each. Aggregate metrics are a direct by-product of the adaptive processes just discussed. Since these processes are the instruments for the execution of each strategic option, they also serve as guidelines to define strategy performance. These metrics reflect an understanding of customer economics and complementor economics, as well as product economics, and stand in contrast to the conventional measures of success, which focus on financial measures.

To fully appreciate the necessity of granular metrics, we should return to the fundamental force enabling new strategic positions: bonding. Bonding is remarkable because it is self-reinforcing. Whereas cost-based competition grows more difficult with each incremental improvement (for example, diminishing returns), bonding is an attractive force that naturally accelerates under its own power. The essential characteristic is a positive feedback loop among market participants (end-users, suppliers, complementors) that is inherent in certain strategic positions. For example, eBay is the beneficiary of buyers wanting to shop at the market exchange with the most sellers, and sellers preferring the exchange with the most buyers. The same feedback can occur in the individual bonding to a customer within a total customer solution position. From feedback emerge three distinctive properties: nonlinearity, concentrations, and sensitive dependence. In a nonlinear world, managing by averages is at best misleading, and at worse dysfunctional. Furthermore, these concentrations are subject to sensitive dependence, as seemingly minor and detailed factors are magnified through a nonlinear system to yield huge consequences.

Granular segmentation is central to the effectiveness of the adaptive processes because it enables one to focus, detect, explain, learn, and act. This in itself constitutes a response mechanism that is an important part of each adaptive process to adapt strategy continually and to self-direct the day-to-day tasks of execution.

The forces of the complex, new economy take us full circle, from bonding to granular metrics. Our research shows that a management framework must integrate the large with the small. There are profoundly new strategic positions to consider for a business, and execution must wrestle with specific details to realize these new sources of profitability.

CONCLUSION

The Delta model answers current challenges by significantly expanding the spectrum of available strategic positions. It recognizes customer-focused options and the emergence of proprietary standards to create an unassailable competitive advantage.

A firm's day-to-day activities need to change to realize the different strategies described by aligning the adaptive processes with the strategic positions. Inherent in the adaptive processes are trade-offs and different priorities critical for intelligent implementation. The role of aggregate and granular metrics is central to define business performance, delineate managerial accountability, monitor progress, and establish the feedback mechanisms necessary to change the course of action as needed.

Because complexity permeates the business environment, it is dangerous to give simple answers to complex questions. The Delta model deals with complexity by providing a rich overall framework that integrates a firm's options and activities without running the risk of oversimplifying the context in which to make decisions.

NOTES

1. M. E. Porter, *Competitive Strategy* (New York: Free Press, 1980).
2. J. M. Utterback, *Mastering the Dynamics of Innovation* (Boston: Harvard Business School Press, 1994).
3. For the concept of complementors, see A. M. Brandenburger and B. J. Nalebuff, *Co-opetition* (New York: Doubleday, 1996).
4. The chief proponents of this thinking were Hammer and Champy. See M. Hammer and J. Champy, *Reengineering the Corporation* (New York: HarperBusiness, 1993).

CHAPTER FOUR

Strategy as Strategic Decision Making

KATHLEEN M. EISENHARDT

M any executives realize that to prosper in the coming decade, they need to turn to the fundamental issue of strategy. What is strategy? To use a simple yet powerful definition from *The Economist,* strategy answers two basic questions: "Where do you want to go?" and "How do you want to get there?"[1]

Traditional approaches to strategy focus on the first question. They involve selecting an attractive market, choosing a defensible strategic position, or building core competencies. Only later, if at all, do executives address the second question. Yet in today's high-velocity, hotly competitive markets, these approaches are incomplete. They overemphasize executives' ability to analyze and predict which industries, competencies, or strategic positions will be viable and for how long, and they underemphasize the challenge of actually creating effective strategies.

Many managers of successful corporations have adopted a different perspective on strategy that Shona Brown and I call "competing on the edge."[2] At the heart of this approach lies the recognition that strategy combines the questions of "where" and "how" to create a continuing flow of temporary and shifting competitive advantages. Executives from a variety of firms echo this perspective. John Browne, CEO of British Petroleum, stated, "No advantage and no success is ever permanent. The winners are those who keep moving."[3] Michael Dell, CEO of Dell, commented, "The only constant in our business is that everything is changing. We have to be ahead of the game."[4] But creating a series of shifting advantages is challenging. It requires effective strategic decision making at several levels: at the unit level to improvise business strategy; at the multibusiness level to create collective strategy and cross-business synergies; and at the corporate level to articulate major inflection points in strategic direction.

This article describes strategy as strategic decision making, especially in rapidly changing markets. Its underlying assumption is that "bet the company" decisions—those that change the firm's direction and generate new competitive advantages—arise much more often in these markets. Therefore, the ability to make fast, widely supported, and high-quality strategic decisions on a frequent basis is the cornerstone of effective strategy. To use the language of contemporary strategy thinking, strategic decision making is the fundamental dynamic capability in excellent firms.

These ideas come from more than a decade of research on strategy in high-velocity markets. During one phase of that research, Jay Bourgeois and I examined top-management teams and their decisions in twelve entrepreneurial firms in Silicon Valley. Using questionnaires and open-ended interview questions, we studied decision speed, conflict over goals and key decision areas, executive power, and politics. In addition, we traced the multiple strategic decisions and firm and decision performance. During a second phase of research, Shona Brown and I studied six matched pairs of European, Asian, and North American multibusiness firms (six dominant and six modestly successful ones) in the broader context of strategy. We gathered data on strategic decision making and other critical processes at multiple levels within these more complex firms.

In both studies, clear differences stood out between the strategic decision-making processes in the more and less effective firms. Strikingly, these differences counter commonly held beliefs that conflict slows down choice, politicking is typical, and fast decisions are autocratic. In other words, these findings challenge the assumption of trade-offs among speed, quality, and support. Instead, the most effective strategic decision makers made choices that were fast, high quality, and widely supported. How did they do it? Four approaches emerged from this research and my other work with executives. Effective decision makers create strategy by

▼ Building collective intuition that enhances the ability of a top-management team to see threats and opportunities sooner and more accurately.

▼ Stimulating quick conflict to improve the quality of strategic thinking without sacrificing significant time.

▼ Maintaining a disciplined pace that drives the decision process to a timely conclusion.

▼ Defusing political behavior that creates unproductive conflict and wastes time.

BUILD COLLECTIVE INTUITION

One myth of strategic decision making in high-velocity markets is that there is no time for formal meetings and no place for the careful consideration of extensive information. Executives, the thinking goes, should consider limited, decision-specific data, concentrate on one or two alternatives, and make decisions on the fly.

Effective strategic decision makers do not follow that approach. They use as much as or more information than ineffective executives, and they are far more likely to hold regularly scheduled, "don't miss" meetings. They rely on extensive, real-time information about internal and external operations, which they discuss in intensive meetings. They avoid both accounting-based information because it tends to lag behind the realities of the business and predictions of the future because these are likely to be wrong. From extensive, real-time information, these executives build a collective intuition that allows them to move quickly and accurately as opportunities arise.

A good example is Hermes (all company names in the study are pseudonyms), a highly successful computer venture whose management team is known for its ability to reposition the firm adroitly as opportunities shift. How do they do it? These managers claim to "measure everything." They examine an array of key operating performance metrics that they collectively track monthly, weekly, and sometimes daily: inventory speed, multiple cash-flow measures, average selling price of products, performance against sales goals, manufacturing yields, customer-acquisition costs, and gross margins by product and geographic region. They prefer operating information to more refined, accounting-based numbers. They also pay attention to innovation-related metrics such as sales from new products, time-related metrics such as trends in average sales size per transaction, rates such as number of new product introductions per quarter, and durations such as the time it takes to launch a product globally.

In addition to internal operations information, the managers at Hermes track external information: new product moves by competitors, competition at key accounts, technical developments within the industry, and industry "gossip." Hermes's top-management team members play key roles in gathering and reporting these data. Each has areas of information for which he or she is responsible. For example, the vice president of marketing tracks product introductions and exits by the competition. The vice president of R&D reports the latest information on the "technical pulse" of the industry.

Sharing information at "must attend" meetings is an essential part of building collective intuition. The interplay of ideas during these meetings enhances managers' understanding of the data. At

Kronos, a global leader in multiple technology-based businesses, the managers of each major business meet every four weeks in a day-long meeting to review the operating basics in their businesses and the state of the industry. Travel is frequent and necessary, but managers do not miss this meeting. As at Hermes, the emphasis is on real-time information, internal and external. In addition, each meeting covers one or two critical strategic issues facing either an individual business or the group of businesses as a whole. The result is a forum for signaling collaborative opportunities across businesses and for shaping the collective strategy.

In contrast, less successful top-management teams rarely meet with their colleagues in a group. Meetings are infrequent or skipped because of travel commitments. These executives typically make fewer and larger strategic choices. When they do turn their attention to important decisions, they rely on market analyses and future trend projections that are idiosyncratic to the particular decision. The result is groups of strangers who have difficulty engaging with one another productively. While they may each be knowledgeable in their own areas of responsibility, they do not develop collective intuition.

For example, at Aspen, a mediocre computer firm, the managers say they communicate frequently with the CEO but not with each other. One executive sketched herself as an "intelligent observer," detached from her colleagues. Another confided, "I don't really know the rest of the team." In one decision that involved a reconfiguration of the product mix in several manufacturing plants, the senior executives delegated the analysis to staff and did not return to the topic for four months. During the interim, the staff painstakingly assembled plant performance metrics that were routine at the more successful firms. The executive team then commissioned more analyses while they familiarized themselves with the issues.

Why do real-time information and "must attend" meetings lead to more effective strategic decision making? Intense interaction creates teams of managers who know each other well. Familiarity and friendship make frank conversation easier because people are less constrained by politeness and more willing to express diverse views. The strategic decision process then moves more quickly and benefits from high-quality information. For example, one manager at Hermes described the interactions as "open and direct." Another explained more graphically, "We get it out on the table and yell about it."

In addition, with intense interaction, managers naturally organize antipodal team-member roles, such as short-term versus long-term or status quo versus change.[5] At Hermes, for example, the vice president of marketing was seen as "constantly thinking about the future," whereas the vice president of engineering was considered to be the keeper of the status quo. Describing the interplay of their relationship, the engineering vice president said, "I depend on her to watch out for tomorrow—I look out for today." A range of perspectives improves decision quality by ensuring that managers consider different sides of the issue.

Most important, when intense interaction focuses on the operating metrics of today's businesses, a deep intuition, or "gut feeling," is created, giving managers a superior grasp of changing competitive dynamics. Artificial intelligence research on championship chess players indicates how this intuition is formed. These players, for example, develop their so-called intuition through experience. Through frequent play, they gain the ability to recognize and process information in patterns or blocks that form the basis of intuition. This patterned processing (what we term *"intuition"*) is faster and more accurate than processing single pieces of information. Consistent with this research, many effective decision makers were described by their colleagues as having "an immense instinctive feel," "a high quality of understanding," and "an intuitive sense of the business." This intuition gives managers a head start in recognizing and understanding strategic issues.

STIMULATE QUICK CONFLICT

In high-velocity markets, many executives are tempted to avoid conflict. They assume that conflict will bog down the decision-making process in endless debate and degenerate into personal attacks. They seek to move quickly toward a few alternatives, analyze the best ones, and make a quick choice that beats the competition to the punch.

Reality is different. In dynamic markets, conflict is a natural feature of high-stakes decision making because reasonable managers will often diverge in their views on how the marketplace will unfold. Furthermore, as research demonstrates, conflict stimulates innovative thinking, creates a fuller understanding of options, and improves decision effectiveness. Without conflict, decision makers commonly miss opportunities to question assumptions and overlook key elements of the decision. Given the value of conflict, effective strategic decision makers in rapidly changing markets not only tolerate conflict, they accelerate it.

One way that executives accelerate conflict is by assembling executive teams that are diverse in age, gender, functional background, and corporate experience. At Venus, a high-growth venture in Silicon Valley, the executive team ranges in age from late twenties to mid-fifties. The group includes several Europeans and a woman. Two members hold PhDs in electrical engineering and computer science, respectively. The president has an economics degree, an MBA, and manufacturing experience. The vice president of engineering came from a competitor, while the senior sales executive is a well-traveled industry veteran who had been at a number of firms before settling at Venus several years ago.

Like their counterparts at other successful firms, these executives say that they argue much of the time. The vice president of finance stated, "We all have different opinions." Another executive observed, "The group is very vocal. They all bring their own ideas."

Particularly striking are the differences in perspectives across the age groups. The older executives usually rely on their expertise from the industry and from other companies to understand strategic choices. They have strong industry connections that pave the way for valuable collaborations with other firms. The younger executives bring in fresh ideas about how to compete and how to exploit the latest technology.

An alliance decision served to demonstrate the difference in outlook. Several of the experienced managers had been involved with both successful and unsuccessful alliances. They described an alliance as a "marriage between equals." The younger managers framed alliances as a way to gain money and credibility. Their take was that alliance partners were temporary "fellow travelers," not lifetime partners. They saw partners simultaneously as friends and foes. The Venus team engaged in extensive debate about alliances. The result was an innovative, alliance-led growth strategy that synthesized the flexible strategic thinking of the younger team members with the realism of the more mature managers. Describing these interactions, the vice president of marketing commented, "We scream a lot, laugh, and resolve the issues."

Another way that effective strategic decision makers accelerate conflict is by using "frame-breaking" tactics that create alternatives to obvious points of view. One technique is scenario planning: Teams systematically consider strategic decisions in the light of several possible future states. Other techniques have executives advocate alternatives that they may or may not favor and perform role-plays of competitors. The details of the techniques are not crucial. Rather, the point is to use and switch among them to prevent stale thinking.

Jupiter, a multibusiness technology firm that has made highly successful acquisitions, provides a good illustration of how the techniques work. One acquisition included a stray business that was not part of the rationale for the purchase. The strategic decision focused on what to do with this business. Managers explored alternatives by creating scenarios of possible futures—such as the Unix operating system prevailing over Microsoft NT or wireless phones becoming more essential than PCs—and then considering how each alternative would play out. They also role-played different competitors to anticipate their responses. In addition, team members used the scenarios to do what is known as "backcasting" to extend their thinking. They envisioned their preferred future (that is, one in which their firm dominated the market) and then thought backwards about how this ideal future might evolve.

Perhaps the most powerful way to accelerate conflict is by creating multiple alternatives. The idea is to develop alternatives as quickly as possible so that the team can work with an array of possibilities simultaneously. As one executive at Jupiter commented, "We play a larger set of options than most people." It is considered entirely appropriate for executives to advocate options that they may not prefer simply to encourage debate.

The executive team at Jupiter, for example, launched its decision-making process to deal with the stray business by quickly developing several alternatives for that business. One called for the acquired business to operate as a new stand-alone division. The second option was to graft the business onto an existing Jupiter strategic business unit; the two businesses could then leverage a common marketing channel. A third option was to combine the business with an existing one with a complementary technology; this combination of businesses would then have sufficient scale to develop the technologies into a more viable business. The final option was to sell the business. Jupiter's executive team quickly compared options, explored them using the frame-breaking tactics noted above, and chose the third. As one executive observed, "There should be three or four solutions to everything." Added another, "We have a preference for working a multiple array of possibilities instead of just a couple."

Why do diverse teams, frame-breaking techniques, and multiple alternatives lead to faster conflict and ultimately more effective decisions? The rationale for diverse teams is clear: These teams come up with more varied viewpoints than homogeneous teams. The value of frame-breaking techniques is more subtle. In addition to the obvious benefit of generating many different perspectives, these techniques establish the norm that constructive conflict is an expected part of the strategic decision-making process. It is acceptable and even desirable to engage in conflict. Furthermore, frame-breaking techniques are intellectually engaging and even fun. They can motivate even apathetic executives to participate more actively in expansive strategic thinking.

The power of multiple alternatives comes from several sources. Clearly, pushing for multiple alternatives speeds up conflict by stimulating executives to develop divergent options. It also enables them to rapidly compare alternatives, helping them to better understand their own preferences. Furthermore, multiple alternatives provide executives with the confidence that they have not overlooked a superior option. That confidence is crucial in rapidly changing markets, where the blocks to effective decision making are emotional as much as cognitive. Finally, multiple alternatives defuse the interpersonal tension that can accompany conflict by giving team members room to maneuver and save face when they disagree. One Jupiter manager told us, for example, that he was strongly against selling the business or setting it up as a stand-alone division. But he could "live with" either of the two combination options.

MAINTAIN THE PACE

Less effective strategic decision makers face a dilemma. On the one hand, they believe that every strategic decision is unique. Each requires its own analytical approach, and each unfolds in its own way. On the other hand, these same decision makers believe that they must decide as quickly as possible. Yet making quick choices conflicts with making one-of-a-kind choices.

Effective strategic decision makers avoid this dilemma by focusing on maintaining decision pace, not pushing decision speed. They launch the decision-making process promptly, keep up the energy surrounding the process, and cut off debate at the appropriate moment. They drive strategic decision-making momentum.

One way that these decision makers maintain decision pace is by following the natural rhythm of strategic choice.[6] They use rules of thumb for how long a major decision should take. Surprisingly, that metric is a fairly constant two to four months. If a decision takes longer, then the management team is trying to decide too big an issue or is procrastinating. If a decision takes less time, then the decision is not strategic enough to warrant management team attention. These decision makers are able to gauge the scale of a decision by recognizing similarities among strategic decisions. That is, each strategic decision is different, but it falls into familiar patterns whose scope and timing are well-known; for example, new product, new technology, or acquisition decisions. They also view a decision as part of a larger web of strategic choices. This allows executives to adjust the scope of a decision to fit the allotted time frame as the process unfolds. Plus, placing strategic decisions in a larger context lowers the emotional stakes of a choice.

The top-management team at Ares, a leading technology firm, uses a rhythm of three to four months for strategic decisions. Typical strategic decisions include entering or exiting markets, investing in new technology, building manufacturing capacity, or forming strategic partnerships. A decision arose concerning how to enter an emerging Internet-based market in e-commerce tools. Although the team had much to learn about the Internet, Ares executives framed the issue as a market-entry decision; as a result, they knew how to begin to gather relevant data. Because they estimated that the decision should take three months, Ares executives could establish milestones and adjust the decision scope as needed to fit the time frame. As the decision-making process progressed, team members realized that the market opportunity fit into a more complex context of e-commerce business than they had originally envisioned. They therefore reconceptualized the immediate strategic choice as part of the larger e-commerce effort and expanded the size of the market under consideration.

In addition, executives maintain pace by prototyping decisions as they analyze them. Instead of merely analyzing options in the abstract, they test them. For example, the Ares executives simultaneously explored relationships with several potential partners to jointly develop e-commerce tools and tested alternative, in-house product designs with several marquee customers. As a result, they were able to hone their understanding of which tools were essential for their e-commerce entry even as they began to implement parts of the final decision.

Effective strategic decision makers skillfully cut off debate, typically using a two-step method called *"consensus with qualification"* to bring decision making to a close. First, managers conduct the decision process itself with the goal of consensus in mind. If they reach consensus, the choice is made. If consensus does not emerge, they break the deadlock using a decision rule such as voting or, more commonly, allowing the manager with the largest stake in the outcome to make the decision. In the case of the e-commerce entry decision, Ares executives were divided over whether to develop a key product in-house or in partnership with another firm. The CEO and the vice president of engineering finally made the call. Not everyone agreed with the choice, but each team member had a legitimate voice in the process. As one executive told us, "Most of the time we reach consensus, but when we can't, Gary [the CEO] pulls the trigger."

In contrast, less successful strategic decision makers stress the rarity and significance of strategic choices. Because the choice then looms so large, they often procrastinate at the start of the decision-making process. Later, they lack a method for pacing their efforts. They oscillate between letting critical issues languish and making "shotgun" strategic choices against deadlines, as the case of Copper, a modestly successful multibusiness computing firm, illustrates. Managers faced a choice over how to organize a sales channel that was to be shared by several businesses. Sharing the channel offered benefits through cost-sharing and cross-selling of products. Although the opportunity had been apparent for some time, the managers did not get around to doing anything for several months. Everyone was avoiding what appeared to be a big task. Once they did get moving, they attempted to come up with a plan that all the major stakeholders would accept. The decision process stretched out over eight months, with most managers becoming frustrated by the seemingly endless meetings to gain consensus. Several disengaged from the process. Eventually, the head of one major business simply implemented his choice with the field sales force, and the rest of the business heads were left scrambling.

Decision-making rhythm helps managers plan their progress and forces them to recognize the familiar aspects of decision making that make the process more predictable. As significant, it emphasizes that hitting decision timing is more critical than forging consensus or developing massive data analyses. As one manager told us, "The worst decision is no decision at all." Prototyping encourages managers to take concrete actions that remove some of the unpredictability that can trigger procrastination. Furthermore, prototyping keeps managers focused on the goal of executing a choice and even begins the implementation process. The result is momentum that lowers the cognitive and emotional barriers to choice and spurs managers toward a conclusion.

Consensus with qualification maintains the pace by taking a realistic view of conflict as valuable and inevitable. Therefore, the endless search for consensus emerges as a fruitless goal. At the same time, consensus with qualification allows decision makers to resolve conflict (and so maintain pace) in a way that team members perceive as equitable. Most managers want a strong voice in the decision-making process but do not believe that they must always get their preferred choice. Consensus with qualification lets decision makers drive decision pace by providing an effective way to reach closure without consensus. For example, at Ares, all the key managers contributed to the market-entry discussion. But when it became apparent that they were stuck in two opposing camps, the CEO and VP of engineering made the call. As one manager observed, "Consensus is nice, but we have to keep up with the train."

DEFUSE POLITICS

Some executives believe that politics are a natural part of strategic choice. They see strategic decision making as involving high stakes that compel managers to lobby one another, manipulate information, and form coalitions. The game quickly becomes a competition among ambitious managers.

More effective strategic decision makers take a negative view of politicking. Since politicking often involves managers' using information to their own advantage, it distorts the information base, leading to a poor strategic decision-making process. Furthermore, these executives see political activity as wasting valuable time. Their perspective is collaborative, not competitive, setting limits on politics and, more generally, interpersonal conflict.

One way in which effective executives defuse politics is by creating common goals. These goals do not imply homogeneous thinking. Rather, they suggest that managers have a shared vision of where they want to be or who their external competitors are. Managers at Neptune, a successful multibusiness computing firm, are highly aware of their external competition. At their monthly meetings, they pay close attention to the moves of the competition and personalize that competition by referring to individual managers in competitor companies, particularly their direct counterparts. They have a clear collective goal for their own ranking and market-share position in the industry: to be number one. At Intel, managers typically contend that "only the paranoid survive." Neptune's managers have their own, more positive rallying cry: "Let's get rich together!"

A more direct way to defuse politics is through a balanced power structure in which each key decision maker has a clear area of responsibility, but in which the leader is the most powerful decision maker. At Venus, the CEO is described as a "team player." Quantitative ratings and qualitative descriptions reveal that he is the most powerful person on the executive team but that he directs decision making only in the arena of corporate organization. Other members of the executive team direct other decisions: The vice president of engineering runs the product development portfolio, the vice president of manufacturing makes the key supply-chain choices, and so on. As one manager pointed out, "Kim [the CEO] believes in hiring great people and letting them run their own shows." Paradoxically, the clear delineation of responsibility makes it easier for managers to help one another and share information because each executive operates from a secure power base. As another manager told us, "We just don't worry much about an internal pecking order."

Humor defuses politics. Effective strategic decision makers often relieve tension by making business fun. They emphasize the excitement of fast-paced markets and the "rush" of competing in these settings. Senior executives at Hermes have articulated "fun" as a management goal. Laughter is common, and practical jokes are popular, especially around April Fool's Day and Halloween.

Less effective strategic decision makers usually have an inward, competitive focus. As a result, they lack the sense of teamwork that characterizes more effective teams. The power structure is typically dysfunctional. A good example is Targhee, a modestly successful Internet firm, where the general manager dominates virtually every aspect of the business. As one manager commented, "Chuck runs the entire show." The result is that the managers who work for Chuck concentrate on impressing him rather than on making smart strategic choices. Another manager observed, "We're all trying to maneuver around to look good in front of Chuck." To make matters worse, Chuck constantly blurs the lines of responsibility, leaving managers insecure and jockeying for position. Noted another manager, "It's like a gun about to go off. I just try to stay out of the cross-fire."

Common goals, clear areas of responsibility, and humor defuse politicking and interpersonal conflict. Goals that stress collective success or common enemies give managers a sense of shared fate. They see themselves as players on the same team, not as competitors. A balanced power structure gives managers a sense of security that dispels the assumption that they need to engage in politicking. For example, at Venus, there was little evidence of politicking. As one manager stated, "We don't have time for politics. I barely get to the meetings." Another said, "We don't have any kind of political stuff. Nobody lobbies behind other people's backs. We just get everything out and talk about it." A third commented, "We're very apolitical." As a result, managers did not hold back information, wasted less time on politics, and made faster, more informed decisions.

Humor strengthens the collaborative outlook. It puts people into a positive mood. Research has shown that people whose frame of mind is positive have more accurate perceptions of each other's arguments and are more optimistic, creative in their problem solving, forgiving, and collaborative. Humor also allows managers to convey negative information in a less threatening way. Managers can say something as a joke that might otherwise be offensive.[7]

TOWARD EFFECTIVE STRATEGIC DECISION MAKING

In high-velocity, hotly competitive markets, traditional approaches to strategy give way to "competing on the edge," where strategic decision making is the fundamental capability leading to superior performance. After all, when strategy is a flow of shifting competitive advantages, the choices that shape strategy matter greatly and occur frequently.

The research data corroborate this view, demonstrating that firms with high performance in profitability, growth, and marketplace reputation have superior (that is, fast, high-quality, and widely supported) strategic decision-making processes. These processes support the emergence of effective strategy. Firms that were more modest performers had strategic decision-making processes that were slower and more political. Their strategies were more predictable and less effective. Executives in these firms often recognized that their strategic decision making was flawed, but they did not know how to fix it.

I have described the four keys to strategy as strategic decision making:

▼ Set the stage by building collective intuition through frequent meetings and real-time metrics that enhance a management team's ability to see threats and opportunities sooner and more accurately.

▼ Stimulate quick conflict by assembling diverse teams, challenging them through frame-breaking heuristics, and stressing multiple alternatives in order to improve the quality of decision making.

▼ Discipline the timing of strategic decision making through time pacing, prototyping, and consensus with qualification to sustain the momentum of strategic choice.

▼ Defuse politics by emphasizing common goals and clear turf, and having fun. These tactics keep decision makers from slipping into destructive interpersonal conflict and time-wasting politics.

Taken together, these approaches direct executive attention toward strategic decision making as the cornerstone of effective strategy.

NOTES

1. "Making Strategy," *The Economist,* 1 March 1997.
2. For a managerial perspective, see S. L. Brown and K. M. Eisenhardt, *Competing on the Edge: Strategy as Structured Chaos* (Boston: Harvard Business School Press, 1998). For an academic perspective, see S. L. Brown and K. M. Eisenhardt, "The Art of Continuous Change: Linking Complexity and Time-Paced Evolution in Relentlessly Shifting Organizations," *Administrative Science Quarterly,* March 1997, 42, 1–34.

3. S. Prokesh, "Unleashing the Power of Learning: An Interview with British Petroleum's John Browne," *Harvard Business Review,* September-October 1997, *75,* 166.

4. D. Narayandas, "Dell Computer Corporation" (Boston: Harvard Business School, case 9–596–058, 1996).

5. For ideas on interaction, see H. Guetzkow, "Differentiation of Roles in Task-Oriented Groups," in D. Cartwright and A. Zander, eds., *Group Dynamics: Research and Theory* (New York: Harper & Row, 1968).

6. For more information on time pacing, see C.J.G. Gersick, "Pacing Strategic Change: The Case of a New Venture," *Academy of Management Journal,* February 1995, *37,* 9–45.

7. For more information on successful negotiation, see R. Pinkley and G. Northcraft, "Conflict Frames of Reference: Implications for Dispute Processes and Outcomes," *Academy of Management Journal,* February 1994, *37,* 193–205; D. Tjosvold, *The Positive-Conflict Organization* (Reading, Massachusetts: Addison-Wesley, 1991); and R. Fisher and W. Ury, *Getting to Yes: Negotiating Agreement Without Giving In* (Boston: Houghton Mifflin, 1981).

PART THREE

The Strategy-Making Process

CHAPTER FIVE

Surfing the Edge of Chaos

RICHARD T. PASCALE

Every decade or two during the past one hundred years, a point of inflection has occurred in management thinking. These breakthroughs are akin to the S-curves of technology that characterize the life cycle of many industrial and consumer products: introduction → acceleration → acceptance → maturity. Each big idea catches hold slowly. Yet within a relatively short time, the new approach becomes so widely accepted that it is difficult even for old-timers to reconstruct how the world looked before.

The decade following World War II gave birth to the "strategic era." While the tenets of military strategy had been evolving for centuries, the link to commercial enterprise was tenuous. Before the late 1940s, most companies adhered to the tenet "make a little, sell a little, make a little more." After the war, faculty at the Harvard Business School (soon joined by swelling ranks of consultants) began to take the discipline of strategy seriously. By the late 1970s, the array of strategic concepts (SWOT analysis, the five forces

---

This article is drawn from R. Pascale, M. Millemann, and L. Gioja, *Surfing the Edge of Chaos: How the Smartest Companies Use the New Science to Stay Ahead* (forthcoming).

framework, experience curves, strategic portfolios, the concept of competitive advantage) had become standard ordnance in the management arsenal. Today, a mere twenty years later, a grasp of these concepts is presumed as a threshold of management literacy. They have become so familiar that it is hard to imagine a world without them.

It is useful to step back and reflect on the scientific underpinnings to this legacy. Eric Beinhocker writes: "The early micro-economists copied the mathematics of mid-nineteenth century physics equation by equation. ['Atoms'] became the individual, 'force' became the economists' notion of 'marginal utility' (or demand), 'kinetic energy' became total expenditure. All of this was synthesized into a coherent theory by Alfred Marshall—known as the theory of industrial organization."[1]

Marshall's work and its underpinnings in nineteenth-century physics exert a huge influence on strategic thinking to this day. From our concept of strategy to our efforts at organizational renewal, the deep logic is based on assumptions of deterministic cause and effect (that is, a billiard ball model of how competitors will respond to a strategic challenge or how employees will behave under a new incentive scheme). And all of this, consistent with Newton's initial conceptions, is assumed to take place in a world where time, space (that is, a particular industry structure or definition of a market), and dynamic equilibrium are accepted as reasonable underpinnings for the formulation of executive action. That's where the trouble begins. Marshall's equilibrium model offered appropriate approximations for the dominant sectors of agriculture and manufacturing of his era and are still useful in many situations. But these constructs run into difficulty in the far from equilibrium conditions found in today's service, technology, or communications-intensive businesses. When new entrants such as Nokia, Amazon.com, Dell Computer, or CNN invade a market, they succeed despite what traditional strategic thinkers would write off as a long shot.

During the 1980s and 1990s, performance improvement (for example, total quality management, *kaizen,* just-in-time, reengineering) succeeded the strategic era. It, too, has followed the S-curve trajectory. Now, as it trails off, an uneasiness is stirring, a feeling that "something more" is required. In particular, disquiet has arisen over the rapidly rising fatality rates of major companies. Organizations cannot win by cost reduction alone and cannot invent appropriate strategic responses fast enough to stay abreast of nimble rivals. Many are exhausted by the pace of change, and their harried attempts to execute new initiatives fall short of expectations.

The next point of inflection is about to unfold. To succeed, the next big idea must address the biggest challenge facing corporations today—namely, to dramatically improve the hit rate of strategic initiatives and attain the level of renewal necessary for successful execution. As in the previous eras, we can expect that the next big idea will at first seem strange and inaccessible.

Here's the good news. For well over a decade, the hard sciences have made enormous strides in understanding and describing how the living world works. Scientists use the term *"complex adaptive systems"* (*"complexity"* for short) to label these theories. To be sure, the new theories do not explain everything. But the work has identified principles that apply to many living things—amoebae and ant colonies, beehives and bond traders, ecologies and economies, you and me.

For an entity to qualify as a complex adaptive system, it must meet four tests. *First,* it must comprise many agents acting in parallel. It is not hierarchically controlled. *Second,* it continuously shuffles these building blocks and generates multiple levels of organization and structure. *Third,* it is subject to the second law of thermodynamics, exhibiting entropy and winding down over time unless replenished with energy. In this sense, complex adaptive systems are vulnerable to death. *Fourth,* a distinguishing characteristic, all complex adaptive systems exhibit a capacity for pattern recognition and employ this to anticipate the future and learn to recognize the anticipation of seasonal change.

Many systems are complex but not adaptive, that is, they meet some of the above conditions, but not all. If sand is gradually piled on a table, it will slide off in patterns. If a wave in a stream is disturbed, it will repair itself once the obstruction is removed. But neither of these complex systems anticipates and learns. Only living systems cope with their environment with a predictive model that anticipates and proacts. Hence, when the worldwide community of strep bacteria mutates to circumvent the threat of the latest antibiotic (as it does rather reliably within three years), it is reaffirming its membership in the club of complexity.

Work on complexity originated during the mid-1980s at New Mexico's Santa Fe Institute. A group of distinguished scientists with backgrounds in particle physics, microbiology, archaeology, astrophysics, paleontology, zoology, botany, and economics were drawn together by similar questions.[2] A series of symposia, underwritten by the Carnegie Foundation, revealed that all the assembled disciplines shared, at their core, building blocks composed of many agents. These might be molecules, neurons, a species, customers, members of a social system, or networks of corporations. Further, these fundamental systems were continually organizing and reorganizing themselves, all flourishing in a boundary between rigidity and randomness and all occasionally forming larger structures through the clash of natural accommodation and competition. Molecules form cells; neurons cluster into neural networks (or brains); species form ecosystems; individuals form tribes or societies; consumers and corporations form economies. These self-organizing structures give rise to emergent behavior (an example of which is the process whereby prebiotic chemicals combined to form the extraordinary diversity of life on earth). Complexity science informs us about organization, stability, and change in social and natural systems. "Unlike the earlier advances in hard science," writes economist Alex Trosiglio, "complexity deals with a world that is far from equilibrium, and is creative and evolving in ways that we cannot hope to predict. It points to fundamental limits to our ability to understand, control, and manage the world, and the need for us to accept unpredictability and change."[3]

The science of complexity has yielded four bedrock principles relevant to the new strategic work:

1. Complex adaptive systems are at risk when in equilibrium. Equilibrium is a precursor to death.[4]

2. Complex adaptive systems exhibit the capacity of self-organization and emergent complexity.[5] Self-organization arises from intelligence in the remote clusters (or "nodes") within a network. Emergent complexity is generated by the propensity of simple structures to generate novel patterns, infinite variety, and often a sum that is greater than the parts. (Again, the escalating complexity of life on earth is an example.)

3. Complex adaptive systems tend to move toward the edge of chaos when provoked by a complex task.[6] Bounded instability is more conducive to evolution than either stable equilibrium or explosive instability. (For example, fire has been found to be a critical factor in regenerating healthy forests and prairies.) One important corollary to this principle is that a complex adaptive system, once having reached a temporary "peak" in its fitness landscape (for example, a company during a golden era), must then "go down to go up" (that is, moving from one peak to a still higher peak requires it to traverse the valleys of the fitness landscape). In cybernetic terms, the organism must be pulled by competitive pressures far enough out of its usual arrangements before it can create substantially different forms and arrive at a more evolved basin of attraction.

4. One cannot direct a living system, only disturb it.[7] Complex adaptive systems are characterized by weak cause-and-effect linkages. Phase transitions occur in the realm where one relatively small and isolated variation can produce huge effects. Alternatively, large changes may have little effect. (This phenomenon is common in the information industry. Massive efforts to promote a superior operating system may come to naught, whereas a series of serendipitous events may establish

an inferior operating system—such as MS-DOS—as the industry standard.)

Is complexity just interesting science, or does it represent something of great importance in thinking about strategic work? As these illustrations suggest, treating organizations as complex adaptive systems provides useful insight into the nature of strategic work. In the following pages, I will (1) briefly describe how the four bedrock principles of complexity occur in nature and (2) demonstrate how they can be applied in a managerial context. In particular, I use the efforts underway at Royal Dutch/Shell to describe an extensive and pragmatic test of these ideas.

The successes at Shell and other companies described here might be achieved with a more traditional mind-set (in much the same way as Newton's laws can be used to explain the mechanics of matter on earth with sufficient accuracy so as to not require the General Theory of Relativity). But the contribution of scientific insight is much more than descriptions of increasing accuracy. Deep theories reveal previously unsuspected aspects of reality that we don't see (the curvature of space-time in the case of relativity theory) and thereby alter the fabric of reality. This is the context for an article on complexity science and strategy. Complexity makes the strategic challenge more understandable and the task of strategic renewal more accessible. In short, this is not a polemic against the traditional strategic approach but an argument for broadening it.

STABLE EQUILIBRIUM EQUALS DEATH

An obscure but important law of cybernetics, the law of requisite variety, states: For any system to survive, it must cultivate variety in its internal controls. If it fails to do so internally, it will fail to cope with variety successfully when it comes from an external source.[8] Here, in the mundane prose of a cybernetic axiom, is the rationale for bounded instability.

A perverse example of this axiom in action was driven home by the devastating fires that wiped out 25 percent of Yellowstone National Park in 1992. For decades, the National Park Service had *imposed* equilibrium on the forest by extinguishing fires whenever they appeared. Gradually, the forest floor became littered with a thick layer of debris. When a lightning strike and ill-timed winds created a conflagration that could not be contained, this carpet of dry material burned longer and hotter than normal. By suppressing natural fires for close to a hundred years, the park service had prevented the forest floor from being cleansed in a natural rhythm. A century's accumulation of deadfall generated extreme temperatures. The fire incinerated large trees and the living components of topsoil that would otherwise have survived. This is the price of enforced equilibrium.

The seductive pull of equilibrium poses a constant danger to successful established companies. Jim Cannavino, a former IBM senior executive, provides an anecdote that speaks to the hazards of resisting change. In 1993, Cannavino was asked by IBM's new CEO, Lou Gerstner, to take a hard look at the strategic planning process. Why had IBM so badly missed the mark? Cannavino dutifully examined the work product—library shelves filled with blue binders containing twenty years of forecasts, trends, and strategic analysis. "It all could be distilled down to one sentence," he recounts. "'We saw it coming'—PC open architecture, networking intelligence in microprocessors, higher margins in software and services than hardware; it was all there. So I looked at the operating plans. How did they reflect the shifts the strategists had projected? These blue volumes (three times as voluminous as the strategic plans) could also be summarized in one sentence: 'Nothing changed.' And the final dose of arsenic to this diet of cyanide was the year-end financial reconciliation process. When we rolled up the sector submissions into totals for the corporation, the growth opportunities never quite covered the erosion of market share. This shortfall, of course, was the tip of an iceberg that would one day upend our strategy and our primary product—the IBM 360 mainframe. But facing these fundamental trends would have pre-cipitated a great deal of turmoil and instability. Instead, year after year, a few of our most senior leaders went behind closed doors and raised prices."[9]

While equilibrium endangers living systems, it often wears the disguise of an attribute. Equilibrium is concealed inside strong val-ues, or a coherent, close-knit social system, or within a company's well-synchronized operating system (often referred to as *"organiza-tional fit"*). Vision, values, and organizational fit are double-edged swords.

Species are inherently drawn toward the seeming oasis of sta-bility and equilibrium—and the further they drift toward this des-tination, the less likely they are to adapt successfully when change is necessary. So why don't all species drift into the thrall of equilib-rium and die off? Two forces thwart equilibrium and promote insta-bility: (1) the threat of death, and (2) the promise of sex.

The Darwinian process, called *"selection pressures"* by natural scientists, imposes harsh consequences on species entrapped in equilibrium. Most species, when challenged to adapt too far from their origins, are unable to do so and gradually disappear. But from the vantage point of the larger ecological community, selection pres-sures enforce an ecological upgrade, insofar as mutations that sur-vive offer a better fit with the new environment. Natural selection exerts itself most aggressively during periods of radical change. Few readers will have difficulty identifying these forces at work in indus-try today. There are no safe havens. From toothpaste to camcorders, pharmaceuticals to office supplies, bookstores to booster rockets for space payloads, soap to software, it's a Darwinian jungle out there, and it's not getting easier.

As a rule, a species becomes more vulnerable as it becomes more genetically homogeneous. Nature hedges against this condi-tion through the reproductive process. Of the several means of reproduction that have evolved on the planet, sex is best. It is deci-sively superior to parthenogenesis (the process by which most plants, worms, and a few mammals conceive offspring through self-induced combination of identical genetic material).

Sexual reproduction maximizes diversity. Chromosome combinations are randomly matched in variant pairings, thereby generating more permutations and variety in offspring. Oxford's evolutionary theorist, William Hamilton, explains why this benefits a species. Enemies (that is, harmful diseases and parasites) find it harder to adapt to the diverse attributes of a population generated by sexual reproduction than to the comparative uniformity of one produced by parthenogenesis.[10]

How does this relate to organizations? In organizations, people are the chromosomes, the genetic material that can create variety. When management thinker Gary Hamel was asked if he thought IBM had a chance of leading the next stage of the information revolution, he replied: "I'd need to know how many of IBM's top 100 executives had grown up on the west coast of America where the future of the computer industry is being created and how many were under forty years of age. If a quarter or a third of the senior group were both under forty and possessed a west coast perspective, IBM has a chance."[11]

Here's the rub: The "exchanges of DNA" attempted within social systems are not nearly as reliable as those driven by the mechanics of reproductive chemistry. True, organizations can hire from the outside, bring seniors into frequent contact with iconoclasts from the ranks, or confront engineers and designers with disgruntled customers. But the enemy of these methods is, of course, the existing social order, which, like the body's immune defense system, seeks to neutralize, isolate, or destroy foreign invaders. "Antibodies" in the form of social norms, corporate values, and orthodox beliefs nullify the advantages of diversity. An executive team may include divergent interests, only to engage in stereotyped listening (for example, "There goes Techie again") or freeze iconoclasts out of important informal discussions. If authentic diversity is sought, all executives, in particular the seniors, must be more seeker than guru.

Disturbing Equilibrium at Shell

In 1996, Steve Miller, age fifty-one, became a member of Shell's committee of managing directors—the five senior leaders who develop objectives and long-term plans for Royal Dutch/Shell.[12] The group found itself captive to its hundred-year-old history. The numbing effects of tradition—a staggering $130 billion in annual revenues, 105,000 predominantly long-tenured employees, and global operations—left Shell vulnerable. While profits continued to flow, fissures were forming beneath the surface.

Miller was appointed group managing director of Shell's worldwide oil products business (known as "Downstream"), which accounts for $40 billion of revenues within the Shell Group. During the previous two years, the company had been engaged in a program to "transform" the organization. Yet the regimen of massive reorganization, traumatic downsizing, and senior management workshops accomplished little. Shell's earnings, while solid, were disappointing to financial analysts, who expected more from the industry's largest competitor. Employees registered widespread resignation and cynicism. And the operating units at the "coal face" (Shell's term for its front-line activities within the 130 countries where Downstream does business) saw little more than business as usual.

For Steve Miller, Shell's impenetrable culture was worrisome. The Downstream business accounted for 37 percent of Shell's assets. Among the businesses in the Shell Group's portfolio, Downstream faced the gravest competitive threats. From 1992 to 1995, a full 50 percent of Shell's retail revenues in France fell victim to the onslaught of the European hypermarkets; a similar pattern was emerging in the United Kingdom. Elsewhere in the world, new competitors, global customers, and more savvy national oil companies were demanding a radically different approach to the marketplace. Having observed Shell's previous transformation efforts, Miller was convinced that it was essential to reach around the resistant bureaucracy and involve the front lines of the organization, a formidable task given the sheer size of the operation. In addition to Downstream's 61,000 full-time employees, Shell's 47,000 filling stations employed hundreds of thousands of mostly part-time attendants and catered to more than 10 million customers every day. In the language of complexity, Miller believed it necessary to tap the emergent properties of Shell's enormous distribution system and shift the locus of strategic initiative to the front lines. He saw this system as a fertile organism that needed encouragement to, in his words, "send green shoots forth."

In an effort to gain the organization's attention (disturb equilibrium), beginning in mid-1996, Miller reallocated more than 50 percent of his calendar to work directly with front-line personnel. Miller states:

> Our Downstream business transformation program had bogged down largely because of the impasse between headquarters and the operating companies, Shell's term for its highly independent country operations. The balance of power between headquarters and field, honed during a period of relative equilibrium, had ground to a stalemate. But the forces for continuing in the old way were enormous and extended throughout the organization. We were overseeing the most decentralized operation in the world, with country chief executives that had, since the 1950s, enjoyed enormous autonomy. This had been part of our success formula. Yet we were encountering a set of daunting competitive threats that transcended national boundaries. Global customers—like British Airways or Daimler Benz—wanted to deal with one Shell contact, not with a different Shell representative in every country in which they operate. We had huge overcapacity in refining, but each country CEO (motivated to maximize his own P&L) resisted the consolidation of refining capacity. These problems begged for a new strategic approach in which the task at the top was to provide the framework and then unleash the regional and local levels to find a path that was best for their market and the corporation as a whole.

Shell had tried to rationalize its assets through a well-engineered strategic response: Directives were issued by the top and driven through the organization. But country heads successfully thwarted consolidation under the banner of host-country objections to the threatened closing of their dedicated refining capacity. Miller continues: "We were equally unsuccessful at igniting a more imaginative approach toward the marketplace. It was like the old game of telephone that we used to play when we were kids: You'd whisper a message to the person next to you, and it goes around the circle. By the time you get to the last person, it bears almost no resemblance to the message you started with. Apply that to the 61,000 people in the Downstream business across the globe, and I knew our strategic aspirations could never penetrate through to the marketplace. The linkages between directives given and actions taken are too problematic." What made sense to Miller was to fundamentally alter the conversation and unleash the emergent possibilities. Midway through the process, Miller became acquainted with core principles of living systems and adopted them as a framework to provide his organization with a context for renewal.

Miller's reports in the operating companies were saying, "Centralization will only bog us down." "They were partly right," he acknowledges. "These are big companies. Some earn several hundreds of millions a year in net income. But the alternative wasn't centralization—it was a radical change in the responsiveness of the Downstream business to the dynamics of the marketplace—from top to bottom such that we could come together in appropriate groups, solve problems, and operate in a manner which transcended the old headquarters versus field schism. What initially seemed like a huge conflict has gradually melted away, I believe, because we stopped treating the Downstream business like a machine to be driven and began to regard it as a living system that needed to evolve."

Miller's solution was to cut through the organization's layers and barriers, put senior management in direct contact with the people at the grassroots level, foster strategic initiatives, create a new sense of urgency, and overwhelm the old order. The first wave of initiatives spawned other initiatives. In Malaysia, for example, Miller's pilot efforts with four initiative teams (called "action labs") have proliferated to forty. "It worked," he states, "because the people at the coal face usually know what's going on. They see the competitive threats and our inadequate response every day. Once you give them the context, they can do a better job of spotting opportunities and stepping up to decisions. In less than two years, we've seen astonishing progress in our retail business in some twenty-five countries. This represents around 85 percent of our retail sales volume, and we have now begun to use this approach in our service organizations and lubricant business. Results? By the end of 1997, Shell's operations in France had regained initiative and achieved double-digit growth and double-digit return on capital. Market share was increasing after years of decline." Austria went from a probable exit candidate to a highly profitable operation. Overall, Shell gained in brand-share preference throughout Europe and ranked first in share among other major oil companies. By the close of 1998, approximately 10,000 Downstream employees have been involved in this effort with audited results (directly attributed to the program) exceeding a $300 million contribution to Shell's bottom line.

SELF-ORGANIZATION
AND EMERGENT COMPLEXITY

Santa Fe Institute's Stuart Kauffman is a geneticist. His lifetime fascination has been with the ordered process by which a fertilized egg unfolds into a newborn infant and later into an adult. Earlier Nobel Prize-winning work on genetic circuits had shown that every cell contains a number of "regulatory" genes that act as switches to turn one another on and off. Modern computers use sequential instructions, whereas the genetic system exercises most of its instructions simultaneously. For decades, scientists have sought to discover the governing mechanism that causes this simultaneous, nonlinear system to settle down and replicate a species.[13]

Kauffman built a simple simulation of a genetic system. His array of a hundred light bulbs looked like a Las Vegas marquee. Since regulatory genes cause the cells (like bulbs) to turn on or off, Kauffman arranged for his bulbs to do just that, each independently of the other. His hypothesis was that no governing mechanism existed; rather, random and independent behavior would settle into patterns—a view that was far from self-evident. The possible combinations in Kauffman's arrangement of blinking lights was two (that is, on and off), multiplied by itself a hundred times (that is, almost one million, trillion, trillion possibilities!).

When Kauffman switched the system on, the result was astonishing. Instead of patterns of infinite variety, the system always settled down within a few minutes to a few more or less orderly states.

The implications of Kauffman's work are far-reaching. Theorists had been searching for the sequence of primordial events that could have produced the first DNA—the building block of life. Kauffman asked instead, "What if life was not just standing around and waiting until DNA happened? What if all those amino acids and sugars and gasses and solar energy were each just doing their thing like the billboard of lights?" If the conditions in primordial soup were right, it wouldn't take a miracle (like a million decks of cards falling from a balcony and all coming up aces) for DNA to randomly turn up. Rather, the compounds in the soup could have formed a coherent, self-reinforcing web of reactions and these, in turn, generated the more complex patterns of DNA.[14]

Emergent complexity is driven by a few simple patterns that combine to generate infinite variety. For example, simulations have shown that a three-pronged "crow's foot" pattern, if combined in various ways, perfectly replicates the foliage patterns of every fern on earth. Similar phenomena hold true in business. John Kao, a specialist in creativity, has observed how one simple creative breakthrough can evoke a cascade of increasing complexity.[15] "Simple" inventions such as the wheel, printing press, or transistor lead to "complex" offshoots such as automobiles, cellular phones, electronic publishing, and computing.

The phenomenon of emergence arises from the way simple patterns combine. Mathematics has coined the term *"fractals"* to describe a set of simple equations that combine to form endless diversity.[16] Fractal mathematics has given us valuable insight into how nature creates the shapes we observe. Mountains, rivers, coastline vegetation, lungs, and circulatory systems are fractal, replicating a dominant pattern at several smaller levels of scale. Fractals, in effect, act like genetic algorithms enabling a species to efficiently replicate essential functions.

One consequence of emerging complexity is that you cannot see the end from the beginning. While many can readily acknowledge nature's propensity to self-organize and generate more complex levels, it is less comforting to put oneself at the mercy of this process with the foreknowledge that we cannot predict the shape that the future will take. Emerging complexity creates not one future but many.

Self-Organization and Emergence at Shell

Building on (1) the principles of complexity, (2) the fractal-like properties of a business model developed by Columbia University's Larry Seldon,[17] and (3) a second fractal-like process, the action labs, Steve Miller and his colleagues at Shell tapped into the intelligence in the trenches and channeled it into a tailored marketplace response.[18] Miller states:

> We needed a vehicle to give us an energy transfusion and remind us that we could play at a far more competitive level. The properties of self-organization and emergence make intuitive sense to me. The question was how to release them. Seldon's model gave us a sharp-edged tool to identify customer needs and markets and to develop our value proposition. This, in effect, gave our troops the "ammunition" to shoot with–analytical distinctions to make the business case. Shell has always been a wholesaler. Yet the forecourt of every service station is an artery for commerce that any retailer would envy. Our task was to tap the potential of that real estate, and we needed both the insight and the initiatives of our front-line troops to pull it off. For a company as large as Shell, leadership can't drive these answers down from the top. We needed to tap into ideas that were out there in the ranks–latent but ready to bear fruit if given encouragement.

At first glance, Shell's methods look pedestrian. Miller began bringing six- to eight-person teams from a half-dozen operating companies from around the world into "retailing boot camps." The first five-day workshop introduced tools for identifying and exploiting market opportunities. It also included a dose of the leadership skills necessary to enroll others back home. Participants returned ready to apply the tools to achieve breakthroughs such as doubling net income in filling stations on the major north-south highways of Malaysia or tripling market share of bottled gas in South Africa. As part of the discipline of the model, every intention (for example, "to lower fuel delivery costs") was translated into "key business activities" (or KBAs). As the first group went home, six more teams would rotate in. During the next sixty days, the first group of teams used the analytical tools to sample customers, identify segments, and develop a value proposition. The group would then return to the workshop for a "peer challenge"—tough give-and-take exchanges with other teams. Then it would go back again for another sixty days to perfect a business plan. At the close of the third workshop, each action lab spent three hours in the "fishbowl" with Miller and several of his direct reports, reviewing business plans, while the other teams observed the proceedings. At the close of each session, plans were approved, rejected, amended. Financial commitments were made in exchange for promised results. (The latter were incorporated in the country's operating goals for the year.) Then the teams went back to the field for another sixty days to put their ideas into action and returned for a follow-up session.

"Week after week, team after team," continues Miller,

> my six direct reports and I and our internal coaches reached out and worked directly with a diverse cross-section of customers, dealers, shop stewards, and young and mid-level professionals. And it worked. Operating company CEOs, historically leery of any "help" from headquarters, saw their people return energized and armed with solid plans to beat the competition. The grassroots employees who participated in the program got to touch and feel the new Shell—a far more informal, give-and-take culture. The conversation down in the ranks of the organization began to change. Guerrilla leaders, historically resigned to Shell's conventional way of doing things, stepped forward to champion ingenious marketplace innovations (such as the Coca-Cola Challenge in Malaysia—a free Coke to any service-station customer who is not offered the full menu of forecourt services. It sounds trivial, but it increased volume by 15 percent). Many, if not most, of the ideas come from the lower ranks of our company who are in direct contact with the customer. Best of all, we learned together. I can't overstate how infectious the optimism and energy of these committed employees was for the many managers above them. In a curious way, these front-line employees taught us to believe in ourselves again.

As executives move up in organizations, they become removed from the work that goes on in the fields. Directives from the top become increasingly abstract as executives tend to rely on mechanical cause-and-effect linkages to drive the business: strategic guidelines, head-count controls, operational expense targets, pay-for-performance incentives, and so forth. These are the tie rods and pistons of "social engineering"—the old model of change. Complexity theory does not discard these useful devices but it starts from a different place. The living-systems approach begins with a focus on the intelligence in the nodes. It seeks to ferret out what this network sees, what stresses it is undergoing, and what is needed to unleash its potential. Other support elements (for example, controls and rewards) are orchestrated to draw on this potential rather than to drive down solutions from above.

Miller was pioneering a very different model from what had always prevailed at Shell. His "design for emergence" generated hundreds of informal connections between headquarters and the field, resembling the parallel networks of the nervous system to the brain. It contrasted with the historical model of mechanical linkages analogous to those that transfer the energy from the engine in a car through a drive train to the tires that perform the "work."

EDGE OF CHAOS

Nothing novel can emerge from systems with high degrees of order and stability—for example, crystals, incestuous communities, or regulated industries. On the other hand, complete chaotic systems, such as stampedes, riots, rage, or the early years of the French Revolution, are too formless to coalesce. Generative complexity takes place in the boundary between rigidity and randomness.

Historically,[19] science viewed "change" as moving from one equilibrium state (water) to another (ice). Newtonian understandings could not cope with the random, near-chaotic messiness of the actual transition itself. Ecologists and economists similarly favored equilibrium conditions because neither observation nor modeling techniques could handle transition states. The relatively inexpensive computational power of modern computers has changed all that. Nonequilibrium and nonlinear simulations are now possible. These developments, along with the study of complexity, have enabled us to better understand the dynamics of "messiness."

Phase transitions occur in the realm near chaos where a relatively small and isolated variation can produce huge effects. Consider the example of lasers: Though only a complex system and not an adaptive one, the infusion of energy into plasma excites a jumble of photons. The more the energy, the more jumbled they become. Still more and the seething mass is transformed into the coherent light of a laser beam. What drives this transition, and how can we orchestrate it? Two determinants—(1) a precise tension between amplifying and damping feedback, and (2) (unique to mankind) the application of mindfulness and intention—are akin to rudder and sail when surfing near the edge of chaos.

Two factors determine the level of excitation in a system. In cybernetics, they are known as *amplifying* (positive) and *damping* (negative) feedback.[20] Damping feedback operates like a thermostat, which keeps temperatures within boundaries with a thermocouple that continually says "too hot, too cold." Amplifying feedback happens when a microphone gets too close to a loudspeaker. The signal is amplified until it oscillates to a piercing shriek. Living systems thrive when these mechanisms are in tension.

Getting the tension right is the hard part. Business obituaries abound with examples of one or the other of these feedback systems gone amok. IT&T under Harold Geneen or Sunbeam under "Chainsaw" Al Dunlap thrives briefly under stringent damping controls, then fades away owing to the loss of imagination and creative energy. At the opposite end, Value Jet thrives in an amplifying phase, adds more planes, departures, and staff without corresponding attention to the damping loop (operational controls, safety, reliability, and service standards).

Psychologists tell us that pain can cause us to change, and this is most likely to occur when we recontextualize pain as the means by which significant learning occurs. When the great Austro-American economist Joseph Schumpeter described the essence of free-market economies as "creative destruction," it could be interpreted as a characterization of the hazards near the edge of chaos. Enduring competitive advantage entails disrupting what has been done in the past and creating a new future.

Hewlett-Packard's printer business was one of the most successful in its portfolio. Observing a downward spiral of margins as many "me too" printers entered the market, HP reinvented its offering. Today, HP's printers are the "free razor blade"—the loss leader in a very different strategy. To maintain scale, HP abandoned its high-cost distribution system with a dedicated sales force, opting instead for mass channels, partnering, and outsourcing to lower manufacturing costs. To protect margins, it targeted its forty biggest corporate customers and formed a partnership to deliver global business printing solutions—whether through low-cost, on-premise equipment, or networked technology. States Tim Mannon, president of HP's printer division: "The biggest single threat to our business today is staying with a previously successful business model one year too long."[21]

Shaping the Edge of Chaos at Shell

Shell moved to the edge of chaos with a multipronged design that intensified stress on all members of the Shell system.[22] First, as noted, Miller and his top team performed major surgery on their calendars and reallocated approximately half their time to teaching and coaching wave after wave of country teams. When the lowest levels of an organization were being trained, coached, and evaluated by those at the very top, it both inspired—and stressed—everyone in the system (including midlevel bosses who were not present). Second, the design, as we have seen, sent teams back to collect real data for three periods of sixty days (interspersed with additional workshop sessions). Pressure to succeed and long hours both during the workshops and back in the country (where these individuals continued to carry their regular duties along with project work) achieved the cultural "unfreezing" effects. Participants were resocialized into a more direct, informal, and less hierarchical way of working. Miller states:

> One of the most important innovations in changing all of us was the fishbowl. The name describes what it is: I and a number of my management team sit in the middle of a room with one action lab in the center with us. The other team members listen from the outer circle. Everyone is watching as the group in the hot seat talks about what they're going to do and what they need from me and my colleagues to be able to do it. That may not sound revolutionary—but in our culture, it was very unusual for anyone lower in the organization to talk this directly to a managing director and his reports.
>
> In the fishbowl, the pressure is on to measure up. The truth is, the pressure is on me and my colleagues. The first time we're not consistent, we're dead meat. If a team brings in a plan that's really a bunch of crap, we've got to be able to call it a bunch of crap. If we cover for people or praise everyone, what do we say when someone brings in an excellent plan? That kind of straight talk is another big culture change for Shell.
>
> The whole process creates complete transparency between the people at the coal face and me and my top management team. At the end, these folks go back home and say, "I just cut a deal with the managing director and his team to do these things." It creates a personal connection, and it changes how we talk with each other and how we work with each other. After that, I can call up those folks anywhere in the world and talk in a very direct way because of this personal connectedness. It has completely changed the dynamics of our operations.

DISTURBING A LIVING SYSTEM

An important and distinct property of living systems is the tenuous connection between cause and effect. As most seasoned managers know, the best-laid plans are often perverted through self-interest, misinterpretation, or lack of necessary skills to reach the intended goal.

Consider the war of attrition waged by ranchers and the U.S. Fish and Wildlife Service to "control" the coyote. A cumulative total of $3 billion (in 1997 dollars) has been spent during the past hundred years to underwrite bounty hunters, field a sophisticated array of traps, introduce novel morsels of poisoned bait, and interject genetic technology (to limit fertility of females)—all with the aim of protecting sheep and cattle ranchers from these wily predators. Result? When white men first appeared in significant numbers west of the Mississippi in the early 1800s, coyotes were found in twelve western states and never seen east of the Mississippi. However, as a direct result of the aggressive programs to eliminate the coyote, the modern-day coyote is 20 percent larger and significantly smarter than his predecessor. The coyote is now found in forty-nine of the fifty states—including suburbs of New York City and Los Angeles. How could this occur? Human intervention so threatened the coyote's survival that a significant number fled into Canada where they bred with the larger Canadian wolf. Still later, these visitors migrated south (and further north to Alaska) and, over the decades, bred with (and increased the size of) the U.S. population. The same threats to survival that had driven some coyotes into Canada drove others to adapt to climates as varied as Florida and New Hampshire. Finally, the persistent efforts to trap or hunt or poison the coyote heightened selection pressures. The survivors were extremely streetwise and wary of human contact. Once alerted by a few fatalities among their brethren, coyotes are usually able to sniff out man's latest stratagem to do them harm.

As the tale of the coyote suggests, living systems are difficult to direct because of these weak cause-and-effect linkages. The best laid efforts by man to intervene in a system, to do it harm, or even to replicate it artificially almost always miss the mark. The strategic intentions of governments in Japan, Taiwan, and Germany to replicate Silicon Valley provide one example. The cause-and-effect formula seemed simple: (1) Identify a region with major universities with strong departments in such fields as microelectronics, genetics, and nuclear medicine and having a geography with climate and amenities suitable to attract professionals, and (2) invest to stimulate a self-reinforcing community of interests. But these and many similar efforts have never quite reached a critical mass. The cause-and-effect relationships proved unclear.[23] A lot depends on chance. One is wiser to acknowledge the broad possibilities that flow from weak cause-and-effect linkages and the need to consider the second- and third-order effects of any bold intervention one is about to undertake.

Disturbing a Complex System at Shell

In today's fast-changing environment, Shell's Steve Miller dismisses the company's old traditional approach as mechanistic. "Top-down strategies don't win ballgames," he states. "Experimentation, rapid learning, and seizing the momentum of success is the better approach."[24] Miller observes:

> We need a different definition of strategy and a different approach to generating it. In the past, strategy was the exclusive domain of top management. Today, if you're going to have a successful company, you have to recognize that the top can't possibly have all the answers. The leaders provide the vision and are the context setters. But the actual solutions about how best to meet the challenges of the moment, those thousands of strategic challenges encountered every day, have to be made by the people closest to the action—the people at the coal face.
>
> Change your approach to strategy, and you change the way a company runs. The leader becomes a context setter, the designer of a learning experience—not an authority figure with solutions. Once the folks at the grassroots realize they own the problem, they also discover that they can help create and own the answers, and they get after it very quickly, very aggressively, and very creatively, with a lot more ideas than the old-style strategic direction could ever have prescribed from headquarters.

A program like this is a high-risk proposition, because it goes counter to the way most senior executives spend their time. I spend 50 percent to 60 percent of my time at this, and there is no direct guarantee that what I'm doing is going make something happen down the line. It's like becoming the helmsman of a big ship when you've grown up behind the steering wheel of a car. This approach isn't about me. It's about rigorous, well-taught marketing concepts, combined with a strong process design, that enable front-line employees to think like businesspeople. Top executives and front-line employees learn to work together in partnership.

People want to evaluate this against the old way, which gives you the illusion of "making things happen." I encountered lots of thinly veiled skepticism: "Did your net income change from last quarter because of this change process?" These challenges create anxiety. The temptation, of course, is to reimpose your directives and controls even though we had an abundance of proof that this would not work. Instead, top executives and lower-level employees learn to work together in partnership. The grassroots approach to strategy development and implementation doesn't happen overnight. But it does happen. People always want results yesterday. But the process and behavior that drive authentic strategic change aren't like that.

There's another kind of risk to the leaders of a strategic inquiry of this kind—the risk of exposure. You're working very closely and intensely with all levels of staff, and they get to assess and evaluate you directly. Before, you were remote from them; now, you're very accessible. If that evaluation comes up negative, you've got a big-time problem.

Finally, the scariest part is letting go. You don't have the same kind of control that traditional leadership is used to. What you don't realize until you do it is that you may, in fact, have more controls but in a different fashion. You get more feedback than before, you learn more than before, you know more through your own people about what's going on in the marketplace and with customers than before. But you still have to let go of the old sense of control.

Miller's words testify to his reconciliation with the weak cause-and-effect linkages that exist in a living system. When strategic work is accomplished through a "design for emergence," it never assumes that a particular input will produce a particular output. It is more akin to the study of subatomic particles in a bubble chamber. The experimenter's design creates probabilistic occurrences that take place within the domain of focus. Period. Greater precision is neither sought nor possible.

NOTES

1. E. D. Beinhocker, "Strategy at the Edge of Chaos," *McKinsey Quarterly,* 1997, *1,* 25.
2. For an entertaining treatment of this inquiry, see M. M. Waldrop, *Complexity* (New York: Simon & Schuster, 1992).
3. A. Trosiglio, "Managing Complexity" (unpublished working paper, June 1995), p. 3; and D. Deutsch, *The Fabric of Reality* (New York: Penguin, 1997), pp. 3–21.
4. See S. Kauffman, *At Home in the Universe* (New York: Oxford University Press, 1995), p. 21; and G. Hamel and C. K. Prahalad, "Strategic Intent," *Harvard Business Review,* May-June 1989, *67,* 63–76.
5. See Kauffman (1995), p. 205; and J. H. Holland, *Hidden Order* (Reading, Massachusetts: Addison-Wesley, 1995), p. 3.
6. See Kauffman (1995), p. 230; and M. Gell-Mann, *The Quark and the Jaguar* (New York: Freeman, 1994), p. 249.
7. See Gell-Mann (1994), pp. 238–239; and Holland (1995), pp. 5, 38–39.
8. W. Ashby, *An Introduction to Cybernetics* (New York: Wiley, 1956).
9. R. Pascale, interviews with James Cannavino, May 1996.
10. See Gell-Mann (1994), pp. 64, 253; and S. J. Gould, *Full House* (New York: Crown Publishing, 1996), p. 138.
11. G. Hamel, "Strategy as Revolution," *Harvard Business Review,* July-August 1996, *74,* 69–82.
12. Information and quotations in this section are drawn from R. Pascale, interviews with Steve Miller, London, The Hague, and Houston, October 1997 through February 1998.

13. Kauffman (1995), pp. 80–86.
14. Waldrop (1992), p. 110.
15. J. Kao, *Jamming: The Art and Discipline of Business Creativity* (New York: HarperCollins, 1997).
16. I. Marshall and D. Zohar, *Who's Afraid of Schrodinger's Cat?* (New York: Morrow, 1997), pp. 16, 19, 153–158.
17. Larry Seldon's work is unpublished. He considers it proprietary and solely for consulting purposes.
18. Information and quotations in this section are drawn from R. Pascale, interviews with Steve Miller, London, The Hague, and Houston, October 1997 through February 1998.
19. Gell-Mann (1994), pp. 228–230.
20. Waldrop (1992), pp. 138–139.
21. R. Hof, "Hewlett-Packard," *Business Week,* 13 February 1995, p. 67.
22. Information and quotations in this section are drawn from R. Pascale, interviews with Steve Miller, London, The Hague, and Houston, October 1997 through February 1998.
23. A. Saxenian, "Lessons from Silicon Valley," *Technology Review,* July 1994, 97(5), 42–45.
24. Information and quotations in this section are drawn from R. Pascale, interviews with Steve Miller, London, The Hague, and Houston, October 1997 through February 1998.

CHAPTER SIX

Robust Adaptive Strategies

ERIC D. BEINHOCKER

In 1988, I was wandering the floor of Comdex, the computer industry's enormous annual trade show, and could feel a palpable sense of anxiety among the throngs of participants. Since the birth of the IBM PC six years earlier, Microsoft's DOS operating system had been the de facto standard of the industry, and the stability it had provided had led to explosive growth for the entire industry. But by 1988, DOS was beginning to show its age, and the big buzz on the floor of the show was, "Are Microsoft's days numbered?"

Apple, then at the peak of its powers, had one of the largest, fanciest booths at the conference. Its dazzling graphical operating system made DOS look like an antique. Aggressive Sun Microsystems had teamed up with AT&T and Xerox to combat Microsoft with a graphical version of Unix called OpenLook. Across the hall, another powerful group of companies, including Hewlett-Packard, Digital Equipment Corporation, Apollo, and Siemens Nixdorf, had combined forces in a consortium called the Open Systems Foundation, which was pushing its version of Unix, also with a slick graphical user interface. Meanwhile, IBM was determined not to let

Microsoft advance on it again. The highlight of its booth was OS/2, a product in which it had invested heavily, and which it claimed combined DOS compatibility with the power of Unix and the Mac's ease of use.

There was something very curious about the Microsoft booth. First, it was by no means the largest or splashiest booth. Microsoft had been quite successful, but was still dwarfed by many of its competitors. More important, the content of the booth was more Middle Eastern bazaar than trade-show booth. In one corner, Microsoft was previewing the second version of its much delayed and much criticized Windows system, which as yet had little significant market share. In another corner, the company was pushing the virtues of its latest release of DOS version 4.0. In yet another area, it was displaying OS/2, which it was codeveloping with IBM. And across from OS/2, it was demonstrating major new releases of Word, Excel, and other applications for the Macintosh. Although Microsoft was a distant second to Lotus and WordPerfect in DOS applications, it had quickly become the leader in applications for the Mac. Finally, in a back corner, it was showing SCO Unix. SCO was the largest provider of PC-based Unix systems at the time, and Microsoft had entered a marketing agreement with the company and would buy a major stake in it a few months later.

A corporate buyer standing next to me grumbled, "What the hell am I supposed to make out of all of this?" It seemed to sum up the situation. Along with the confused customers, the press was also grumbling. Columnists claimed that Microsoft was adrift and Gates had no strategy. The press also reported that tension and infighting inside the company was caused by the fact that groups on one part of the Redmond campus were furiously working on Windows and DOS, while others down the hall were pouring their energies into OS/2, the Mac, and Unix.

The ending to this story is well known, and the success of Windows has helped make Microsoft one of the most valuable companies in the world. But Windows's success was not preordained. Standing on the Comdex floor in 1988, it was far from obvious who would win. But whether it was by intent, instinct, or luck, Bill Gates created a very robust strategy for securing Microsoft's position. Clearly, his preferred outcome was Windows's success, but he could see that this was by no means certain. His strategy was aimed at those uncertainties. If customers wanted evolution in DOS and not revolution with Windows, he could provide that. If OS/2 won, he would share the wealth with IBM. If the Mac won, he would lose the operating system but win in applications. If Unix won, he would no longer be the major player, but at least with SCO, he could be a contender. In addition to making bets on multiple horses, he also took steps that would pay off no matter what the outcome. So, for instance, he invested heavily in building skills in graphical user interface design and object-oriented programming—two technologies that would be a factor no matter which operating system won.

This scenario is playing itself out again as Microsoft makes a bid to lead the Internet. Microsoft's constantly shifting portfolio of development projects, investments, acquisitions, and joint ventures with software, cable TV, telecommunications, and media companies looks quite confusing if we ask, "What is Microsoft's strategy?" It makes a lot more sense if we ask, "What are Microsoft's strategies?"

UNRELIABLE MINDS
IN AN UNPREDICTABLE WORLD

Strategy development inherently requires managers to make a prediction about the future. Based on this prediction, managers make big decisions about company focus, the investment of resources, and how to coordinate activities across the company. Big decisions are hard to reverse. They usually involve serious commitments of capital and people, and once a company is heading down a particular path, it may be very costly, time consuming, or simply impossible to change.[1] This is why managers often have that pit-in-the-stomach, "I really hope I'm doing the right thing," feeling when they make strategic decisions.

Developing strategies based on narrow predictions about the future is entirely the wrong mindset for an inherently uncertain world. Recent scientific work suggests that, in fact, our intuition about uncertainty may be understated, the business world is even less predictable than we think, and that our minds are even worse at forecasting than we might hope.

Scientists have gained an understanding of *complex systems,* systems made up of many parts in which the parts dynamically interact with each other. Examples of complex systems include galaxies, ecosystems, insect colonies, brains, the Internet, cities—and business markets. Although on the surface these systems may seem quite different, they have some deep commonalities, just as the laws of statistics apply to phenomena as diverse as gas clouds and poker games.[2]

Most importantly for strategists, scientists have discovered that complex systems are difficult and often impossible to predict because they exhibit *punctuated equilibrium* and *path dependence.* Punctuated equilibrium occurs when a system's behavior is characterized by periods of relative quiescence interspersed with episodes of dramatic change. This means that occasional major upheavals (like stock market crashes) are inherent in the dynamics of the system and not the result of some unusual external shock.[3] Path dependence means that small, random changes at one point in time can lead to radically different outcomes down the road—something usually illustrated by the overused metaphor of a flapping butterfly causing a hurricane.[4]

A particularly insidious consequence of punctuated equilibrium and path dependence is that the past is *not* a reliable guide to the future, as illustrated by our limited success in predicting both the weather and the stock market. The problem, however, is that people tend to recognize patterns. Research shows that people try to interpret situations in the context of patterns they have seen before ("Oh, this is just like the Latin American banking crisis of the early eighties") and then take action based on rules of thumb associated with those historical patterns.[5] People also have a strong tendency to extrapolate current trends into the future; so, for example, we are usually more comfortable buying a rising stock than a falling one. Our drive to see patterns and trends is so strong that we will even see them in perfectly random data.[6]

So complex systems are almost perversely designed to trick our minds. We like to make predictions from patterns, yet in complex systems, the patterns do not have great predictive value. Punctuated equilibrium lulls us into thinking that we really do understand the world and then suddenly throws an earthquake at us. And we tend to assume linear relationships between cause and effect and extrapolate current trends into the future; yet in a path-dependent world, extrapolation can be quite wrong.

Strategy, then, requires good predictions, but the world is inherently unpredictable, and our minds are often tricked by the patterns we see. What is a strategist to do?

Nature faces a similar problem in designing species that can survive in constantly changing and unpredictable environments. There are many examples of ingenious survival strategies that are incredibly robust and have proved quite adaptive to complex environments. Yet nature lacks even our limited forecasting abilities and relies solely on the blind process of evolution to create its strategies.

In this article, I argue that we should take a cue from nature and change the way we develop business strategy, relying less on our ability to make accurate predictions and more on the power of evolution. Specifically, I suggest that precisely because business evolution, like biological evolution, is a complex adaptive system, we can employ some of the tools scientists have used to better understand biological evolution to understand business strategy.[7] Businesses should not have singular focused strategies, but instead should cultivate and manage *populations of multiple strategies that evolve over time.*

By harnessing the forces of evolution acting on a population of strategies, those strategies will be more robust and more adaptive than a traditional, singular focused strategy. A *robust* population of strategies will produce positive results under a variety of circumstances, even though it may not be optimal in some scenarios. An *adaptive* population of strategies keeps an array of options open over time, minimizing long-term and irreversible commitments. Robust, adaptive strategies willingly sacrifice the focus, apparent certainty, efficiency, and coordination that traditional strategies provide for the sake of flexibility and a higher probability of success. Microsoft's population of operating system strategies was neither focused, certain, efficient, nor always coordinated. Nor is its population of Internet strategies today. But the first represents the greatest business success since Rockefeller and Carnegie, and the second may prove greater still.

STRATEGY AS EVOLUTIONARY SEARCH

Let's perform a thought experiment.[8] Imagine a very large flat grid. Each point on the grid represents a possible strategy your company could pursue. So one point might represent "Focus on U.S. customers with a narrow product offering that is differentiated on technology and has cost advantages achieved through vertical integration." Another point on the grid might be "Sell globally with a broad one-stop-shop product line, competing on price, and using a network of suppliers, distributors, and joint venture partners." Say, further, that the profitability or *fitness* of each possible strategy on the grid is represented by its height, taking the grid to three dimensions. The grid is now a mountainous landscape of profitable peaks and loss-making valleys (see Figure 6.1).

Scientists use just such an imaginary grid, called a *fitness landscape,* to understand patterns of evolution in nature.[9] In a biologist's landscape, the points on the grid represent possible gene combinations rather than business strategies, and the heights of the points represent fitness for survival rather than profits.[10] We can think of evolution as the process by which species (or businesses) search for the high points in their fitness landscapes. Fitness landscapes have a number of regular properties, and by understanding those properties, we can better understand how evolution works and how it finds good survival strategies on the landscape.[11]

Fitness landscapes can take various shapes. Stuart Kauffman, a researcher at the Santa Fe Institute and the Bios Group, suggests that one can imagine a "Mt. Fuji" landscape with a single high point representing a strategy superior to all others. We can also imagine a random landscape with lots of jagged peaks and valleys. In most complex systems, whether biological or business, the landscapes have lots of peaks and valleys, but the heights of different points on the landscapes are correlated so that strategies differing slightly are near each other and have similar fitness levels. High mountains thus tend to be near other high mountains, and low valleys near other low valleys, thereby creating a complex landscape of "Rocky Mountain" highlands and "Death Valley" lowlands.[12]

The landscape is not fixed, like a mountain range, but is constantly bucking and heaving. As the environment and the strategies of competitors change, the fitness attributable to any given potential strategy will also change. So the height of any particular point on the landscape is moving up or down over time. What is successful today may not be successful tomorrow.

If formulating business strategy is an evolutionary search for high points in a fitness landscape, then you, as a strategist, are an alpine hiker whose goal is to reach and stay on the highest possible peaks. However, you face several challenges. First, there is food only

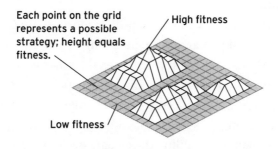

Figure 6.1. A Fitness Landscape.

on the higher peaks and you can carry only a limited amount on the journey; if you get stuck in a low valley for too long, you might die of starvation. Second, you have no map of the region and must rely only on sight. Third, it is very foggy and you can see only a few feet ahead. And fourth, this region of the Alps experiences periodic earthquakes. How would you survive in such an unfriendly landscape? What would your strategy be for searching for the high peaks?

PROSPERING IN THE WILDERNESS

If we accept that the search for profitable business strategies can be described by a fitness landscape, then it follows that the rules for success in fitness landscapes in general also apply to business problems.

One caveat: while I contend that these rules hold true generally, their specific application will vary significantly by company and situation. They are also not perfect recipes for success and will not yield the right answer under all circumstances. However, just as they increase the odds of survival in nature, they can increase the odds of survival in business.

Three elements are vital for finding high peaks in fitness landscapes: Keep moving, deploy platoons of hikers, and mix short and long jumps across the landscape.

Keep Moving

Stasis is death. If you are not constantly exploring, you'll never find new peaks. Even if you are fortunate enough to be on a high peak, at some point, that peak will collapse as the environment changes or competitors' actions deform the landscape. In the biological world, species respond to a constantly changing environment and relentless selection pressures through mutation and sexual recombination, constantly reshuffling the genetic deck in search of higher fitness. Since every individual in a species is slightly different from all others, even species that are relatively stable over time are constantly testing the value of that stable strategy with millions of individual experiments.

Collins and Porras, in a set of detailed case studies of successful companies, identify a common attitude they describe as "good enough never is."[13] In the language of fitness landscapes, this attitude describes a desire to try always to find higher peaks, never settle for the current peak, and always keep moving. Collins and Porras describe how companies such as Procter & Gamble, Merck, and Hewlett-Packard, which have remained successful for many years, create a culture of restlessness, discomfort with the status quo, and constant striving for improvement.

Deploy Platoons of Hikers

Another key to searching fitness landscapes effectively is parallelism: The more places you are simultaneously exploring, the more likely you are to find a new higher peak or to know where good spots are when your peak begins to collapse. You will find the high peaks more quickly with a platoon of hikers than with a single explorer (see Figure 6.2). Natural evolution is massively parallel, in that each member of a species is a different experiment on the fitness landscape, some closer and some farther from the average location of the group. Parallelism has three benefits:

▼ Innovation and progress require experiments, yet experiments by their nature are risky; parallelism in experiments increases the odds that one or more will work out.

▼ What is fit today may not be fit tomorrow; having a population of strategies allows some diversity, which increases the odds of survival when the environment changes.

▼ Parallelism breeds boldness; having multiple experiments allows you to take a few risks without "betting the farm."

The highly successful credit card company Capital One uses parallelism.[14] At any one time, it is running scores of experiments with various product market strategies. The company rapidly develops many new ideas, tries them out in the marketplace, sees what works and what doesn't, backs the winners, and unsentimentally kills off the losers. In this way, it generates more hits than its less prolific competitors, is better prepared to shift its focus when a particular product strategy starts faltering, and can afford to try things that more traditional competitors would shy away from.

High-performing pharmaceutical companies such as Merck apply a similar philosophy in drug discovery. They understand the uncertainty inherent in finding a new drug and improve their odds by creating populations of initiatives in new therapy design that range from incremental to radical. Although their short-term performance may be highly dependent on one or two blockbuster products, their pipeline of future opportunities always contains many possibilities.

Markets themselves are highly parallel. In the packaged goods, banking, industrial equipment, biotech, or energy markets, for example, at any time, there are scores of experiments going on with different types of strategies in places ranging from Fortune 500 boardrooms to entrepreneurs' garages. Thus markets deploy platoons of hikers, with different companies trying out different spots, which results in tremendous innovation in strategy, technologies, products, and processes. Most companies, however, pursue relatively singular strategies and thus occupy only one spot on the landscape. Although

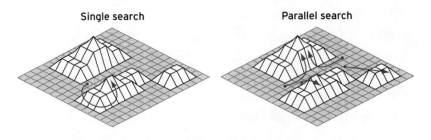

Figure 6.2. Deploy Platoons of Hikers.

no one company can replicate the parallelism of the entire market-place, it is important that companies be more like the market and simultaneously explore multiple areas of the landscape.

Mix Short and Long Jumps

So you need to keep moving in the fitness landscape and deploy a platoon of hikers. How do you decide where your hikers should go? Although it is foggy, they can see some of the surrounding area. Sometimes the fog lifts a bit; sometimes it thickens. So the first thing to do is to look for a path leading upward in the landscape, taking incremental steps. Biologists and mathematicians call such a process of incremental upward steps in the landscape an *adaptive walk*.

Adaptive walks are a very efficient method for searching fitness landscapes, especially if the peaks are correlated; that is, high peaks are near other high peaks. However, adaptive walks have an important flaw: You might arrive on a peak that is a local maximum—the highest point in its immediate vicinity but not the highest in a larger region—and get stuck, because every direction will lead down. You may get stuck on a peak where, just across a narrow valley but not visible through the fog, lies a much higher peak.

So let's consider a second strategy. Imagine a very powerful pogo stick that lets you spring to points far away in the landscape. In nature, this ability to jump to new spots is provided by sexual reproduction, which shuffles the genetic deck more radically than point mutations of DNA, nature's mechanism for adaptive walks. The advantage of the pogo stick is that you can get away from a local maximum and find higher peaks. The disadvantage is that, because of the fog, there's no way to predict where your pogo hop will take you. You might land in a low valley. In nature, this is represented by the occasional appearance, through sexual reproduction, of much less fit offspring than would likely occur with a single mutation. Given that high peaks tend to be near other high peaks and low valleys near other low valleys, the farther you jump, the greater the probability you will land someplace significantly lower than where you started.

The best strategy for searching a correlated fitness landscape is really a mixture of an adaptive walk with the occasional medium and long pogo jump (see Figure 6.3). This can be proven mathematically and through computer simulation but makes intuitive sense as well.[15] The adaptive walk ensures that most of the time you are heading toward a higher fitness level, while the jumps keep you from getting stuck on local peaks and occasionally yield significant improvements, though at the cost of occasional drops in fitness.

McKinsey & Company, in a study of thirty of the leading growth companies in the world, found that their actions are consistent with the notion of mixing short and long jumps.[16] In general, successful growth companies manage a portfolio of strategic initiatives across three horizons:

- Horizon 1 initiatives are efforts to extend and defend existing businesses (adaptive walks).
- Horizon 2 initiatives seek to build off existing capabilities to create new businesses (medium jumps).
- Horizon 3 initiatives plant the seeds for future businesses that do not yet exist (long jumps).

The study found that most companies focus on Horizon 1 activities but not on Horizon 2 and 3. Distinctive growth compa-

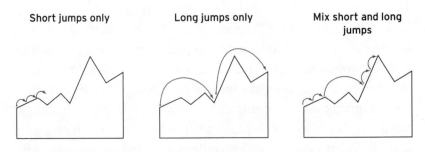

Short jumps only   Long jumps only   Mix short and long
                                                jumps

Figure 6.3. Mix Short and Long Jumps.

nies, in contrast, had much more balanced portfolios across all three horizons (see Figure 6.4). For example, Bombardier, the Canadian aerospace, transportation, and recreational vehicles company, has achieved more than 20 percent annual revenue and earnings growth for ten years by constantly creating and harvesting strategic initiatives that cover all three horizons. Current initiatives include a new class of ultra long-range business jets (Horizon 1), military aircraft maintenance services (Horizon 2), and electric vehicles for neighborhood transportation (Horizon 3).[17]

Hence, in creating a population of strategies, it is essential that the population contain a balanced mixture of initiatives ranging from short-jump incremental extensions of the current business to long-jump initiatives that have longer time frames, are higher in risk and farther afield, but have the potential to build capability and create opportunity.

Having a mixture of jumps not only increases the odds of discovering high peaks, but by providing some diversity to current strategies it also provides some protection when the landscape unexpectedly changes. In nature, genetic diversity is critical to species survival. If a species has a diverse portfolio of genetic experiments, and the environment changes and reduces the fitness of typical members, the existence of atypical members, some of whom have a quality useful in the new environment, makes the species' survival more likely.

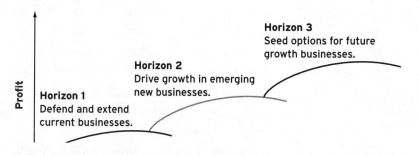

Figure 6.4. Three Horizons of Growth.

Source: McKinsey & Company Growth Initiative.

By mixing short and long jumps, the population of strategies will include a greater diversity of experiments, which will undoubtedly produce some unfit mutants; more importantly, however, the diversity may contain the seeds for success in an unknown future.

How different is this way of thinking about strategy? While some companies excel in individual elements of these three imperatives, few beside Microsoft and some others have put all three together to manage their strategies as an evolving population. Companies more commonly pursue singular, focused strategies that are either explicitly or implicitly based on a particular view of the world and prediction of the future. (For questions to help you determine the status of your company's strategy, see box, "Is Your Strategy Robust and Adaptive?")

Can We Create Populations of Strategies?

While the notion of creating evolving populations of strategies may sound appealing in theory, some practical issues and questions come to mind:

▼ *We can't afford to do everything. Won't we spread ourselves too thin?* A common objection to parallelism is "we cannot bet on everything." But an equally valid truism is "we should not put all our eggs in one strategy basket." So the best course likely lies somewhere in the middle. Nature is also frugal with resources: In the population of a species, we find significant variation, but not wild random diversity.

If we turn back to the notion of growth horizons discussed earlier, the really big dollars are committed to Horizon 1 investments, to the extension and defense of existing businesses. For Horizon 2 and Horizon 3 businesses, the dollars involved tend to scale down. Thus Bombardier is investing significantly more in the success of its new Global Express airplane than in its experiments with electric vehicles. What distinguishes Bombardier from many of its competitors is not the specific amount invested in its Horizon 3 experiments; it is the fact that it has these experiments at all.

▼

Is Your Strategy Robust and Adaptive?

1. In your company, is there a sense of constant experimentation and a restlessness with the status quo?

2. How many strategies is each business simultaneously pursuing? Are they truly different strategies or just different initiatives pursuing the same strategy?

3. What is the mix of short-term and long-term, low-risk and high-risk, and closely related and less related strategies in your company's population of strategies? Does the population include shaping, hedging, and no-regrets moves?

4. How diverse are the backgrounds and experiences of senior people in the organization? Is there a mix of "lifers" and newcomers, different industry backgrounds, functional knowledge, and geographic experience? Is diversity cultivated and welcomed or is group-think the norm?

5. Is the option value of a strategy an important and explicit criterion in making decisions? Does your company use real-options techniques to supplement net present value for valuing strategic decisions?

6. What are the major scenarios for your industry? Which might constitute significant threats or create large opportunities? Which scenarios does your population of strategies cover? Where is the company exposed?

7. Does your company have effective processes for dynamically managing a population of strategies and initiatives over time, encouraging the start-up of new initiatives, monitoring performance, cultivating successes, and weeding out failures?

8. Do your company's personnel evaluation processes and incentives distinguish between good ideas that were well executed but unsuccessful and people who are unsuccessful?

9. Does your company have mechanisms for getting the market "inside" to drive decisions on investments and commitments to strategies? Or are such decisions driven more by the political power and influence of the executives? Do dollars tend to flow to historical revenue producers or to future value creators?

10. Do your company's performance metrics distinguish between legacy businesses and future growth options? Does the company measure future growth options as a venture capitalist would?

A company will also want to bet more on a preferred outcome than on a hedging bet. So, for example, Microsoft invested more in developing Windows than it did in OS/2 or Unix. Again, what distinguished it from competitors was not the amount of money it could spend (IBM and AT&T at the time had far deeper pockets), but rather that, in addition to its preferred outcome, it had a set of hedging bets at all. A lack of money rarely keeps companies from creating a true population of strategies. Rather, issues having to do with organization, culture, incentives, and mindset prevent it.

▼ *Diversity sounds great, but what about sticking to core competencies?* History is littered with companies that got too far from what they knew how to do and failed. Although the population of strategies should contain a diversity of strategies, they should be built from a common base of knowledge and capabilities. Bombardier's Horizon 3 initiatives, though bold, build on its capabilities in systems integration, composite technologies, and knowledge of certain customer groups. Likewise, Microsoft's hedging moves, while diversifying its strategy, built on its software competencies. However, while long jumps should build on existing skill platforms, they should also provide opportunities to create new skill platforms. Thus Microsoft's population of Internet initiatives is helping the company add new skills in communications technologies and media. Remember that in nature, the population of a species may be diverse, but all are related in the end.

▼ *Can a company achieve competitive advantage without real commitment?* Many strategy theorists have noted that a decision is strategic when the company makes a commitment to irreversible investments in assets or resources that are difficult for others to copy and thus lead to competitive advantage.[18] Microsoft has made enormous commitments to Windows, but the decision was not all or nothing at one point in time. Rather, the commitment built up over time, as Microsoft experimented with Windows, sometimes in fits and starts, and as it hedged its bets with other investments. If necessary, Microsoft could have shifted its commitment into OS/2: It would have lost much of its Windows investment (except for its "no regrets" investments in interface design and object-oriented programming), but at least it would not have completely lost the desktop operating system market. And again, Microsoft was not successful because of deeper pockets with which to make commitments; its pockets at the time were shallower than most of its competitors.

Competitive advantage does not come from the act of commitment itself; rather, it comes from the strategy ideas and innovations that eventually lead to commitments. A company needs a portfolio of ideas or innovations it might want to commit to as the future unfolds and uncertainties begin to resolve themselves. My approach does not negate the need for commitments; rather, it makes available a larger stream of choices to which a company can possibly commit over time.

▼ *Does this approach differ by industry or company?* Many of my examples come from software or other industries with low economies of scale. The approach may be fine for Microsoft, but how many strategies can Boeing, for example, afford to pursue? Or a small start-up? Exactly what constitutes a robust population of strategies will be different from industry to industry and company to company. The mix of short and long jumps or of shaping and hedging moves will all be highly specific. Capital One can probably maintain a larger population of strategies than can Boeing. Likewise, Monsanto, in the fast-moving biotech world, probably needs to make more effort in Horizon 3 initiatives than a commodity chemicals producer. But these are matters of degree; the general principles still hold. Both Boeing and the commodity chemicals producer should be cultivating a portfolio of strategies that contains near-term strategies, the seeds of future growth businesses, and hedges against key uncertainties, rather than pursuing singularly focused strategies that presume predictability.

So, if we believe that it is at least possible in principle to create evolving populations of strategies, how do we make them work?

CREATING ROBUST ADAPTIVE STRATEGIES

The lessons of fitness landscapes offer an untraditional picture of what is needed for successful strategy development. Strategists need to build and manage an evolving population of strategies (see Figure 6.5). New ideas and innovation create new strategies that are added to the population. Those strategies are cultivated and their performance monitored as they evolve over time, and decisions are made on levels of commitment or abandoning a strategy.

However, shifting an organization to this way of thinking about strategy is not easy. Often the organizational processes, measurement metrics, and incentives are geared toward a linear view of strategy and must change to support the new mindset. In this section, I briefly discuss six actions that can reinforce the robust adaptive mindset. This is by no means a comprehensive discussion: for example, stimulating creativity in strategy development is itself a significant issue. The individual tools are not themselves new. However, viewed through the lens of fitness landscapes and the imperatives for successful strategic search discussed in the previous section, it becomes clearer that these tools, which many companies do not use, are essential to good strategy formulation.

Invest in Diversity

In order to build and manage a diverse population of strategies, a company needs a diverse population of people. New strategy ideas are developed through inductive insights drawing on past experiences, analogies from other industries and situations, and mixing and matching elements of other successful strategies. Strategy creation is thus highly dependent on people's experiences and frames of reference; group-think is the death of strategic diversity. This is not just demographic diversity (age, sex, race, national origin, and

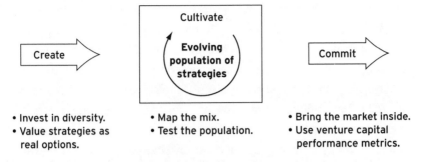

Figure 6.5. Building and Managing a Population of Strategies.

so on) but a diversity of experience. A McKinsey & Company study describes how companies such as General Electric create diversity by deliberately hiring from diverse talent pools and then giving employees varying experiences in different businesses, functions, and geographies.[19] While many companies would see all this moving people around as inefficient, the dangers of not doing so are the same as those created by inbreeding. Diversity must be viewed as an investment and actively cultivated.

Value Strategies as Real Options

Most companies assign a critical role to the financial valuations of potential strategies. But unfortunately the most frequently used measures for evaluating new investments, net present value (NPV), payback period, operating profit, and return on capital, discourage strategic experimentation. All these measures share a common flaw: they fail to account for the uncertainty of the future and the probability distribution of different potential outcomes. One investment might open up entirely new avenues of exploration and another might be a dead end, but traditional analysis gives them the same value. Evaluating investments as *real options* can compensate for this bias and reveal the true value of experimentation.[20]

In the financial world, an option is a right, but not an obligation, to buy an asset within a certain time at a certain price. Options have value because they create and preserve an opportunity to do something ("the right") for a period of time, without commitment if it later becomes unattractive ("not an obligation"). A strategy also has option value because of what it *could* lead to, as well as what it is intended to lead to. The strategy may open *future* possibilities (not certainties) that the company did not have available to it before. A strategy that locates a company in the fitness landscape so that it has many potential routes up the mountain range is worth more than a strategy that puts it in a dead-end canyon, even if the strategies have the same immediate level of fitness. Not only is there value in having lots of choices, there is also value in having a choice available over time, as it provides *flexibility* in an uncertain world.

Real option techniques help a company appropriately value flexibility as well. Adoption of tools for incorporating real options into decision making can influence the behavior of managers and remove the biases built into traditional measures that undervalue experimentation and flexibility.

Map Jumps on the Landscape

Most companies quite naturally make incremental moves in their strategy and are occasionally willing to make a big bet. But few companies step back, look at their population of strategies, and ask whether the mix is right. The population of strategies needs to be diversified along three dimensions: length of time frame, risk, and relatedness to the current business. Often these attributes will correlate; for example, long-term initiatives and those farther afield from the current business tend to be riskier. But sometimes they do not correlate—for example, a high-risk but near-term investment in a brand in a current business or a low-risk but long-term joint venture in a new business. Managers should categorize their strategies and initiatives as to whether they are near-, medium-, or long-term in their payoff, whether they are low, medium, or high risk, and whether they are extending or defending the current business, building a new business, or laying the foundations for future possible businesses. This provides a simple but useful map of the population of strategies.

Test the Population of Strategies

In addition to ensuring that the mix of jumps is appropriate, the company needs to ensure that the population of strategies has enough initiatives covering a sufficiently diverse but promising area of the landscape. Most companies resist parallelism; it is expensive, seems inefficient, and can put people at cross-purposes when there is internal competition. One way to see the value of parallelism is to test the population against potential scenarios by asking

▼ What are the major likely future scenarios?
▼ Which scenarios, whether likely or unlikely, could present major threats or provide major opportunities? Have we covered ourselves for these eventualities or do we accept the risk?
▼ What is the preferred scenario—the one we'd like to shape?
▼ How will we adapt in the other potentially likely scenarios?

Classical scenario analysis, system dynamics modeling, and new frameworks for categorizing and managing uncertainty are all helpful tools for identifying areas where parallel exploration is important.[21]

Bring the Market Inside

In making decisions on whether to commit to strategies in the population or to abandon them, it is critical that the selection pressures on the internal population of strategies reflect as far as possible the selection pressures operating on the population of strategies in the marketplace. In many companies, investment dollars often flow to the politically powerful or to those who have yesterday's revenues instead of tomorrow's possibilities. In the marketplace, venture capitalists and stock market investors all try to invest in the most exciting Horizon 3 opportunities, whereas in most companies, big Horizon 1 businesses get all the attention. Thermo-Electron avoids this pitfall by inviting outside venture capitalists to participate in its early stage investments and by spinning out parts of new businesses to the stock market in IPOs, thus providing market validation to its commitment decisions.

Similarly, most companies find it difficult to abandon poorly performing strategies. Egos, career concerns, and turf battles can keep poor strategies alive. Capital One carefully distinguishes between failed experiments and failed people to encourage greater risk taking and more objectivity, and to make it easier to abandon unsuccessful strategies. It even shuts down successful efforts simply to free up good people and resources for high-potential experiments.[22]

Use Venture Capital Performance Metrics

Many companies apply the same performance metrics to a mature plant making widgets in Ohio and a start-up Internet operation in India. It may be entirely appropriate to measure the performance of short-jump initiatives on things like near-term operating profit or return on capital. But if a company applies these metrics to long-jump growth options, it will never allow any to survive. In addition to using real options to evaluate the initial investment decision, the metrics for evaluating the performance of the various strategies in the portfolio over time need to be different. In evaluating long-term growth options, a company needs to be more like a venture capitalist. It needs to monitor financial measures, but such measures as meeting the milestones against a business plan, progress in technology development, establishing key relationships, building talent, and market acceptance are often better indicators of value creation.

▼ ▼

Evolution provides a powerful and effective recipe for solving problems and creating strategies in an unpredictable environment. Fitness landscapes demonstrate how evolutionary search creates robustness and adaptability through constant experimentation, parallel search, and a mix of adaptive walks and long jumps. By creating and cultivating evolving portfolios of strategies, managers can make it more likely that their company will stay out of the strategy wilderness and enjoy the high fitness peaks.

Acknowledgments

I would like to thank Bill Barnett, Kevin Coyne, Renee Dye, Dick Foster, Sarah Kaplan, Saul Rosenberg, my colleagues in McKinsey's Strategy Theory Initiative, and Costas Markides for their comments on earlier drafts. I would also like to thank Stuart Kauffman of the Santa Fe Institute and the Bios Group, and Brian Arthur of the Santa Fe Institute for their many contributions to my thinking on this topic. All shortcomings are mine.

NOTES

1. P. Ghemawat, *Commitment: The Dynamic of Strategy* (New York: Free Press, 1991).

2. For a discussion of complex adaptive systems and business, see E. D. Beinhocker, "Strategy at the Edge of Chaos," *McKinsey Quarterly,* 1997, *1*, 24–39. For a general overview of the science behind complexity, see M. M. Waldrop, *Complexity* (New York: Simon & Schuster, 1992). For technical discussions of complexity and economics, see P. W. Anderson, K. J. Arrow, and D. Pines, eds., *The Economy as an Evolving Complex System* (Redwood City, California: Addison-Wesley, 1988); and W. B. Arthur, S. N. Durlauf, and D. A. Lane, eds., *The Economy as an Evolving Complex System II* (Redwood City, California: Addison-Wesley, 1997).

3. For a discussion of punctuated equilibrium in complex systems, see P. Bak, *How Nature Works* (New York: Springer-Verlag, 1996).

4. For a discussion of path dependence as applied to economics, see W. B. Arthur, *Increasing Returns and Path Dependence in the Economy* (Ann Arbor, Michigan: University of Michigan Press, 1994).

5. J. H. Holland, K. J. Holyoak, R. E. Nisbett, and P. R. Thagard, *Induction: Processes of Inference, Learning, and Discovery* (Cambridge, Massachusetts: MIT Press, 1986).

6. D. Kahneman, P. Slovic, A. Tversky, *Judgment Under Uncertainty: Heuristics and Biases* (Cambridge, England: Cambridge University Press, 1982); and M. Bazerman, *Judgment in Managerial Decision Making,* third edition (Chicago: Northwestern University Press, 1994).

7. J. H. Holland, *Adaptation in Natural and Artificial Systems* (Cambridge, Massachusetts: MIT Press, 1992). As such, biological evolution is just one sub-class of a universal class of evolutionary processes. I take the position in this article that the search for business strategies is another sub-class of this more general class. So, although there are differences in biological and business evolution, both sub-classes are subject to the same general principles that govern all evolutionary systems. This is stronger than saying that business is metaphorically like biology, and there are some interesting analogies to be made. Rather, this position claims that any principles that make for effective or ineffective evolutionary searches in general will also apply to business strategy.

8. This thought experiment is borrowed from D. C. Dennett, *Darwin's Dangerous Idea* (New York: Touchstone, 1995), pp. 107–113.

9. For general discussions of fitness landscapes, see S. Kauffman, *At Home in the Universe* (New York: Oxford University Press, 1995); and Dennett (1995). For a technical discussion, see S. Kauffman, *The Origins of Order* (New York: Oxford University Press, 1993).

10. A real fitness landscape would have a very large number of dimensions, but a three-dimensional space is easier to visualize, so I have discussed the landscape in three dimensions, although the same principles apply in higher-dimensional spaces. See Kauffman (1993) and (1995).

11. Fitness landscapes can be represented mathematically and exhibit regularities that provide insights into how evolution works. For example, Kauffman and others have borrowed the mathematics of spin-glasses from physics to explore the characteristics of evolutionary searches on fitness landscapes. See Kauffman (1995).

12. Kauffman (1995).

13. See J. C. Collins and J. I. Porras, *Built to Last: Successful Habits of Visionary Companies* (New York: HarperCollins, 1994).

14. From presentations by J. Donehey and G. Overholser, Capital One (Boston: Ernst & Young Embracing Complexity Conference, 2–4 August 1998).

15. Kauffman (1993) and (1995).

16. M. A. Baghai, S. C. Coley, and D. White, *The Alchemy of Growth: Kickstarting and Sustaining Growth in Your Company* (London: Orion Business, 1999).

17. M. A. Baghai, S. C. Coley, R. H. Farmer, and H. Sarrazin, "The Growth Philosophy of Bombardier," *McKinsey Quarterly,* 1997, 2, 4–29.

18. P. Ghemawat and P. Del Sol, "Commitment vs. Flexibility," *California Management Review,* Summer 1998, 40, 26–43.

19. C. Fishman, "The War for Talent," *Fast Company,* August 1998, pp. 104–107.

20. K. Leslie and M. Michaels, "The Real Power of Real Options," *McKinsey Quarterly,* 1997, 3, 4–22. See also A. K. Dixit and R. S. Pindyck, *Investment Under Uncertainty* (Princeton, New Jersey: Princeton University Press, 1994); and T. A. Luehrman, "Strategy as a Portfolio of Real Options," *Harvard Business Review,* September-October 1998, 76, 89–99.

21. See, for example, P. Schwartz, *The Art of the Long View* (New York: Doubleday, 1991); K. van der Heijden, *Scenarios: The Art of Strategic Conversation* (New York: Wiley, 1996); P. M. Senge, *The Fifth Discipline* (New York: Doubleday, 1990); and H. Courtney, J. Kirkland, and P. Viguerie, "Strategy Under Uncertainty," *Harvard Business Review,* November-December 1997, 75, 66–79.

22. Donehey and Overholser (1998).

CHAPTER SEVEN

Strategy as Options on the Future

PETER J. WILLIAMSON

It is a great piece of skill to know how to guide your luck even while waiting for it.

—Baltasar Gracián (1601–1658)

In 1984, *The Economist* asked sixteen people—four finance ministers, four chairmen of multinational companies, four Oxford University economics students, and four London dustmen (or garbage collectors)—to generate ten-year forecasts. They were the kinds of forecasts that underpin many long-term, strategic plans: the average growth rate in Organization for Economic Cooperation and Development (OECD) countries over ten years, the average inflation rate in OECD countries, the exchange rate between pound sterling and the U.S. dollar, the price of oil, and the year when Singapore's GDP per capita would overtake Australia's (double Singapore's at the time). In 1994, *The Economist* checked the sixteen people's forecasts against what had actually happened.

On average, the forecasts were more than 60 percent too high or too low. The average forecasted price of oil, for example, was $40 compared with an actual price of just $17. All the respondents said

Singapore's GDP per capita would never overtake Australia's, but that had actually happened in 1993. The most accurate forecasters were the London dustmen and the chairmen of multinational companies (a tie for first place); the finance ministers came in last. But the performance of every group was quite abysmal. The unpalatable fact is that no one can predict the long-term economic and market environment with any real accuracy.

Yet many strategic plans are meticulously constructed on these foundations of sand, perched on top of forecasts that, in all probability, will prove to be hopelessly off the mark. Consider how many companies approach strategic planning: The numbers in the long-term plan are dominated by a sales forecast that is produced by product and customer type or region (often a projection of around five years); the companies then allocate the investment to business units consistent with achieving the long-term sales forecast. Then they compute the implied costs and profits, and the process iterates until they produce an acceptable "long-term plan." The plans often include erudite SWOT analysis (strengths, weaknesses, opportunities, and threats) or other market and trend analyses, but the decisions are made on the basis of forecast sales, investments, and costs.[1] The forecasts are often heavily influenced by straight-line projections with forecasts of sales growth of existing products in existing markets. This implies that the company will maintain significant percentages of its costs as fixed, so that when these are spread over the greater sales volume, profits will grow.

The large forecast error in projecting variables like those in *The Economist* experiment and, hence, sales levels over the long run creates problems for the kind of strategic planning I described above. Companies will tend to overinvest in building assets and capabilities that are highly specific to a particular strategy, relative to what would be optimal if the planning approach explicitly acknowledged that its forecasts would most likely be off the mark. A framework that encourages planners to optimize the configuration of investments on the assumption that they know the sales volume for particular products and markets will underinvest in flexibility.

By making investment decisions on "single line" forecasts, a company risks becoming a prisoner of its existing investments in capabilities and market understanding. Rapidly repositioning a company when investments in the capabilities and market knowledge necessary have not been made in advance will leave it like "an aircraft carrier turning on a dime." The company will suffer "diseconomies of time compression" (extra costs of trying to accelerate the rate of change).[2] Contrast this with a company that has invested in experiments to understand potential new markets and in seeding new capabilities (such as a small-scale project to supply a particular product direct to customers). These investments, and the learning they produce, effectively create a portfolio of strategic options on the future, a series of alternative "launching pads" that the company can use to rapidly change its strategic direction in response to market developments. A competitor that has aligned its investments with a single, and different, trajectory will struggle to catch up in the race to reposition.

For example, in 1990, USX (formerly United States Steel) had the choice of investing in new equipment to gain experience in a new steel-casting technology—compact strip production (CSP)—or in equipment using its traditional hot-rolling technology. USX chose to invest further in the hot rolling. A competitor, Nucor Steel, piloted the CSP technology and, in the process, created an option not available to USX. Commenting on USX's ability to catch up once CSP had proven successful, Nucor's CEO remarked: "It will take them two years to build a plant and another year to get it running properly. We've got at least three-and-a-half to four years on them."[3]

My message is that while companies may focus on executing a single strategy at any point in time, they must also build and maintain a portfolio of strategic options on the future. Building that portfolio of options requires investments in developing new capabilities and learning about new, potential markets. By putting in place a set of strategic options on the future, a company will be able to reposition itself faster than competitors that have focused all their investments on "doing more of the same." But this requires changes to traditional strategy processes and a new way of thinking about how planning and opportunism interact in determining strategy.

Next I discuss a strategy that embodies a coherent portfolio of options, sketch a process managers can use to develop this kind of strategy, and explain how planning and management opportunism can reinforce each other. Establishing a portfolio of future options involves four main steps:

▼ Uncovering the hidden constraints on the company's future
▼ Establishing processes for building new strategic options
▼ Optimizing the portfolio of strategic options
▼ Combining planning and opportunism

STEP 1. UNCOVER THE HIDDEN CONSTRAINTS

Successful companies often get ahead of competitors by focusing on a particular segment of customers or geographic market and learning more about their behavior and needs than anyone else. The companies design a profit-generating engine, based on a particular price, margin, and cost structure, that is underpinned by investments in the capability to source, produce, distribute, and support a product or service that these customers value. Over time, this profit engine is continually fine-tuned, often reaping economies of scale, scope, and learning. For example, Frank Winfield Woolworth, who founded Woolworth Corporation in 1879, pioneered the idea of selling merchandise at no more than five cents. He refined this "five and dime" profit engine to become a finely-tuned general merchandising machine. Initial concepts of "no frills" service, cheap products, and items that were nonperishable formed the core. The Woolworth Corporation subsequently developed competencies in managing a wide product range while keeping stock turnover high, competencies in site selection and development, and logistics to reap economies of scale from a chain of stores.

When its founder died in 1919, Woolworth boasted a chain of 1,081 stores with sales of $119 million (an incredible figure for its day). The power of the formula was reflected in the company's New York headquarters building at 233 Broadway: at 792 feet, it was the world's tallest building until the Chrysler building was completed in 1930. After World War II, the company continued to improve on the winning formula, adding new competencies in the management of advertising, consumer credit, and self-service and in site selection and management in the new retailing environment of U.S. suburbs.

Woolworth's strategy had the advantages of focus: It was able to deepen its existing competencies and incrementally expand both its competency base and its knowledge of different market environments. However, competitors were developing retail formats that required both competencies and market knowledge that were outside the "box" in which Woolworth was operating. Competitors like Wal-Mart (general-merchandise, discount superstores) attacked on one flank, while specialty "category killers" like Toys-R-Us attacked on the other.

Despite a decline in its overall sales figures in real terms, Woolworth failed to invest in creating new capabilities or understanding the behavior of shoppers using the new retail format so it could expand into either superstores or specialty retailing. When, in the late 1980s, Woolworth eventually tried to respond with its own discount and specialty stores, it ran into a hidden constraint: Although the strategy made sense, Woolworth didn't really have the option to change its strategy quickly, because it had not invested in creating new capabilities and knowledge outside its existing formula. Thus, by 1995, Woolworth was forced to sell its new specialty stores, "Kids Mart" and "Little Folks," established in the early 1990s, because of poor profitability. The company had become a prisoner of its past.

In 1993, Woolworth closed 400 stores in the United States and sold its 122 Canadian Woolco stores to Wal-Mart. In 1997, Woolworth shut down its last general-merchandise store in the United States. It had refined and polished its economic engine and deepened its narrow range of competencies into almost perfect extinction. The company had invested in new strategic options too late to build the competencies and knowledge necessary to pursue a new strategy.

In the quest to achieve challenging new missions, Woolworth managers kept bumping up against two constraints: They didn't really understand the customers they needed to attract to achieve a new, broader strategy, and they didn't have the capabilities to compete with rivals that were already established. When they decided to respond to lost sales caused by market changes, well-established Woolworth managers kept hitting the dual constraints. They had not invested in real options soon enough to replace their dying profit engine and were caught in a box (see Figure 7.1).

Woolworth did, however, invest in one new strategic option that partially saved it when, in 1974, it backed an experiment in specialty retailing—Foot Locker. Using new capabilities in the retailing of athletic footwear and its market knowledge, Woolworth exercised this option to build a chain of athletic-shoe stores when growth in the market took off in the 1980s. It subsequently introduced new formats, including Lady Foot Locker in 1982 and Kids Foot Locker in 1987. Over time, Woolworth opened more than

Figure 7.1. Hidden Constraints: Narrow Capabilities and Market Knowledge.

7,100 specialty stores, and in June 1998, it changed its corporate name to Venator Group. In some ways, this is an example of successfully repositioning a company whose core business had become obsolete. But Woolworth paid a high price for failing to recognize the hidden constraints on its strategy choices and underinvestment in new strategic options. Venator is a much smaller company; it now occupies only half the floors in that famous New York skyscraper, which it sold in April 1998.

To avoid becoming a prisoner of hidden constraints, a company must build new capabilities and simultaneously expand its knowledge of new market segments and customer behavior. If the outcome of uncertain market developments falls within the range of that portfolio of options, the company will then be able to exercise one or more relevant options. The company will thus be able to outperform the competitors that have not made these investments. Alternatively, it will be able to close the competitive gap with rivals that already possess the necessary capabilities and market knowledge.

Companies should distinguish between capability constraints and market knowledge constraints (see the "existing" box in Figure 7.1). Some companies' options are not seriously constrained by their market knowledge. Through various processes I describe later, they have created a large internal pool of knowledge about new customers and competitive behavior. This may include knowledge about new potential users of the company's products or services, new geographic segments, existing users with changed needs and buying behavior, or competitors changing the rules of the game. The dilemma these companies face is that market knowledge itself can still leave them with few ways to exploit that knowledge (other than, perhaps, selling it to someone else). The *"trader"* is a company with potentially valuable market information, but no capability to use it to create value except by trading the information or using it to arbitrage a commodity (see Figure 7.2). Obviously, some profitable companies are based on trading information, but for most, this option

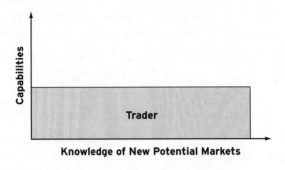

Figure 7.2. The Trader (Aware but Incapable).

does not allow them to leverage their existing competence base and therefore support an adequate return on their asset and skill bases.

To avoid having capabilities that are too narrow to exploit the knowledge of different markets and customer behaviors, such a company needs systematically to expand its pool of value-creating capabilities (adding, for example, the capability to manufacture products or deliver services that use that market knowledge). For example, the British trading house, Inchcape, had a geographic reach extending from Southeast Asia to the Americas, the Caribbean, India, Europe, and Africa, with interests in more than 500 companies in forty-four countries. It became a professional distributor, marketer, and seller of the products and technologies of its "principals" (the owners of the branded products and services it traded) and a provider of specialist services. As a trader, it successfully expanded its options into new markets (the horizontal dimension in Figure 7.2). But as the principals for whom Inchcape acted as agent became more familiar with the local markets, they wanted more control over their market positioning and built the scale to cover the fixed costs of local operations. They began to invade Inchcape's business. As a traditional trader, it had few places to turn. With finely honed trading skills, but lacking the breadth of capabilities to add value in other ways, its strategic options were tightly circumscribed. Some of Inchcape's competitors, like Swire Pacific, for example, had invested more in creating options by developing new capabilities in areas such as property development and airline management. By the time that pure trading as a mechanism for extracting profit from local knowledge came under serious threat, Swire used these expanded capabilities to extract an increasing proportion of total profit from its local knowledge in new ways.[4]

Some companies have the opposite problem: They have created formidable capabilities but are prisoners of their lack of market knowledge (see Figure 7.3). AT&T, immediately after deregulation, had capabilities in technology and communications infrastructure and experience in sales and customer service. As a result of domestic regulation and government monopolies overseas, however, the potential of AT&T's capabilities was imprisoned by a lack of market experience outside the long-distance, voice, and data sector in the United States. These constraints meant that AT&T could not fully utilize its existing capabilities so that it had underutilized capacity for value creation (in the sense that the marginal costs of using these capabilities would have been less than the marginal revenues earned had AT&T had the option to broaden its offering and the range of markets it served). Gradually, AT&T has opened new strategic

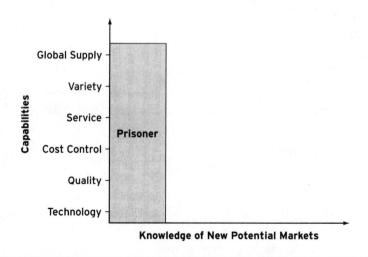

Figure 7.3. The Prisoner (Capable but Unaware).

options by building its knowledge base of the markets for new domestic service and users in national markets overseas. It is thus able to increase the effective capacity utilization of its existing capabilities.

To develop new strategic options, therefore, two sets of processes are required: (1) processes that fundamentally expand the company's capabilities, and (2) processes that expand the company's knowledge of new markets and market behavior. However, opening new options does not necessarily imply unrelated, or even related diversification in the traditional sense.[5] Strategic options on the future are not full-fledged new businesses. Instead, they are the "doors to the future" that are created when a company undertakes pilot projects, reconnaissance, and experiments that expand its knowledge of alternative market segments and value propositions and that seed new organizational capabilities.

In the case of Woolworth, the relevant options turned out to be experiments with new retailing formats, which can be seen as a type of related diversification. But alternatively, new options can often involve finding new ways to either deliver enhanced value to or reduce the costs of serving an existing customer segment, as in Monsanto's use of biotechnology to replace traditional chemicals in its weed-control business or Schwab's introduction of "E-Schwab." In almost every case, however, creating new options involves some combination of fundamentally extending the company's existing capabilities and, at the same time, its knowledge of customer and market behavior. E-Schwab, for example, requires new capabilities in the design and management of an Internet interface between the customer and Schwab's internal systems. Many E-Schwab customers use the existing telephone trading system, but they are likely to behave differently in electronic trading. Schwab needed to understand, for example, which customers would pay a price premium and how it could change its ability to build customer loyalty.[6]

I am not arguing that companies should develop an infinite number of capabilities or exploit them across every possible market. Such approaches would eventually drown in diseconomies of complexity as the variety of activities increased.[7] There is an optimal portfolio of options that a company can create in order to strike the right balance between the cost of creating and maintaining an option and the payoffs in the ability to reposition itself more rapidly and at lower costs.

What do these processes look like? How broad a range of options should a company create? Woolworth, for example, continually expanded its capabilities and knowledge of customer behavior within its existing retailing format; its error was to limit the range of new options, given the rate and nature of changes occurring in its industry.

STEP 2. ESTABLISH PROCESSES

As we have seen, creating new strategic options combines expansion of the company's knowledge about new, potential markets or customer behaviors with simultaneous development of new capabilities. The processes need to minimize the costs of building and maintaining the portfolio of strategic options—a particularly important factor given that many options are likely to remain unexercised.

Cost-effective methods of expanding knowledge about new potential markets and customer behavior include leveraging customers' and suppliers' knowledge and learning from "maverick" competitors and related industries. Market research is perhaps the most obvious way to leverage customers' knowledge. Traditional market research is limited by the current perceptions and orthodoxies of existing consumers. Companies should focus on customers' complaints to understand their perceptions of the existing offering. In some industries, companies can become partners with customers that have articulated an unserved need.

The geographic periphery of the company's existing markets or concentrations of highly sophisticated customers can also supply knowledge about potential new customer segments or emerging customer behavior. The company must ensure the right environment for the broad potential of these adaptations. It may enter a new market simply to learn what is potentially relevant for its global operations, rather than earn profits from that market directly. The costs of such a market are an investment in expanding the portfolio of strategic options.

Partnerships with leading-edge suppliers, exchange of technical information, or purchase of minority equity stakes in suppliers with potentially innovative technologies are processes that can provide the raw material to generate new options. Likewise, the company can scan related industries for potentially applicable technologies, service systems, or patterns of changing customer behavior as a way to form new options.

Companies should continually ask which companies are breaking the rules in the industry. A company with a single strategy, from which sales and efficiency must be optimized, dismisses these competitors as irrelevant or as following a different strategy. However, the behavior of maverick competitors can be a source of ideas for creating a portfolio of strategic options.

Analogous processes build the new capabilities that allow a company to expand its strategic options. Leonard-Barton analyzed the processes, including building a company's capabilities base through problem solving, experimentation, importing knowledge, and implementing and integrating new capabilities.[8] The combination of capability-building initiatives involved in a total quality management system includes physical and technical systems, managerial systems, and values and norms, all aligned to the process of building a new capability, in this case, "quality."

Acer used these processes to grow from a small electronics company in Taiwan to becoming the third largest supplier of personal computers in the world (see Figure 7.4). Just like its competitors, Acer lacked a reliable crystal ball to forecast the future, but had a broad sense of which markets it should learn about to expand its strategic options. Acer recognized that because Americans are

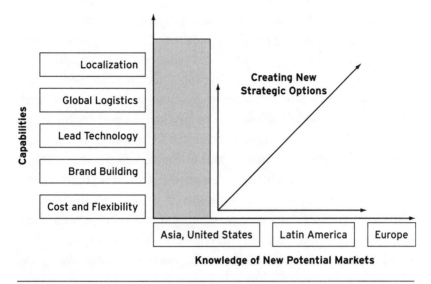

Figure 7.4. Creating Strategic Options at Acer.

sophisticated PC buyers, understanding these customers would give it a head start against competitors in other global markets. That understanding would open many options for Acer both to respond more rapidly and to lead change as other markets followed the U.S. lead. According to Acer's Chairman Stan Shih, this is why Acer has maintained its presence in the United States despite sometimes extended periods of local financial losses.[9]

Acer also knew it would be suicidal to attack the established PC giants across a broad front, so it concentrated on understanding the Asian consumers. Most of the major PC suppliers had traditionally sold only to the high-end, high-price segment of Asian markets. Acer developed capabilities, products, and consumer understanding so it could access the much lower-price mainstream markets in Asia. After rounds of redesigns to cut costs, interspersed with test marketing, Acer learned how to sell computers to the mass-market segment in emerging Asian economies ahead of competitors. This opened new options to enter other low-price, emerging markets like Mexico, South Africa, and Russia.

Acer didn't follow a strategy of straight-line forecasting based on its existing products and procedures. When it entered a new market, it didn't always know exactly what product it would sell to whom. Its initial investment in entering a market amounted to buying an option. Rather than simply selling its products to the kinds of customers it served at home, Acer invested in partnerships with local distributors and suppliers designed to maximize its opportunities to learn about the market and further develop its capabilities. In the United States, partnerships with discount retailers taught Acer how to use a previously underserved channel. Its alliance with California-based Frog Design built its capability to develop non-traditional computer designs and ergonomics. It subsequently exercised this option when it launched the unconventional, sleek, gray "Aspire"—a multimedia home PC.

In Mexico, competitors like IBM and HP believed that only large corporations could afford branded personal computers, while private consumers bought low-quality clones. Acer invested with its local partner in working with small- and medium-sized companies to discover a gap in the market of smaller businesses. It then used its capabilities to create a suitable product. Having established a new option, it moved aggressively to exercise it, building its market share in Mexico to 32 percent by 1996.

Acer did not exercise all the options it created. In 1996, Acer built an assembly plant in Lappeenranta, Finland, from which it could efficiently supply computers to Russian distributors. Developments in Russia during 1996 and 1997, including the rapid emergence of strong, domestic competitors, meant that the Russian market became less attractive than when Acer had made the investment. However, given Finland's membership in the European Union, Acer could easily transfer resulting excess capacity into other European markets.[10] Its experience points to another important factor: A company should design an option to minimize the costs incurred, should it decide not to exercise it.

Acer's approach was that strategy is creating options and exercising them in new markets. It expanded its capabilities in successive waves, by first exploiting its basic capabilities in low-cost man-ufacturing and flexibility to rapidly introduce new technology as a supplier of components and sub-assemblies to other PC suppliers. Each wave of Acer's initiatives opened new, broader options for posi-tioning. No amount of planning could enable it to pinpoint exactly which option it would exercise in an uncertain future. Unlike Woolworth or Inchcape, however, it created an expanded strategic space in which it could maneuver.

STEP 3. OPTIMIZE THE PORTFOLIO

How does a manager know if he or she has created the right port-folio of strategic options for the future? First, by setting aside tradi-tional spreadsheets. Instead, managers need to consider two factors:

1. What alternative capabilities might profitably meet probable customers' needs? (For example, digital or analog technology, localization or individual customization, high levels of variety, reduced lead times, bundled products and services, and so on.)
2. Which potential future markets (geographic, customer, or nonuser segments) or new customer behavior (such as effects of e-commerce) does the company need to know about?

If they stay at the level of future capabilities and potential new markets, far above the detail of unit sales and prices, companies can probably forecast with reasonable accuracy. In 1984, the same year as *The Economist* forecasting competition, John Naisbitt analyzed 6,000 U.S. newspapers to isolate ten "megatrends." They were devel-opments such as "customers would demand a combination of high-tech combined with high-touch," "globalization would mean a combination of more shared production with more cultural assertiveness in individual markets," or customers would demand an "option explosion," not just chocolate or vanilla, but a huge variety of alternative product or services.[11] Most of these broad "predictions" came to pass, largely because they were not predictions at all, but trends already under way that simply gathered pace over time. They are exactly the views that companies need to assess the capabilities necessary to generate a sound portfolio of strategic options. What kind of capabilities does a company need to increase options and provide future customers with more variety? What does this mean for operations, for inventory systems, for salesforce training? The answers will obviously differ by industry and by company.

Various techniques exist to develop needed alternative capabilities and to understand market environments or customer behavior. One approach is scenario planning.[12] Hamel and Prahalad suggest isolating potential "discontinuities" by looking for the likely collision of different trends that will create a step-change in the environment.[13] An example of such discontinuity is the combination of a twenty-four-hour demand for news broadcasts, emergence of a new cable media distribution channel, and development of low-cost satellite communications.

Once a company lists alternative new capabilities and market environments and behavior, it can create a table of its main alternatives (see Table 7.1). Not all combinations of future potential discontinuities and possible capabilities required to underpin competitive advantage will be technically feasible (Internet-mobile telephony convergence and analog technology, for example). Once planners identify the feasible options, they must decide whether to make the necessary investment to include a particular option in the portfolio. In looking at Table 7.1, for example, each competitor has to decide whether to include option 3 and option 8 in its portfolio by investing in the continued development of analog technology. These decisions should result from three considerations:

▼ The costs of creating and maintaining the option
▼ The estimated probability that the company will exercise the options
▼ The probability that creating the option will itself spawn future options, even if it remains unexercised (for example, a company

Table 7.1. Portfolio of Options for the Mobile Telephone Business.

	Capability Requirement		
Market Discontinuity	**Analog Engineering**	**Digital GSM Engineering**	**Other Digital Engineering**
Mobile telephones competing to replace fixed-line services inside large corporations		Option 1	Option 2
Emergence of lifestyle uses and the mobile telephone as a "fashion accessory"	Option 3	Option 4	Option 5
Internet, voice, and data applications converge		Option 6	Option 7
Entertainment media and mobile telephony converge	Option 8		Option 9

may value option 3 or option 8, not for its direct profit-making potential, but because of its capacity to open future options that rely on analog technology)

When strategy is viewed as the creation of options on the future, minimizing the costs of creating and maintaining them becomes a critical managerial concern. The costs can be reduced by careful design of efficient experiments, test marketing, and proto-typing; by sharing the costs in partnership with interested customers or suppliers; and by leveraging new information sources.

In attempting to optimize the company's portfolio of options, management must clearly distinguish between the cost of investing in the option and the cost of exercising that option (the latter being the cost of scaling up the option into a profit-generating business). In the case of Woolworth, for example, the cost of its initial exper-iment to establish its first Foot Locker store was the cost of creating an option to move into specialty retailing. If Woolworth had not exercised this option, the cost would have amounted to writing off the cost of the experiment. The cost of exercising the option included all the investments required to establish and operate a competitive chain of stores that achieved the minimum efficient scale. The cost of Acer's option on the Russian market amounted to the investment in its Finnish plant less the expected present value of cash it could obtain from selling the product elsewhere in Europe if it decided not to exercise the option to enter Russia. The costs of exercising its Russian option, meanwhile, would have included the costs of investing in brand building and distribution capacity in Russia, and so on. This distinction is critical because the decision whether to include a particular option in a portfolio should be made by comparing the estimated value of that option with the *cost of cre-ating the option,* not with the costs of exercising it.[14]

By viewing the first role of good strategy as the creation of a portfolio of options for the future, that strategy's success does not rest on the ability to predict continuing trends. Depending on the future environment, not all options will be exercised. However, those discarded are not wasted, but serve the useful purpose of insurance against an uncertain future.

STEP 4. COMBINE PLANNING AND OPPORTUNISM

Planning and opportunism both have an essential role in the strategy process. A company can plan the successive capabilities needed and new potential markets in order to create sufficient strategic space— the room to maneuver in the future. It can plan the proactive creation of strategic options.

A company cannot plan the precise options to select: Exactly which products and services will it sell to which customers in which markets at what prices? That is the purview of opportunism. For example, as part of building its "localization" capability, Acer began assembling its product in a suburb of Mexico City in 1993. By careful planning, it expanded its strategic options in respect of the market. During the peso crisis in December 1994, Acer exploited one of these strategic options. Having shifted a significant part of its cost structure to Mexico, it broke with the industry custom of quoting U.S. dollar prices and listed its products in pesos. When the computer market shrank by 40 percent, it launched a new model, continued to buy TV time, and targeted new customers, winning prestigious contracts to supply the national, state-owned power company and the main public university. Its market share rocketed, allowing it to retain a 32 percent market share when the market improved by 1996. Through timely opportunism, Acer decisively exercised its option to its advantage. It didn't predict the peso crisis, but when unexpected events unfolded, it had the strategic option to turn adversity to its advantage.

Another example of the interplay between strategic options and unexpected opportunities is the introduction of Acer's "fast food" model of PC supply. When Acer began to build its original localization capability, it didn't need to know exactly how to use it.

It knew that localization would become an important capability and that, having analyzed the possibilities, the investment in this option was justified. Having this strategic option allowed Acer to outpace its competitors when the market moved toward "customized" PCs. Opportunism guided Acer's tactics for using its localization capability and market knowledge to gain a specific competitive advantage.

A critical element is to keep tactical opportunism within the bounds of the company's overall direction and to rule out the options that would cause it to wander from its long-term mission. The selection and management of a portfolio of options, with some options expiring and new ones added, based on the decision rules I discussed earlier, is a good way to set bounds. To make "bounded opportunism" work in practice, every manager should ask the following question about each tactical opportunity: "Is it a weed or a flower?" An unexpected opportunity that diverts the company from pursuing its long-term mission is a "weed." Meanwhile, opportunities that allow it to take advantage of its options to accelerate progress toward long-term goals are "flowers." In this way, top management can set bounds that are sensitively applied without crushing the organization's entrepreneurial spirit.

CONCLUSION

Traditional strategic planning draws from forecasts of parameters like market growth, prices, exchange rates, and input costs. As *The Economist* experiment aptly demonstrates, we are unable to predict those variables five or ten years in advance with any accuracy. Spreadsheets try to predict exactly what products and services to sell to which customers in what volumes at what prices. In the process, these traditional frameworks lead to betting everything on straight-line strategies and risk boxing the company into a corner when reality inevitably turns out differently from predictions.

The trends we can predict with reasonable confidence—more localization, increased variety, and faster response times—can't be acted on by classic strategic planning systems driven by forecasts of sales, prices, and costs. Strategic planning systems deploy exactly the input we have no way to accurately predict, while discarding the new capabilities and knowledge of new market segments that will give companies the option to respond to broad, long-term trends.

To break from this trap, companies need to understand that successful strategy must combine both planning and opportunism. Planning builds new capabilities and augments knowledge of new, potential markets and customer behavior. Because investing in these options costs money, however, the number of strategic options must be optimized and managed. Actively managing a portfolio of strategic options allows a company room to maneuver and reposition. Short-term opportunism must determine which precise option a company chooses to exercise.

Acknowledgments

I would like to thank José F. P. dos Santos, Constantinos Markides, and the anonymous referees for their helpful comments on an earlier draft. Remaining errors are, of course, the responsibility of the author.

NOTES

1. These techniques are well described in R. M. Grant, *Contemporary Strategy Analysis,* second edition (Oxford: Blackwell Business, 1995).
2. See I. Dierickx and K. Cool, "Asset Stock Accumulation and Sustainability of Competitive Advantage," *Management Science,* December 1989, *35,* 1504–1514.
3. R. Wrubel, "The Ghost of Andy Carnegie?" *Financial World,* September 1992, *1,* 50.

4. P. Lasserre and C. Butler, "The Inchcape Group (A): The End of an Era" (Fontainebleau, France: INSEAD, case 04/93–317, 1993); and C. Kennedy, "Can Two Hongs Get It Right?" *Director,* February 1996, pp. 34–40.

5. See, for example, M. Lubatkin and S. Chetterjee, "Extending Modern Portfolio Theory to the Domain of Corporate Strategy: Does It Apply?" *Academy of Management Journal,* September 1994, *37,* 109–36.

6. A. DeMeyer, "E*Trade, Charles Schwab, and Yahoo!: The Transformation of On-line Brokerage" (Fontainebleau, France: INSEAD, case 05/98–4757, 1998).

7. P.J.H. Schoemaker, "Strategy, Complexity, and Economic Rent," *Management Science,* October 1990, *36,* 31–43.

8. D. Leonard-Barton, *Wellsprings of Knowledge* (Boston: Harvard Business School Press, 1995).

9. P. J. Williamson and D. Clyde-Smith, "The Acer Group: Building an Asian Multinational" (Fontainebleau, France: INSEAD, case 01/98–4712, 1998).

10. "Laptops from Lapland," *The Economist,* 6 September 1997, pp. 89–90.

11. J. Naisbitt, *Megatrends* (New York: Simon & Schuster, 1984).

12. See, for example, C.A.R. McNulty, "Scenario Development for Corporate Planning," *Futures,* April 1977; or A. de Geus, "Planning as Learning," *Harvard Business Review,* March-April 1988, *66,* 70–74.

13. G. Hamel and C. K. Prahalad, *Competing for the Future* (Boston: Harvard Business School Press, 1994), p. 145.

14. The subject of valuing real options is a large topic in its own right. There is insufficient space to cover it here. For relevant techniques and methods, see, for example, M. Amram and N. Kulatilaka, *Real Options: Managing Strategic Investment in an Uncertain World* (Boston: Harvard Business School Press, 1999).

PART FOUR

Strategic Innovation and Growth

CHAPTER EIGHT

Strategy Innovation and the Quest for Value

GARY HAMEL

Profound change in the competitive environment has produced a Cambrian explosion of new organizational forms, institutional relationships, and value-creating possibilities. Schumpeter's gale has become a hurricane. Whether you call it the "digital" economy, the "knowledge" economy, or just the "new" economy, it seems clear that we are on the cusp of an industrial revolution as profound as that which gave birth to the modern age. But, of course, we already know this. We've all read Alvin Toffler, Nicholas Negroponte, and *Wired*. The deeper question is, who will profit from this sea change? Which companies will sail on the new winds of change and which will be driven onto the rocks of irrelevance? I believe that only those companies that are capable of reinventing themselves and their industry in a profound way will be around a decade hence. The question today is not whether you can reengineer your processes; the question is whether you can reinvent the entire industry model—as Amazon.com has been attempting to do in book selling, as Enron has done in the energy business, or as $(TC)^2$ hopes to do in the clothing industry.

In industry after industry, it is the revolutionaries—usually newcomers—who are creating the new wealth. Of course, there are examples of incumbents like Coca-Cola and Procter & Gamble that are able to continually reinvent themselves and their industry, but all too often, industry incumbents fail to challenge their own orthodoxies and succumb to unconventional rivals.

The point seems incontestable: *In a discontinuous world, strategy innovation is the key to wealth creation.* Strategy innovation is the capacity to reconceive the existing industry model in ways that create new value for customers, wrong-foot competitors, and produce new wealth for all stakeholders.[1] Strategy innovation is the only way for newcomers to succeed in the face of enormous resource disadvantages, and the only way for incumbents to renew their lease on success. And if one redefines the metric of corporate success as *share of new wealth creation* within some broad opportunity domain—for example, energy, transportation, communication, computing, and so on—the innovation imperative becomes inescapable.

Today, many companies are worrying about EVA (economic value added), but EVA—earning more than your cost of capital—is just the starting point. The goal is not to earn more than your cost of capital; the goal is to capture a disproportionate share of industry wealth creation. There are many semiconductor companies that earn more than their cost of capital, but it is Intel that has created and captured much of the new value in the microprocessor industry during the past decade. Of course Intel earns its cost of capital, but it earns much more than that.

One way of measuring share of wealth creation is to compare a company's current share of the total market capitalization of all firms in a particular competitive domain with its share of market capitalization ten years earlier. For example, at Strategos, we have calculated that in 1988 IBM's share of total market capitalization within the computing and office equipment domain amounted to 45.9 percent. By 1997, this figure had fallen to 14.2 percent. During the same period, DEC's share fell from 10.3 percent to 1.1 percent. Microsoft's share soared from zero to 22.7 percent. If IBM had maintained its share, it would be worth approximately $140 billion more than its current value. When, in the late 1980s and early 1990s, IBM unwittingly surrendered its historic role as the architect of industry transformation, it also surrendered billions of dollars in future wealth creation.

Kmart, a pioneer in discount retailing, saw its share of total wealth within the retailing domain plummet from 8.2 percent in 1988 to 2.8 percent in early 1997. Wal-Mart's share surged from 19.2 percent to 28.1 percent during the same decade. Although IBM, Kmart, and other tarnished leaders may be able to prop up the price of their shares through massive stock repurchases, they are unlikely to create fundamentally new wealth unless they regain their capacity for strategy innovation.

Shareholders love strategy innovation. Again, let's look at the evidence. Between 1985 and 1995, there were fewer than forty companies of the Fortune 1,000 that grew total shareholder returns by more than 25 percent per annum. This is the most exclusive club in U.S. industry. These companies averaged a compounded annual growth in revenues of 25.3 percent during this time frame, while operating margins improved at a rate of just 6.7 percent per year. Given these growth rates, revenues will increase by almost ten times during a decade, while margins will nearly double. So, if the goal is to dramatically improve shareholder returns, where is the leverage going to come from? Clearly, it will come from revenue growth, not from improvement in operating margins. Most companies are simply running out of headroom on margin improvement.

Twenty-five percent revenue growth, less than 7 percent margin growth—that's a ratio of 3.5 to 1. But how many managers, during the past few years, have put 3.5 times the amount of effort into revenue growth that they invested in margin improvement? The obsession of most senior managers has been cost reduction, not growth.

But hold on, I am not suggesting that growth is the antidote to the pain wrought by downsizing and reengineering. There is always a tendency to mistake the scoreboard for the game. Growth is the scoreboard, but it is definitely not the game. Focusing on growth, rather than on the game of strategy innovation, is likely to destroy wealth rather than create it. The reason is simple. There are as many stupid ways to grow as there are to cut: acquisitions that destroy value (Sony and Matsushita in Hollywood), market share battles that lower industry profitability (the airlines' perennial favorite), and megabucks blue-sky projects (think Apple and the Newton) are just a few examples that should illustrate the danger of go-for-broke growth strategies. Needless to say, companies pursuing value-destroying growth won't make it onto any list of star performers.

When we dig deeper, we find that those extraordinarily successful companies that managed 25 percent-plus growth rates in shareholder returns grew by radically changing the basis for competition in their industries. They either invented totally new industries or dramatically reinvented existing ones. This is true for Home Depot, Amgen, Nike, Intel, Compaq, the Gap, and most of the other companies on the superstar list. They all developed nonlinear strategies.

IS STRATEGY IRRELEVANT?

So if strategy innovation is key to creating new wealth, why is "strategy" no longer a "big idea" in most companies? Why does it seem to command so little of top management's time and attention? And why are planners an increasingly endangered species?

It has been at least ten years since strategy was the brightest star in the firmament of management ideas. It was the work of Bruce Henderson and the Boston Consulting Group, as well as the PIMS research project, that pushed strategy's star above the managerial horizon in the mid-1970s—this and General Electric's pioneering use of planning within its "strategic business units." With the publication of Michael Porter's profoundly insightful book, *Competitive Strategy,* in 1980, strategy's star rose farther still.

But by the mid-1980s, the strategy star was beginning to dim, as managers turned their attention to quality, cycle time reduction, and the other operational improvement challenges foisted on them by global competitors and impatient shareholders. Strategy's star was finally eclipsed in 1993, with the publication of Michael Hammer and James Champy's *Reengineering the Corporation*. Big thinking was out, euphemisms for downsizing were in.

Many consulting companies that had been designing corporate futures in the 1980s suddenly found themselves two levels down in their clients' companies, grinding away at the coal face of operational inefficiency or slicing away at layers of bureaucratic flab. Consultants became masters of corporate liposuction. Their revenues were up, but fewer and fewer of their minions could claim to be working on big strategy problems or to be helping their clients invent the future.

The competitive environment faced by companies today is far, far different from that which gave birth to the concept of strategy some thirty years ago. But while the rapidly shifting strategy environment has partially devalued some traditional strategy concepts, such as industry structure analysis, it has also provided the impetus for much new thinking. Indeed, the changing context for strategy has provoked a huge amount of new thinking on the *content* of strategy. The new themes in the strategy world include: foresight, knowledge, competencies, coalitions, networks, extra-market competition, ecosystems, transformation, renewal. All these subjects are intensely contemporary.

So strategists certainly can't be accused of being ignorant of the new competitive realities. But as informed as they may be, impactful they are not. Why? Because managers simply do not know what to do with all the wonderful concepts, frameworks, and buzzwords that tumble from the pages of the *Harvard Business Review,* jam the business aisles of bookstores, and glisten in the slickly edited pages of business magazines.

Strategists may have a lot to say about the context and content of strategy, but in recent years they have had precious little to say about the *conduct* of strategy—that is, the task of strategy making. No one seems to know much about how to create strategy. Managers today know how to embed quality disciplines, how to reengineer processes, and how to reduce cycle times, but they don't know how to foster the development of innovative wealth-creating strategies.

So, while there has been enormous innovation around the content of strategy—management has an ever-expanding list of "strategic" issues to address—there has been no corresponding innovation around the conduct of strategy. Let's face it, the annual strategic planning process in most companies has changed hardly at all during the past decade or two.

It's ironic; never has a capacity for deep strategic thinking been so necessary as in today's turbulent times, and yet never, in the past two decades, has strategy's "share of voice" been lower in the corridors of corporate power. Some argue that the tide is turning. In summer 1996, *Business Week* ran a cover story proclaiming that "strategic planning is back."[2] But the tide has not changed; there are just a few hopeful souls swimming against the flow.

For the tide to turn, the practice of strategy must be reinvented. Sorry, did I say reinvented? Let's not pretend. There's little that's worth reinventing. Surely, we're not going to start with the traditional planning process in our quest to increase the value added of strategy! No, we must start from scratch. The challenge is to invent anew the conduct of strategy in ways that make it intensely important to companies struggling to maintain their vitality in the innovate-or-die environment of the new economy.

WHAT ARE THE SECRETS
OF STRATEGY CREATION?

The strategy industry—all those consultants, business school professors, authors, and planners—has a dirty little secret. Everyone knows a strategy when they see one—be it Microsoft's, Nucor's, or Virgin Atlantic's. We all recognize a great strategy after the fact. In the case study method, professors hold strategies up to be admired, or ridiculed, by preternaturally wise MBA students. Their post hoc explanations of the competitive success and failure that ensue are stunningly beautiful. We are great at pinning down butterflies. But our case libraries and business magazines, with their stories of corporate success and failure, are museums filled with dead specimens. Simply put, we all know strategy as a "thing"—once someone else has bagged it and tagged it. We also understand planning as a "process." But the planning process doesn't produce strategy, it produces plans—a point that Henry Mintzberg has made on more than one occasion.

Anyone who claims to be a strategist should be intensely embarrassed by the fact that the strategy industry doesn't have a theory of strategy creation! It doesn't know where bold, new value-creating strategies come from. There's a gaping hole in the middle of the strategy discipline. No, let me put that differently: There's no foundation to the strategy discipline. I mean, really! Maybe a general manager hungry for a new strategy should eat a fiery vindaloo curry at eleven o'clock at night and hope that, when the inevitable indigestion interrupts his or her slumber, it succeeds in provoking a strategy insight. Gastric upset is at least as likely to produce a strategy insight as attendance at another interminable planning review.

What we need is a deep theory of strategy creation. Think about the amount of progress that has been made during the past fifteen years on the *content* of strategy: competitive rivalry, the resource-based view of the firm, hypercompetition, coalitions, knowledge management, etc. Now ask, how much progress has been made on the practice of strategy? Or compare the rate of innovation during the past twenty years in how companies develop products, manage the supply chain, or build quality into products with the rate of innovation in how they *do* strategy. Case closed.

The questions we must address are these: How can we create a Cambrian explosion of innovative strategies inside the firm? What does it take to invent new strategy "S curves"? To answer these questions, we must have a theory of strategy innovation. Developing such a theory is a grand project. All I can do here is to offer a few starting propositions.

I agree with Mintzberg that strategy "emerges." But I don't believe the emergent nature of strategy creation prevents us from aiding and abetting the process of strategy innovation. We are not helpless. The reason I don't believe we're helpless is because strategy doesn't simply emerge—rather, it is *emergent*, in the same full-bodied sense that life itself is emergent. One of the things we're learning from complexity theorists is that by creating the right set of preconditions, one can provoke emergence. Stuart Kauffman, a pioneer in complexity theory, has suggested that life began with an "autocatalytic" system—a self-reinforcing set of chemical reactions.[3] Whether you agree or disagree, the analogy may be useful. What, we must ask, would catalyze the emergence of new, viable strategies in a successful, though complacent, organization? My guess is that the answer, while perhaps subtle, will nevertheless be easier to come by than the mystery of life.

Once you start thinking of strategy as an emergent phenomenon, you realize that we have often attacked the wrong end of the problem. Strategists and senior executives have too often worked on "the strategy," rather than on the preconditions that could give rise to strategy innovation. In essence, they've been trying to design complex, multicell organisms, rather than trying to understand and create the conditions from which such organisms will emerge.

So we must start with a search for the deep rules of emergence. I think the fundamental challenge is to discover, and make explicit, the linkages among

The rules of strategy emergence → strategy innovation →
industry revolution → the creation of new wealth

Emergence is not a random walk; neither, it has been suggested, was biological evolution. There are many who now believe that if evolution had been an entirely random process, we would still be amoebas. It is asserted that the time frame of life on earth has been too short for blind experimentation to get us to our present stage of biological order. Life evolved toward order, as do all emergent systems.[4]

Two great forces of nature seem to be counterposed. On one hand, there is the general trend toward entropy. When we convert fossil fuel into heat to power our cars or heat our homes, we are turning highly ordered energy—complex carbon molecules—into "disordered" energy—heat, as well as a variety of pollutants. These things can never be "put back together." The second law of thermodynamics suggests that we are sliding inevitably toward chaos. Not only does the law characterize physical systems, it often seems to characterize human systems. Many organizations seem to be affected by a kind of "institutional entropy" in which energy, enthusiasm, and effectiveness slowly dissipate over time.

On the other hand, we see order all around us: the New York Stock Exchange, Toyota's supplier network, a great university, or, most miraculous of all, ourselves. A human being is an almost infinitely more ordered thing, and a much, much more complex system, than a single-celled organism. Order seems to be the second great force in nature. And while entropy may be inevitable in physical systems, there is nothing to suggest that it is inevitable in biological or human systems. Of course, perfect order is never achieved; disruptive change always intervenes. Nevertheless, the impulse for order is everywhere visible in the world around us—with the notable exception of a teenager's bedroom!

While a complex living system, and the order it possesses, is probably not the product of random variation, neither can it be designed top-down. The New York Stock Exchange couldn't be designed top-down. Neither could life on the Internet, nor a human being, nor a complex but internally consistent strategy. What is going on in all these cases is what Kauffman calls "order without careful crafting." "Order *without* careful crafting"—I'd like to suggest that this is the goal of strategizing.

Order arises from simple, deep rules. Craig Reynolds has shown that with three simple rules, one can richly simulate the behavior of a flock of birds in flight.[5] So it's not that there is *no* crafting, *no* design, only that it works at the level of preconditions and broad parameters—not at the level of a detailed design. So while there was a simple architecture underlying the Internet, no one could have envisioned all the rich permutations of Net-based life that would emerge in the new on-line biosphere. Likewise, although there was a simple, overarching intent to the U.S. space program in the 1960s, the strategies for getting a human to the moon were deeply emergent.

Like all forms of complexity, strategy is poised on the border between perfect order and total chaos, between absolute efficiency and blind experimentation, between autocracy and complete *ad hocracy*. Now if you believe even some of this, it has profound implications for how we think about strategy—and where we should focus our attention if the goal is to develop a capacity for strategy innovation deep within organizations. Let me illustrate with this old story of how humans acquired a taste for cooked meat. One day, a wild pig wandered into a hut; lightning struck the hut; the hut burned down; a human poked through the charred remains, touched the pig, sucked on a finger, and voila! Yummy (at least, for carnivores).

Business school researchers from the "process school" of strategy, along with business journalists, have expended much effort in studying the "accidents" of strategy making. Process researchers pick through the ashes: "So this is how an idea fights its way up through a sclerotic organization over months or years and finally succeeds in changing the company's strategy." "Wow, what a great story!" remarks the journalist. But maybe we could do something to make the path from insight to strategy less arduous. Maybe we could dramatically improve the odds of an insight occurring and then being translated into purposeful action. Maybe those who study the complicated, emergent nature of strategy creation can be more than mere reporters.

On the other hand, researchers in the "content school" (Michael Porter, first and foremost) have given all would-be pig eaters a set of elaborate criteria to determine whether or not they really have a pig, versus something much less palatable. "Will this particular strategy make money?" is the question here. Strategy professors and consultants have produced elaborate guides to pig spotting but typically know little about pig farming and much less about the culinary arts required to turn that pig into *terrine de rillettes*. Industrial economists and traditional consultants are not strategy chefs.

For their part, planners assure everyone that with the right incantations you can get lightning to strike twice in the same place. Ultimately, after much trial and error, humankind discovered the principles of cooking and the oven. Later came the principles of animal husbandry. Human beings still cannot make a pig out of nothing— only a pig can make a pig—but they have learned how to construct a system that dramatically increases the probability of getting pork on the plate on any given night of the week.

Let me ask a question of those who've ever sat through a business school case study: Have you ever gotten halfway through a brilliant exposition of a company's strategy and thought to yourself, "Did they really have this thing figured out ahead of time? Isn't this just luck? Isn't this 20/20 hindsight? What about all the failures?" Sure, you have. These impertinent questions lie at the heart of our search for a theory of strategy creation. Is a great strategy luck, or is it foresight? Of course, the answer is that it is both. Circumstance, cognition, data, and desire converge, and a strategy insight is born. The fact that strategy has a significant element of serendipity to it shouldn't cause us to despair. The alternatives are not the "big brain" design school of strategy, nor the "muddle along" process school. The question is, how can we increase the odds that new wealth-creating strategies emerge? How can we make serendipity happen? How can we prompt emergence?

HOW DOES STRATEGY EMERGE?

The most fundamental insight of complexity theory is that "complex behavior need not have complex roots," as Christopher Langton has so succinctly put it.[6] So what are the simple roots of strategy creation? My experience, and that of my colleagues at Strategos, in helping companies improve their capacity for strategizing suggests that there are five preconditions for the emergence of strategy. (Vindaloo curry is not on the list.)

1. *New voices.* Bringing new "genetic material" into the strategy process always serves to illuminate unconventional strategies. Top management must give up its monopoly on strategy creation, and previously underrepresented constituencies must be given a larger share of voice in the strategy creation process. Specifically, I believe that young people, newcomers, and those at the geographic periphery of the organization deserve a larger share of voice. It is in these constituencies where diversity lurks. So strategy creation must be a pluralistic process, a deeply participative undertaking.

2. *New conversations.* Creating a dialogue about strategy that cuts across all the usual organizational and industry boundaries substantially increases the odds that new strategy insights will emerge. All too often, in large organizations, conversations become hardwired over time, with the same people talking to the same people about the same issues year after year. After a while, individuals have little left to learn from each other. Opportunities for new insights are created when one juxtaposes previously isolated knowledge in new ways.

3. *New passions.* Unleashing the deep sense of discovery that resides in almost every human being, and focusing that sense of discovery on the search for new wealth-creating strategies, is another prerequisite. I believe the widespread assumption that individuals are against change is flat wrong. People are against change when it doesn't offer the prospect of new opportunity. There is much talk

today about return on investment, but I like to think in terms of return on emotional investment. Individuals will not invest emotionally in a firm and its success unless they believe they will get a return on that investment. All my experience suggests that individuals will eagerly embrace change when given the chance to have a share of voice in inventing the future of their company. They will invest when there's a chance to create a unique and exciting future in which they can share.

4. *New perspectives.* New conceptual lenses that allow individuals to reconceive their industry, their company's capabilities, customer needs, and so on substantially aid the process of strategy innovation. To increase the probability of strategy innovation, managers must become the merchants of new perspective. They must search constantly for new lenses that help companies reconceive themselves, their customers, their competitors, and thereby their opportunities.

5. *New experiments.* Launching a series of small, risk-avoiding experiments in the market serves to maximize a company's rate of learning about just which new strategies will work and which won't. The insights that come from a broad-based strategy dialogue will never be perfect. While much traditional analysis can be done to refine those insights into viable strategies, there is much that can be learned only in the marketplace.

So where does this leave us? We should spend less time working on strategy as a "thing" and more time working to understand the preconditions that give rise to the "thing." Executives, consultants, and business school professors must rebalance the attention given to context, content, and conduct in favor of conduct.

In focusing on the conduct of strategy, not only are we trying to *discover* something—the hidden properties of strategy emergence—we are also trying to *invent* something. Like those long-ago Neanderthals trying to figure out the principles of cooking ("Why can't we have pork every night, rather than only after electrical storms?"), we need to invent an oven—*a strategy oven.*

In our quest for the strategy oven, our most valuable insights will probably come from far beyond the traditional strategy disciplines. Personally, I believe we will discover the strategy oven at the juncture of concepts like emergence, self-organization, cognition, and organizational learning. Science is closing in on the deep secrets of life. And we, as strategists, are finally beginning to close in on the deep secrets of corporate vitality.

WORDS TO THE WISE

For those of you who, like me, have found employment within the strategy industry, I have a final comment.

To Professors. If you're a strategy professor and you want to have a role in inventing the strategy oven, you'd better roll up your sleeves and get involved in the world of practice. You can no longer be a mere observer. You must create laboratories, inside real institutions, where you can study the phenomenon of emergence. Like particle physicists, strategy researchers must develop their hypotheses, build their particle accelerators, and then see if their musings about the deep structures of strategy creation really are valid. We must do more than merely study strategy emergence; we must become active experimenters in the realm of strategy creation.

I have long admired Peter Senge's approach to action research with the MIT Center for Organizational Learning. Through Senge's work, thousands of "application labs" (my term, not his) have been built in companies around the world. From these laboratories, learning about learning emerges. Where is the strategy field's equivalent set of social experiments? I'm not suggesting that strategy professors become consultants. I am suggesting that they stop being dilettantes.

To Consultants. If you're a traditional strategy consultant, watch out. If I'm a senior executive, why should I pay your twenty-nine-year-old to teach me about my industry? Wouldn't it be better to get my own twenty-nine-year-olds, and everybody else in my company, to help teach me about the future? So stop trying to create dependency and start trying to embed a deep capability for strategy innovation. Work to put yourselves out of business!

To Planners. Unless you get involved in the quest for the deep secrets of strategy emergence, the best you can hope for is honorable mention in a Dilbert cartoon.

NOTES

1. I first introduced this concept in "Strategy as Revolution," *Harvard Business Review,* July-August 1996, 74, 69–82.
2. "Strategic Planning," *Business Week,* 26 August 1996, pp. 46–52.
3. S. Kauffman, *At Home in the Universe: The Search for the Laws of Self-Organization and Complexity* (New York: Oxford University Press, 1995).
4. I will leave the terribly profound question of where the "rules of order" come from to others. My personal belief, though, is that since the rules of order drive the system, they cannot emanate from within the system.
5. M. M. Waldrop, *Complexity: The Emerging Science at the Edge of Order and Chaos* (New York: Simon & Schuster, 1992), pp. 241, 242.
6. C. Langton, in Waldrop (1992), p. 279.

CHAPTER NINE

Strategy, Value Innovation, and the Knowledge Economy

W. CHAN KIM
RENÉE MAUBORGNE

For the past twenty years, competition has occupied the center of strategic thinking. Indeed, one hardly speaks of strategy without drawing on the vocabulary of competition—competitive strategy, competitive benchmarking, competitive advantages, outperforming the competition. In fact, most strategic prescriptions merely redefine the ways companies build advantages over the competition. This has been the strategic objective of many firms and, in itself, nothing is wrong with this objective. After all, a company needs some advantages over the competition to sustain itself in the marketplace. When asked to build competitive advantage, however, managers typically assess what competitors do and strive to do it better. Their strategic thinking thus regresses toward the competition. After expending tremendous effort, companies often achieve no more than incremental improvement—imitation, not innovation.[1]

Consider what happened in the microwave oven and VCR industries. As a result of competitive benchmarking, product offerings were nearly mirror images of each other and, from the customer's perspective, they were overdesigned and overpriced. Most buyers had no use for most of the features and found them confusing and irritating. These companies may have outdone one another, but they missed an opportunity to capture the mass market by offering microwaves and VCRs that were easy to use at accessible prices.

Another classic example is the battle of IBM versus Compaq in the PC market. In 1983, when Compaq launched its IBM-compatible machines with technologically superb quality at a 15 percent lower price than IBM's, it rapidly won the mass of PC buyers. Once roused by Compaq's success, IBM started a race to beat Compaq; Compaq likewise focused on beating IBM. Trying to outperform one another in sophisticated feature enhancements, neither company foresaw the emergence of the low-end PC market in which user-friendliness and low price—not the latest technology—were keys to success. Both companies created a line of overly designed and overpriced PCs, and both companies missed the emerging low-end market. When IBM walked off the cliff in the late 1980s, Compaq was following closely.

These cases illustrate that strategy driven by the competition usually has three latent, unintended effects:[2]

▼ *Imitative, not innovative, approaches to the market.* Companies often accept what competitors are doing and simply strive to do it better.
▼ *Companies act reactively.* Time and talent are unconsciously absorbed in responding to daily competitive moves, rather than creating growth opportunities.
▼ *A company's understanding of emerging mass markets and changing customer demands becomes hazy.*

Over the past decade, we have studied companies of sustained high growth and profits vis-à-vis their less successful competitors. Regardless of size, years of operation, industry conditions, and country of origin, the strategy these companies pursue is what we call *value innovation.*[3] Value innovation is quite different from building layers of competitive advantages and is not about striving to outperform the competition. Nor is value innovation about segmenting the market and accommodating customers' individual needs and differences. Value innovation makes the competition irrelevant by offering fundamentally new and superior buyer value in existing markets and by enabling a quantum leap in buyer value to create new markets. (For details of our research process, see box, "Researching the Roots of Profitable Growth.")

Take, for example, Callaway Golf, the U.S. golf club manufacturer, which in 1991 launched its "Big Bertha" golf club. The product rapidly rose to dominate the market, wresting market share from its rivals and expanding the total golf club market. Despite intense competition, Callaway did not focus on its competitors. Rival golf clubs looked alike and featured sophisticated enhancements, a result of attentive benchmarking of the competitors' products. In the meantime, Callaway pondered the "country club" markets of golf and tennis. Many people play tennis because they find the task of hitting a little golf ball with a little golf club head too daunting. Recognizing a business opportunity, Callaway made a golf club with a larger head that made playing golf less difficult and more fun. The result: Not only were new players drawn into the market, but Callaway captured an overwhelming share of existing players as well.

Similar examples of value innovation arise in diverse industries. Consider Enron in energy, CNN in news broadcasting, Wal-Mart in discount retailing, Compaq in computers (after its turnaround), Kinepolis in cinema, IKEA in home products retail, Charles Schwab & Co. in investment and brokerage account management, Home Depot in home improvement retail, SAP in business application software, Barnes & Noble in book retailing, Southwest Airlines in short-haul air travel, and others. Their steady growth and high profits are not a consequence of daring young organizational members, being a small entrepreneurial start-up, being in attractive industries, or making big commitments in the latest technology. Instead, the superperforming companies that we

Researching the Roots of Profitable Growth

Almost a decade ago, we researched the growth problems of a particular company. Our interviews with the company's managers revealed a typical story. They were suffering from bad industry conditions—stagnant growth, overcapacity, and intense competition. They could do little about these factors, so they were trying to create some advantages over the competition by improving their products, services, and cost structure. Nevertheless, their performance was not improving greatly because the competition was also moving forward.

Not long after, we studied another company with a record of sustained profitable growth despite bad industry conditions. Managers of this company told us a different story. To them, bad industry conditions were excuses for tired executives. The competition was not the reference point for their strategy because they were striving to go far beyond the competition. They were searching for new ideas that could grab the market by providing exceptional value for customers.

As we pondered these two companies, we became interested in further developing and testing our initial observations on firm growth. Since a company's profits must support its growth to be sustainable, we targeted companies with sustained high growth in both revenues and profits. Through our professional and personal network, we systematically identified national and global growth champions from many industries and built strategic, organizational, and performance profiles of them. During this process, we also identified their less successful competitors. We targeted companies in more than thirty industries; their diversity includes hotel, cinema, retailing, airline, energy, computer, broadcasting, home construction, automobile, and steel manufacturing. We then interviewed managers from profitable high-growth companies and those from their less successful competitors. We also spoke with investment and private research group analysts, who track these companies regularly, to gain further insight into their strategic approaches.

We first examined whether industry or corporate characteristics could explain the distinction between these two groups. Are certain industry or corporate characteristics common to companies with high profitable growth, distinguishing them from their less successful competitors? We failed to find any systematic differences. Robust profitable growth was achieved by small and large companies, by young and old managers, by companies in high- and low-growth industries, by new entrants and established incumbents, by private and public companies, and by companies of diverse national origins.

Next, we decided to explore our original insights on possible divergent approaches to strategy. We analyzed the content of managers' remarks about their strategic approach to the market. We analyzed comments from interviews, speeches to analysts or shareholders, and statements gleaned from print media to find examples of implicit and explicit strategic thinking. To further validate our analyses, major business launches (as manifestations of strategic thinking) were reviewed for consistency with management statements and real actions in the marketplace. As we searched for convergence within each group and divergence across the two groups, we found that the focus of corporate strategy differed. Less successful companies were racing to beat the competition; highly successful companies did not use the competition as their strategic reference. Rather than building advantages over their competitors, companies with high profitable growth aimed to make competition irrelevant by providing buyers with a quantum leap in value. We have come to call their way of strategic thinking *value innovation*.

studied are united in their pursuit of innovation outside a conventional context. That is, they do not pursue innovation as technology but as value. The companies cited above created quantum leaps in some aspect of value; many have nothing to do with new technology. This is why we call these companies value innovators.[4]

Many high achievers excel despite bad industry conditions. Instead of falling victim to industry conditions, these value innovators focus on creating opportunities in their fields. They ask, "How can we offer buyers greater value that will result in soaring profitable growth irrespective of industry or competitive conditions?" Because they question everything about a particular industry and their competitors, they explore a far wider range of strategic options than other companies. This broadens their creative scope, allowing them to find opportunities where other companies can see only constraints imposed by external conditions.[5]

To achieve sustained profitable growth, companies must break out of the competitive and imitative trap. Rather than striving to match or outperform the competition, companies must cultivate value innovation. Emphasis on value places the buyer, not the competition, at the center of strategic thinking; emphasis on innovation pushes managers to go beyond incremental improvements to totally new ways of doing things.

Consider a recent study of the profitable growth consequences of more than a hundred new business launches.[6] We found that while 86 percent of these business launches were "me too" businesses or businesses with value improvements over the competition, they generated only 62 percent of total revenues and 39 percent of total profits. In contrast, the remaining 14 percent of the business launches—those that were value innovations—generated 38 percent of total revenues and a whopping 61 percent of total profits. The performance of value innovators far exceeds that of companies focusing on matching or beating their competitors. Companies pursuing value innovation are on the rise. Value innovation fuels small companies to grow profitably and regenerates the fortunes of big companies.

SHIFTING THE BASIS OF STRATEGY

Why has competition been the key building block of strategy in theory and practice? Think of the competitive penetration of Japanese companies into U.S. industries that awakened U.S. companies to the reality of global competition. After a period of denial, U.S. companies vigorously responded, making competition the centerpiece of their strategic thinking. Concurrently, under the strong influence of old economics—especially in the form of industrial organization—academics were comfortable with competition-based strategy, too.[7] In neoclassical economics, firms and innovations are treated as "black boxes." What firms do is determined by market conditions because market conditions are assumed to be beyond the influence of individual companies.[8] In such a setting, innovations are random events exogenous to firms. If market conditions and innovations are treated as given sets of the external environment, a firm strategically chooses a distinctive cost or differentiation position that best fits with its internal systems and capabilities to counter the competition in that particular environment. In such a situation, innovation is not endogenous to its system, so cost and product performance are seen as trade-offs.

Competition-based strategy, however, has waning power in today's economy, in which, in many industries, supply exceeds demand. Competing for a share of contracting markets is a marginal and *"second-best"* strategy. Such a zero-sum strategy is cutthroat and does not create new wealth. A *"first-best"* strategy in today's economy stimulates the demand side of the economy. It expands existing markets and creates new markets.[9] Such a non-zero-sum strategy generates new wealth and has high payoffs. In regard to profitable growth, creating shareholder value, and generating new jobs and wealth for society, companies pursuing the first-best strategy through value innovation far outperform companies following the second-best strategy. In our studies, we see this happening in the business world today.

During the past two decades, for example, we have seen a rapid change in the Fortune 500 list, both in rankings and those who qualify for the list; some 60 percent have disappeared from the list. Value innovators are now among the most rapidly growing companies. In less than forty years, a value innovator like Wal-Mart, for example, has become the world's eighth largest company in revenues and the world's second largest employer (825,000 people).

Shareholder value and wealth created by value innovators are equally compelling. The market value of SAP, for example, exceeds that of 150-year-old Siemens; Microsoft's market value towers over the combined values of General Motors and Ford. In 1995, with $6 billion in revenues and $7 billion in assets, the market value of Microsoft was 1.5 times that of GM with $168 billion in revenues and $217 billion in assets.

Why do value innovators such as SAP have such high market valuations despite their much smaller physical and fiscal assets? What do investors value in these companies that is not reflected on their balance sheets? As far as the market is concerned, their high stock of *knowledge* portends tremendous wealth-creating potential despite their much smaller sizes. In creating wealth, knowledge is increasingly taking a front seat to the traditional factors of production, that is, physical and fiscal assets.[10] The gap between a company's market value and its tangible asset value is widening; the key variable explaining this gap is a firm's stock of knowledge. Unlike land, labor, and capital—the economist's traditional, finite factors of production—knowledge and ideas are infinite economic goods that can generate increasing returns through their systematic use, as SAP and Nintendo prove.

What we observe in the real world of business is consistent with the theory of new economics. New economics proposes endogenous growth theory, in which growth and innovation come from within a system.[11] While its unit of analysis is primarily the nation-state, the principal argument in endogenous growth theory is applicable to the firm. The theory informs us of the arrival of the knowledge economy and argues that innovations are no longer exogenous and can be created with the ideas and knowledge within a system.

In a world in which industry conditions no longer dictate corporate well-being because companies can transcend these conditions through the systematic pursuit of innovation, a firm need not compete for a share of given demand—it can create new demand. Moreover, low cost and differentiation do not have to be an either-or choice because innovation can be a sustainable strategy.[12] In fact, to innovate in this knowledge economy, companies employing the first best strategy often pursue low cost and differentiation simultaneously. Indeed, our field observations support the prediction of new growth theory. Rising companies, small or large, that have achieved sustained high growth and profits are those that have pursued value innovation. Their strategic focus was not on outcompeting within given industry conditions, but on creating fundamentally new and superior value, thereby making their competitors irrelevant. They went beyond competing in existing markets to expanding the demand side of the economy.

VALUE AND INNOVATION

Value innovation places equal emphasis on *value* and *innovation*. Value without innovation tends to focus on improving the buyer's net benefit or value creation on an incremental scale. Innovation without value can be too strategic or wild (by betting on a company's long-term industry foresight) or too technology-driven or futuristic (shooting far beyond what buyers are ready to accept). Value innovation anchors innovation with buyer value. Hence, value innovation is not the same as *value creation*. Value creation as a concept of strategy is too broad because no boundary condition specifies the direction a company should follow to bring about successful strategic actions. Value creation on an incremental scale, for example, still creates some value but is not sufficient for high performance.

Value innovation also differs from *technology innovation*. As previously mentioned, technology innovation is not a requisite for value innovation; value innovation can occur with or without new technology. Moreover, technology innovation does not necessarily produce value innovation. For example, although Ampex innovated video recording technology in the 1950s, the company failed to convert this new technology into a value innovation cheap enough for mass buyers. As a result, later value innovators, such as Sony and JVC, profited greatly by unlocking the mass market at almost 1 percent of Ampex's initial price. Value innovators are not necessarily first entrants to their markets in technological terms. In this sense, they are not necessarily technology pioneers, but they are value pioneers.

Value innovation links innovation to what the mass of buyers value. To value innovate, companies must ask two questions: (1) Are we offering customers radically superior value? (2) Is our price level accessible to the mass of buyers in our target market? High-growth companies understand that offering a new and superior product or service at a price that most buyers cannot afford is like laying an egg that other companies will hatch. (See Figure 9.1 for the relationships among value creation, value innovation, and technology innovation.)

Although technology innovators such as Ampex failed to capture profits for themselves, their technological discoveries often benefited the overall economy because later value innovators eventually used these technological discoveries successfully. In light of this, the distinction between technology innovation and value innovation may not be relevant to economists whose main concern is a theory of growth at the macro level. Such a distinction, however, is important to those whose interest is in building a theory of firm growth. Who will capture the profit is a pertinent and critical issue to individual firms.

Many innovation and creativity studies have focused on improving or redefining solutions to problems with technology as a central component of the discussions. Researchers attempted to explain how an organization develops technological solutions to customers' problems.[13] Because technologies are seen as solutions to problems, most innovation studies have been solution driven.[14]

Unlike technology innovation, value innovation focuses on redefining the problems themselves. This is how value innovation makes the competition irrelevant. By redefining the problem an industry focuses on, a value innovator shifts the performance criteria that matter to customers. This creates new market space. To redefine customers' problems, market insights are needed to discover existing but "hidden" demand or to create totally new demand. Value innovation is a consequence of such market insights gained from creative strategic thinking.[15]

Callaway Golf, for example, created its Big Bertha golf club after redefining the consumer's need, that is, a desire to hit the ball more easily. Rivals focused on offering better solutions to hitting the ball farther—some were cost leaders and some were differentiators in solving this particular problem. By addressing a redefined problem, Big Bertha expanded the total market by attracting new customers who had not previously played golf. The company gained this market insight by thinking in terms of alternative industries—golf versus tennis—as opposed to thinking in terms of its industry competitors. Its main strategic question was why people choose tennis over golf in the country club market; Callaway Golf did not concentrate on how to outperform other golf club manufacturers by offering a better solution to the conventional goal of hitting the ball farther.

The concept of value innovation is consistent with the Schumpeterian notion of "creative destruction" in the sense that it is about

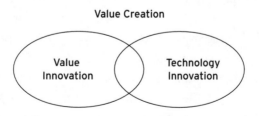

Figure 9.1. Relationships Among Value Creation, Value Innovation, and Technology Innovation.

creating fundamentally new and superior value, hence making existing things and ways of doing things irrelevant.[16] But whereas the entrepreneur is the major input in creating Schumpeterian innovation, knowledge and ideas are the major inputs for value innovation. Whether an executive or a factory worker, anyone can have a good idea; value innovation can occur in any organization and at any time in a sustainable manner with the proper process. In contrast, the realization of Schumpeterian innovation is subject to the availability of entrepreneurs, who are in short supply. Hence, while an understanding of entrepreneurship and the entrepreneur as an economic hero are critical to Schumpeterian innovation, it is not with value innovation.

Unlike the old economics, in which monopoly power is the enemy of economic development, both new growth theory and Schumpeter argue for the importance of the innovators' monopoly profits to bolster future discovery that stimulates economic growth.[17] They argue that monopolies must be tolerated to a degree. Value innovators in the new knowledge economy, however, act quite differently from the typical monopolists portrayed in economics.

MARKET DYNAMICS OF VALUE INNOVATION

Consider Enron, the Houston-based energy company. Enron's roots are traceable to one of the oldest, capital-intensive commodity industries in the world—gas and utilities. Yet for three consecutive years, *Fortune* has ranked Enron the most innovative company in the United States. During the past fifteen years, Enron has struck upon repeated value innovations, thereby lowering the cost of gas and electricity to customers by as much as 40 percent to 50 percent. Enron did so while dramatically reducing its own cost structure by, for example, creating the first national spot market for gas in which commodity swaps, future contracts, and other complex derivatives effectively stripped the risk and volatility out of gas prices. Today,

Enron has as many traders, analysts, and scientists—including a rocket scientist from the former Soviet Union—employed at Enron's headquarters as gas and pipeline personnel. Enron exemplifies the transition from the production to the knowledge economy. The proportion and value of knowledge to land, labor, and capital—even in this most basic industry—are rising dramatically. Think also of IKEA in furniture, Starbucks in coffee, Wal-Mart in discount retail, or Borders and Barnes & Noble in bookstores—all are offering buyers fundamentally new and superior value in traditional businesses through innovative ideas and knowledge.

The transition from a production to a knowledge economy has two new consequences. First, it creates the potential for increasing returns.[18] This is easy to understand in the software industry in which, for example, producing the first copy of the Windows 95 operating system cost Microsoft millions, whereas subsequent copies involved no more than the near trivial cost of a diskette. In capital-intensive businesses such as Enron's, after paying the fixed cost of developing sophisticated risk management financial tools, the company can apply the tools to infinite transactions at insignificant marginal cost. Second, it creates the potential for free-riding. This relates to the nonrival and partially excludable nature of knowledge, a discussion of which follows.[19]

The use of a *rival good* by one firm precludes its use by another. So, for example, Nobel Prize-winning scientists employed by IBM cannot simultaneously be employed by another company. Nor can scrap steel consumed by Nucor be simultaneously consumed for production by other minimill steel makers. In contrast, the use of a *nonrival good* by one firm does not limit its use by another. Ideas fall into this category. So, for example, when Virgin Atlantic Airways launched its "Upper Class" value innovation—a new concept in business class travel that essentially combined the huge seats and leg room of traditional first class with the price of business class tickets—other airlines could apply this idea to their own business class service without limiting Virgin's ability to use it.

This makes competitive imitation not only possible but less costly, as the cost and risk of developing the innovative idea is borne by the value innovator, not the follower. This challenge is exacerbated when the notion of *excludability* is considered.

Excludability is a function of both the nature of the good and the legal system. A good is excludable if the company can prevent others from using it due, for example, to limited access or patent protection. So, for example, Intel can exclude other microprocessor chipmakers from using its manufacturing facilities through property ownership laws. Starbucks Coffee can prevent coffee chain start-ups from using its coffee beans by refusing to sell to would-be copycats, that is, by strategically limiting access. However, Starbucks cannot exclude others from walking into any store, studying its layout, atmosphere, and product range, and mimicking the chic coffee bar concept in which exotic coffee is sold by the cup in elite locations. The highest value-added element of Starbucks's formula is not excludable. Once ideas are "out there," knowledge naturally spills over to other firms. This lack of excludability reinforces the risk of free-riding.

Of course, were it possible to get a patent and formal legal protection for innovative ideas, the risk of free-riding would be considerably lower. Pharmaceutical companies, for example, have long enjoyed the benefit of formal patent protection to prevent the free-riding of other drug companies on their scientific discoveries for a specified time. But how do you patent a radically superior concept for a coffee store such as Starbucks, which has tremendous value but in itself consists of no new technological discoveries? It is the arrangement of the items that adds fundamentally new value, that is, the way they are combined, not the items themselves. While collectively this represents a new, creative, and explosive concept, little about the Starbucks's concept is scientifically new and, hence, patentable and excludable. Starbucks, like The Body Shop, Home Depot, Schwab, Virgin Atlantic Airways, Amazon.com, Borders, and Barnes & Noble, is not about patentable technology innovation, but value innovation.

Even value innovations in software run the risk of free-riding. Although computer software companies can obtain copyrights to prohibit others from copying program code, the look, feel, and functionality of software is not patentable.[20] Thus, any successful program can be copied. Competing firms need only write their own code; the software functionality, the structure of the internal programming components, and the software's look and feel can be imitated, as Netscape painfully learned. The same can be said for Wal-Mart's valuable inventory replenishment system. In other words, the ideas that contain the real value are usually not excludable or are only partially so.

The question is how best to maximize profits from value innovation ideas that have the potential for both increasing returns and free-riding. Should value innovators follow the conventional practice of technology innovators: set high prices, limit access, initially engage in price skimming to earn a premium on the innovation, and only later focus on lowering price and costs to retain market share and discourage imitators?

In a world of nonrival and nonexcludable goods that are imbued with the potential of economies of scale, learning, and increasing returns, the importance of volume, price, and cost grows in unprecedented ways. From the outset, the aim is to capture the mass of buyers and expand the size of the market by offering radically superior value at price points accessible to a mass market. This means that value innovators should not follow conventional practices for maximizing profits. First, by charging a high premium and restricting supply, unmet demand combined with a high price ceiling is a huge incentive for others to free-ride to undercut the price of the innovator and capture the market. Second, high prices and limited volume that create an image of exclusivity and uniqueness do not allow the innovator to exploit either economies of scale and learning or the potential for increasing returns. This undermines the innate profit advantage of knowledge-intensive goods.

In our studies, we observed successful value innovators using a distinctly different market approach from that of conventional monopolists. Their approach has two components:

▼ *Strategic pricing for demand creation.* Strategic pricing leads to high volume and rapidly establishes a powerful brand reputation.
▼ *Target costing for profit creation.* Target costing leads to attractive profit margins and a cost structure that is hard for potential followers to match.

Consider how Nicholas Hayek, the chairman of SMH, used this new market approach with the launch of the Swatch, a value innovation that revived the Swiss watch industry. The Swatch transformed the wristwatch from a functional item used to tell time to a mass-market fashion accessory. The company innovated the concept of a watch by combining mechanical punctuality with creative designs that conveyed a powerful emotional message.

To profit from this value innovation, Hayek set up a project team to determine the strategic price for the Swatch. At the time, cheap (about $75), high-precision quartz watches from Japan and Hong Kong were capturing the mass market. To entice these customers and to quickly build a strong brand name, SMH aggressively set the Swatch's price at $40, a price at which customers could buy several Swatches as fashion accessories. The low price left no profit margin for Japanese or Hong Kong-based companies to copy Swatch and undercut its price. Directed to sell the Swatch for that price and not a penny more, the SMH project team had worked backwards to arrive at the target cost, which involved determining the margin SMH needed to support marketing and services. On this basis, the project team then devised a suitable production system. SMH was compelled to innovate the design of the Swatch's mechanics, production, and assembly, which produced an unbeatable cost structure in the worldwide watch industry.

How can a value innovator like Swatch sustain its profitable growth over time? Value innovation radically increases the appeal of a good, shifting the demand curve from D1 to D2 (see Figure 9.2). However, recognizing the nonrival and only partial excludable nature of its innovative good, the value innovator strategically prices the product from the outset to capture the mass of buyers in the expanded market, in the case of Swatch shifting the price from P1 to P2. This increases the quantity sold from Q1 to Q2 and builds strong brand recognition for unprecedented value. The value innovator, however, engages in target costing to simultaneously reduce the long-run average cost curve from LRAC1 to LRAC2 to expand its ability to profit and to discourage free-riding and imitation.

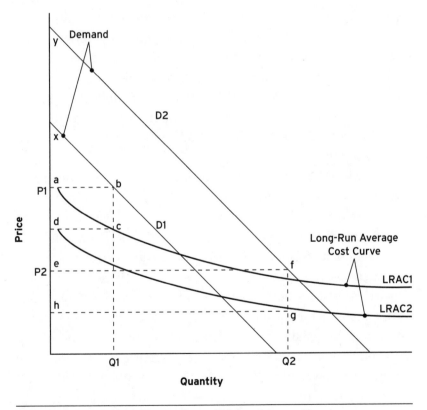

Figure 9.2. Market Dynamics of Value Innovation.

Hence, buyers receive a quantum leap in value, shifting the consumer surplus from *axb* to *eyf*. And the value innovator earns a leap in profit and growth, shifting the profit zone from *abcd* to *efgh*. The rapid brand recognition built by the value innovator as a result of the unprecedented value offered in the marketplace combined with the simultaneous drive to lower costs makes the competition nearly irrelevant and hard to catch up with as economies of scale, learning, and increasing returns kick in. Hence the emergence of the new phenomena such as category killers and winner-take-most markets where companies earn dominant positions while customers simultaneously come out big winners.

While value innovators do not always exercise low strategic pricing as Swatch did, attracting a mass of buyers is, in many respects, at odds with the tactics of conventional monopolists.[21] In the production economy, firms with dominant market positions have been associated with two social welfare loss activities. First, to maximize their profits, companies set high prices, which prohibited the mass of customers who, though desiring the product, could not afford it. Second, lacking viable competition, firms with monopolistic positions did not focus on efficiency and hence consumed more of society's resources.

However, in the knowledge economy, innovative companies engage less in the exorbitant price skimming common in the production economy. The focus shifts from restricting output at a high price to creating new aggregate demand through a leap in value and introduction at an accessible price. This creates a strong incentive to reduce costs to the lowest possible level. Perhaps this explains why the antitrust actions against Microsoft proceed slowly despite its dominant market position. Microsoft is not acting as a monopolist in the traditional sense; customers are winning, and innovation in its industry has not slowed but is accelerating as others strive to capture the powerful profitable growth consequences of being a market leader in the knowledge economy.

SHIFTING STRATEGY FOCUS

The underlying foundation of business is shifting in unprecedented ways. Consider the emergence of the Internet, the rise of multimedia, the speed of globalization, and the advent of the euro. The rate of change seems to increase as new knowledge, idea creation, and global diffusion accelerate. This new reality requires new strategic responses. Companies that continue to focus on the competition, on leveraging and extending their current capabilities, and on retaining and extending their existing customers are off the mark.[22] As has been argued, the competition provides a sticky starting point for strategic thinking. A focus on matching and beating the competition leads to reactive, incremental, and often imitative strategic moves—not what is needed in a knowledge economy. The irony of competition is this: Intense competition makes innovation indispensable, but an obsessive focus on the competition makes innovation difficult to attain.

At the same time, thinking beyond a company's boundaries is necessary. Since the field of strategy emerged, its focus has been on building and leveraging a company's strengths. The basic argument here is that firms possess unique resources, reputation, and skills—capabilities that should be nurtured and leveraged to guide their strategic decisions. Extended and refined over time, this basic argument persists in theory and practice. An inwardly driven focus on capabilities within a company, however, significantly limits a company's opportunity horizon and introduces resistance to change if the market is evolving away from a company's forte.[23] As we enter an era of the modular society in which networks become more prevalent, companies can increasingly pursue strategic relations with other firms to capture emerging opportunities on the basis of their respective strengths.

The central quest of a value innovator's strategic mindset is to create radically new and superior value. The conventional focus on retaining and better satisfying existing customers tends to promote hesitancy to challenge the status quo for fear of losing or dissatisfying existing customers.[24] However, companies must focus on capturing the mass of buyers, even if that means losing some existing customers. Value innovators monitor existing customers but, more importantly, follow noncustomers closely because they provide deep insights into trends and changes.

After radically superior value is discovered, value innovators deploy capabilities that exist both inside and outside their companies to actualize an opportunity. Value innovators often have a network of partners that provide complementary assets, capabilities, products, and services.

The strategic responses of value innovators illustrate how the three basic building blocks of strategy—competition, customers, and corporate capabilities—must shift to thrive in this rapidly changing knowledge economy (see Figure 9.3).

SMH's innovative Swatch idea did not originate with the competition. The company did not have a core competency in mass-market watches, in plastic molding, or in contemporary design. At the time of the Swatch introduction, the young mass-market customers were not SMH customers. What did SMH have in its favor? Hayek had a relentless desire to offer buyers radically superior value, an idea (to create a watch exuding *joie de vivre*), and the insight to create, buy, or borrow the expertise needed to produce the watches. Likewise, SAP possessed no core competencies or distinctive resources. At the time of its founding more than twenty-five years ago, SAP did not own computers to use in writing its software. Yet SAP not only created its first value innovation, R/2 business application software for the mainframe environment, but repeatedly launched value innovations, including R/3, client-server business application software. As Hasso Plattner, SAP cofounder, put it: "The only resource we had was our brains and the idea of how to build powerful software." Later SAP leveraged the resources and capabilities of others, including Andersen Consulting, which served as SAP's marketing and implementation arm; Oracle, which supplied the necessary sophisticated

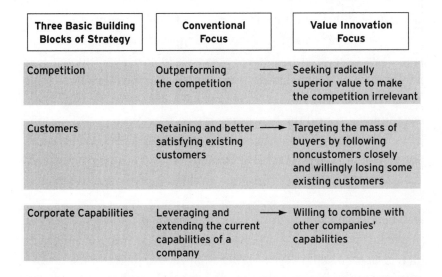

Three Basic Building Blocks of Strategy	Conventional Focus	Value Innovation Focus
Competition	Outperforming the competition ⟶	Seeking radically superior value to make the competition irrelevant
Customers	Retaining and better satisfying existing customers ⟶	Targeting the mass of buyers by following noncustomers closely and willingly losing some existing customers
Corporate Capabilities	Leveraging and extending the current capabilities of a company ⟶	Willing to combine with other companies' capabilities

Figure 9.3. Shifting Strategy Focus.

database; and IBM, which supplied hardware. SAP has continuously renewed its customer base by moving aggressively from mainframe users to client-server users and to midsized and small companies to capitalize on emerging market opportunities. "Noncustomers often offer the greatest insights into where the market is moving and what we should be doing fundamentally differently," remarked Plattner. "We never look at what the competition is doing." As a result, SAP is the global leader in business application software.

MAKING VALUE INNOVATION HAPPEN

To make value innovation happen, top management must clearly communicate the company's commitment to value innovation as the key strategy component by articulating its underlying logic.[25] The aim is to drive out of the organization conventional, competition-based thinking that usually leads only to incremental market improvements. The CEO and his or her top management team play a critical role in initiating this change.[26] Through strategic retreats and corporate communications, and by continuously challenging proposed strategic plans on the basis of value innovation, staff members will gradually orient themselves toward the principles of value innovation.[27] Five key questions, which contrast conventional competition-based logic with that of value innovation, can serve as a guide to reframing strategic thinking toward the new mindset (see Table 9.1).

What type of organization best unlocks the ideas and creativity of its employees to achieve this end? In our studies, two structural characteristics are common to value innovation companies:

▼ *Small autonomous units or teams focusing on a common business or product goal* rather than organization on the basis of function, region, or channel type.[28] Although top managers must clearly specify that the strategic goal is to value innovate (as opposed to benchmarking the competition), teams must freely explore how to achieve these objectives. Some degree of freedom heightens a sense of ownership among team members, promotes creativity, and ensures that individual expertise is fully exploited.[29]

▼ *Team members of diverse backgrounds and perspectives.* This seems most conducive to higher levels of creativity.[30]

When putting value innovation strategies into action, structural conditions create only the *potential* for individuals to share their best ideas and knowledge. To *actualize* this potential, a company must cultivate a corporate culture conducive to willing collaboration.

How to promote voluntary cooperation among organizational members is critical to value innovation efforts. An organization must supply and create knowledge and ideas effectively, because these are the primary inputs for value innovation. Unlike traditional production factors, such as land, labor, and capital, knowledge and ideas are intangible assets locked in the human mind. Even in ideal organizational conditions, creating and sharing knowledge—intangible activities—cannot be supervised or forced; they happen only when individuals cooperate voluntarily.

Table 9.1. Five Key Questions to Reframe Strategic Thinking.

	Conventional Logic	Value Innovation Logic
Question 1	Does your company allow industry conditions to dictate the realm of what is possible, probable, and profitable?	Does your company challenge the inevitability of industry conditions?
Question 2	Does your company focus on outpacing the competition?	Does your company focus on dominating the market by introducing a major advance in buyer value?
Question 3	Does management start by considering current assets and capabilities?	Does management consider starting anew?
Question 4	Does your company focus on customer segmentation, customization, and retention?	Does your company search for key value commodities that can unlock the mass market even if some existing customers will be lost?
Question 5	Does your company strive to improve the products and services of your industry?	Does your company think in terms of a total customer solution even if this pushes beyond the industry's traditional offerings?

The distinction between compulsory and voluntary cooperation is worth noting. Compulsory cooperation is in accordance with organizational rules, regulations, and acceptable standards, whereas voluntary cooperation goes beyond the call of duty: Individuals exert effort, energy, and initiative to the best of their abilities on behalf of the organization.[31] Companies can mandate compulsory cooperation by using organizational force; voluntary cooperation is not achievable without trust and commitment that can only be cultivated purposefully. Compulsory cooperation alone cannot effectively supply and generate the knowledge required to formulate value innovation plans.[32]

Voluntary cooperation is also essential because effectively executing planned value innovation usually involves major changes in how a company functions. This often requires behavioral changes. The collaborative initiative and spontaneity that are characteristic of voluntary cooperation are key to adapting to change.

As we studied successes and failures in this area, one central theme repeatedly emerged whether we were working with senior executives or shop floor employees: Individuals are most likely to share ideas and cooperate voluntarily when the company acknowledges their intellectual and emotional worth. Individuals are gratified when the company solicits and thoughtfully considers their ideas and shares opinions with them. Recognizing individuals as human beings worthy of respect regardless of hierarchical level rather than "labor," "personnel," or "human resources" engenders loyalty and willingness to collaborate for the welfare of the company.

We found that exercising *fair process*—fairness in the process of making and executing decisions—is a powerful way to recognize people's intellectual and emotional worth.[33] Fair process brings forth trust and commitment, whereas treatment perceived as unfair elicits idea hoarding and foot dragging. The three bedrock principles of fair process are: (1) *engaging* people in decisions that affect them, (2) *explaining* final decisions, and (3) *establishing clear expectations* of actions and deliverables. Fair process is a key organizational practice for effectively conceiving and executing any strategy but is particularly efficacious when companies wish to break from the status quo to value innovate.

Consider the recent successes of Compaq Computer. In 1991, Compaq saw tremendous opportunity in the low-end PC market. Because its existing production systems and logistics had neither the cost dynamics nor distribution reach to capture this burgeoning market, Compaq swiftly reinvented itself to serve the low-end PC market. In several months, for example, the company moved from 3,000 value-added resellers to more than 30,000 dealers, including mass-market merchandisers like Wal-Mart and Circuit City. In six years, its sales increased from $3 billion to $25 billion, and it is the world's top-ranked desktop computer maker, sporting a world-class line of portables, servers, and workstations. Compaq Chairman Eckhard Pfeiffer clearly articulated and never wavered from his intention to value innovate. Beyond autonomous teams populated with diversity, use of fair process methods defined a working mode that built trust and voluntary cooperation around the corporation's strategic goal.

Fair process and value innovation create a positively reinforcing cycle (see Figure 9.4). Each success in implementing a general value innovation strategy based on fair process strengthens group cohesiveness and people's belief in the process, which perpetuates the collaborative and creative modes inherent to value innovation.

Most companies strive to deliver *fair outcomes* without distinguishing this concept from fair process. Delivering fair outcomes ensures that individuals receive power, resources, or material rewards in exchange for compulsory cooperation.[34] To induce knowledge creation and voluntary cooperation between individuals, however, companies must go beyond fair outcome to fair process.

People possessing knowledge are the key resource of companies pursuing value innovation; this cherished resource is independent and mobile. Today's knowledge economy traffics actively in this key resource. As a result, companies must meet fair outcome expectations *and* fair process expectations to produce fulfilling work environments.

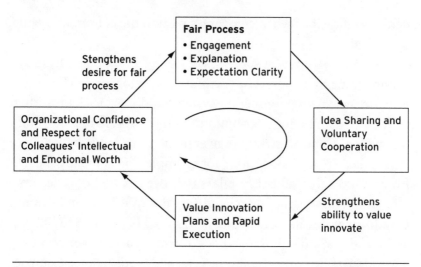

Figure 9.4. The Positively Reinforcing Cycle of Fair Process.

This is how many successful value innovation companies, such as SAP, retain their talented employees. In an industry notorious for its lack of employee loyalty, the annual staff turnover rate of SAP, for example, is 4 percent—about half the industry average.

VALUE INNOVATION AS STRATEGY

In the coming decade, what is the key strategic agenda for corporate giants like Microsoft, Intel, Compaq, Enron, SAP, Procter & Gamble, Johnson & Johnson, Motorola, Chrysler, SMH, 3M, Sony, Toyota, and Samsung? For example, Procter & Gamble's strategic goal for the next decade is to double its $35 billion business through assertive efforts to achieve business breakthroughs. As we participated in, heard, and read about their management training, strategic planning discussions, and executive retreats, we unfailingly noted that all these companies aspire to attain breakthroughs in their markets.

We believe that value innovation is the essence of strategy in the knowledge economy. It must be supported by the proper tactics to prolong and maximize an innovation's profit-making potential, distancing it from emulators. After a value innovation is created, business line extensions and continuous improvements can maximize profits before another value innovation is launched. However, these business and operational improvements are not strategies; they are tactics.[35] Value innovation as strategy creates a pattern of punctuated equilibrium, in which bursts of value innovation that reshape the industrial landscape are interspersed with periods of improvements, geographic and product line extensions, and consolidation.

In some industrial and regional sectors of the economy, however, many companies will still be successful on the basis of competition-driven strategy without spurts of value innovation. We predict that these dormant sectors of the economy will increasingly dwindle as value innovation and its globalization penetrate farther into the economy. Nevertheless, other successful strategies exist. Along with value innovators, cost leaders and differentiators can achieve profitable growth. In markets where value innovation occurs, however, the space for success of cost leaders and differentiators narrows as value innovators occupy the core of markets by attracting the mass of buyers. For example, since Wal-Mart has grown to dominate the discount retail market by capturing its core, successful cost leaders and differentiators in this market are those pursuing a rock-bottom pricing strategy (Dollar General, Family Dollar, Dollar Tree) or targeting high-end segments (specialty stores). As value innovation further penetrates into markets, strategies of cost leadership and differentiation are likely to succeed best at the low end (cost leaders) and the high end (differentiators). As happened in discount retailing, cost leaders and differentiators may become peripheral players relative to value innovators that emerge to capture the core of expanded markets. It is important to note here that value innovators do capture the core of the market but not at the direct expense of other market players, since they expand the market by creating new demand.

NOTES

1. W. C. Kim and R. Mauborgne, "When Competitive Advantage Is Neither," *Wall Street Journal,* 21 April 1997a, p. 22.
2. W. C. Kim and R. Mauborgne, "On the Inside Track," *Financial Times,* 7 April 1997b, p. 10.
3. W. C. Kim and R. Mauborgne, "Value Innovation: The Strategic Logic of High Growth," *Harvard Business Review,* January-February 1997c, *75,* 102–112.
4. W. C. Kim and R. Mauborgne, "Opportunity Beckons," *Financial Times,* 18 August 1997d, p. 8.
5. W. C. Kim and R. Mauborgne, "How to Leapfrog the Competition," *Wall Street Journal Europe,* 6 March 1997e, p. 10.
6. Kim and Mauborgne (1997c).
7. R. P. Rumelt, D. Schendel, and D. J. Teece, "Strategic Management and Economics," *Strategic Management Journal,* Winter 1991, *12,* 5–29.
8. R. R. Nelson, "Why Do Firms Differ, and How Does It Matter?" *Strategic Management Journal,* Winter 1991, *12,* 61–74.
9. For a discussion on the importance and patterns of creating new markets, see W. C. Kim and R. Mauborgne, "Creating New Market Space," *Harvard Business Review,* January-February 1999, *77,* 83–93; also see G. Hamel and C. K. Prahalad, *Competing for the Future* (Boston: Harvard Business School Press, 1994).
10. W. C. Kim and R. Mauborgne, "Value Knowledge or Pay the Price," *Wall Street Journal Europe,* 29 January 1998a, p. 6; and T. A. Stewart, *Intellectual Capital* (New York: Currency/Doubleday, 1997).
11. P. Romer, "Endogenous Technological Change," *Journal of Political Economy,* October 1990, *98,* S71-S102; P. M. Romer, "The Origins of Endogenous Growth," *Journal of Economic Perspectives,* Winter 1994, *8,* 3–22; and G. M. Grossman and E. Helpman, *Innovation and Growth* (Cambridge, Massachusetts: MIT Press, 1995).
12. C.W.L. Hill, "Differentiation Versus Low Cost or Differentiation and Low Cost," *Academy of Management Review,* July 1988, *13,* 401–412. Hill argues that low cost and differentiation do not have to be an either-or choice.

13. For the most recent research on this, see A. Hargadon and R. Sutton, "Technology Brokering and Innovation in a Product Development Firm," *Administrative Science Quarterly,* December 1997, 42, 716–749.

14. For an excellent discussion on this, see E. M. Rogers, *Diffusion of Innovations* (New York: Free Press, 1995).

15. For more discussion on this, see Kim and Mauborgne (1999).

16. For a discussion of "creative destruction," see J. A. Schumpeter, *The Theory of Economic Development* (Cambridge, Massachusetts: Harvard University Press, 1934).

17. For discussion of the importance of innovators' monopoly profits, see Schumpeter (1934); Romer (1990); and W. B. Arthur, "Increasing Returns and the New World of Business," *Harvard Business Review,* July-August 1996, 74, 100–109.

18. P. Romer, "Increasing Returns and Long-Run Growth," *Journal of Political Economy,* October 1986, 94, 1002–1037; and Arthur (1996).

19. K. J. Arrow, "Economic Welfare and the Allocation of Resources for Inventions," in R. R. Nelson, ed., *The Rate and Direction of Inventive Activity* (Princeton, New Jersey: Princeton University Press, 1962), pp. 609–626; and Romer (1990). It is worth noting that both Arrow and Romer limited their discussions of nonrival and nonexcludable goods to technological innovations as is the tradition of economics. When the concept of innovation is redefined as value innovation, which is more relevant at the microeconomic firm level, the importance of the nonrival and nonexcludable notion is even more striking. This is because technological innovation often has a greater excludable component due to the possibility and relative ease of obtaining patent protection.

20. For a brilliant discussion of this issue, see L. C. Thurow, "Needed: A New System of Intellectual Property Rights," *Harvard Business Review,* September-October 1997, 75, 94–103.

21. The extent to which the idea behind a value innovation is nonexcludable affects the strategic price set by the value innovator. As we have argued, while innovative ideas and processes are usually nonexcludable or only partially so, some value innovators have patentable ideas that are excludable for a given time. In these cases,

value innovators may be inclined to price their product the same as or higher than rivals' products and services. However, recognizing the powerful economies of scale, learning, and increasing returns that come with high volumes of knowledge-intensive goods, the strategic price will still be set from the outset with an aim to capture the mass of buyers. In the United Kingdom, Dyson Appliances, for example, created a value innovation in vacuum cleaners with its launch of the Dyson Dual Cyclone, which eliminated vacuum cleaner bags and the hassle of replacing bags for the life of the vacuum. In doing so, Dyson also increased the suction power of its vacuum cleaner dramatically over the industry average. Given the radically superior value of its product and the fact that its value innovation was patentable, Dyson strategically set its price relatively high while still capturing the mass of buyers. Although the vacuum cleaner was priced higher than the competition, it was a leap in value and within the economic reach of the mass of buyers. In this instance, Dyson did not use the conventional monopolist's practice of restricting supply by establishing a high price.

22. W. C. Kim and R. Mauborgne, "A Corporate Future Built with New Blocks," *New York Times*, 29 March 1998b, Section 3, p. 14.

23. For thought-provoking discussions on the implications of a focus on a company's current capabilities, see M. E. Porter, "Towards a Dynamic Theory of Strategy," *Strategic Management Journal*, Winter 1991, *12*, 95–117; and M. L. Tushman and P. Anderson, "Technological Discontinuities and Organizational Environments," *Administrative Science Quarterly*, September 1986, *31*, 439–465.

24. That a focus on current customers can be detrimental to a firm's long-run viability is also discussed in J. L. Bower and C. M. Christensen, "Disruptive Technologies: Catching the Wave," *Harvard Business Review*, January-February 1995, *73*, 43–53.

25. For a more thorough discussion on this, see Kim and Mauborgne (1997c).

26. The critical importance of top management setting clear expectations is highlighted in the works of Kanter and Amabile. See R. M. Kanter, "When a Thousand Flowers Bloom: Structural, Collective, and Social Conditions for Innovation in Organizations," in P. S. Myers,

ed., *Knowledge Management and Organization Design* (Boston: Butterworth-Heinemann, 1996), pp. 169–211; and T. M. Amabile, "A Model of Creativity and Innovation in Organizations," in *Research in Organizational Behavior* (Greenwich, Connecticut: JAI Press, 1988), pp. 123–167.

27. This is consistent with the work of Amabile (1988), who argues that the most important elements of motivating innovation are concise and compelling articulation of the value of innovation, orientation away from the status quo, and activating an offensive leadership strategy aimed at the future, rather than simply trying to protect an organization's past.

28. Kanter (1996) also argues for the importance of smaller units organized around common business objectives as a catalyst for innovative thinking in organizations.

29. The important work on creativity conducted by Amabile clearly establishes the importance of autonomy in achieving strategic goals to foster creativity. See T. M. Amabile, "How to Kill Creativity," *Harvard Business Review,* September-October 1998, *76,* 76–87.

30. The need for diversity or cross-disciplinary contact to spark innovation is also well articulated in the excellent works of Kanter (1996) and Amabile (1998).

31. The roots of our distinction between voluntary and compulsory cooperation originate with P. Blau and W. R. Scott, *Formal Organizations* (San Francisco: Chandler Publishing Company, 1962); and O. E. Williamson, *Markets and Hierarchies* (New York: Free Press, 1975).

32. Kim and Mauborgne (1998a); and W. C. Kim and R. Mauborgne, "Building Trust," *Financial Times,* 9 January 1998c, p. 25.

33. W. C. Kim and R. Mauborgne, "Fair Process: Managing in the Knowledge Economy," *Harvard Business Review,* July-August 1997, *75,* 65–75; W. C. Kim and R. Mauborgne, "Procedural Justice, Strategic Decision Making and the Knowledge Economy," *Strategic Management Journal,* April 1998, *19,* 323–338; and W. C. Kim and R. Mauborgne, "A Procedural Justice Model of Strategic Decision Making: Strategy Content Implications," *Organization Science,* January-February 1995, *19,* 44–61.

34. W. C. Kim and R. Mauborgne, "Procedural Justice and Managers' In-role and Extra-role Behavior," *Management Science,* April 1996, 42, 499–515.

35. For an excellent discussion of how strategy differs from operational improvements, see M. E. Porter, "What Is Strategy?" *Harvard Business Review,* November-December 1996, 74, 61–78.

CHAPTER TEN

A Dynamic View of Strategy

CONSTANTINOS C. MARKIDES

In late 1988, the newly appointed CEO of the Nestlé subsidiary, Nespresso, was trying to decide how to rejuvenate his subsidiary's financial fortunes. Jean-Paul Gaillard had just taken over a subsidiary that, despite selling one of Nestlé's most innovative new products, was facing serious financial problems.

The Nespresso product was a system that allowed the consumer to produce a fresh cup of espresso coffee at home. Though simple in appearance and use, it took Nestlé more than ten years to develop it. The system consisted of two parts: a coffee capsule and a machine. The coffee capsule was hermetically sealed in aluminum and contained five grams of ground roast coffee. The machine consisted of a handle, a water container, a pump, and an electrical heating system. These four parts were cast into a body to form the machine.

The use of the Nespresso system was straightforward. The coffee capsule was placed in the handle, which was then inserted into the machine. The act of inserting the handle into the machine pierced the coffee capsule at the top. At the press of a button, pressurized hot water passed through the capsule. The result was a creamy, foamy, high-quality cup of espresso.

The new product was introduced in 1986. Nestlé's original strategy was to set up a joint venture with a Swiss-based distributor, called Sobal, to sell the new product. This joint venture (named Sobal-Nespresso) would purchase the machines from another Swiss company (called Turmix) and the coffee capsules from Nestlé, after which it would distribute and sell everything as a system—one product, one price. Offices and restaurants were targeted as the customers and a separate unit called Nespresso S.A. was set up within Nestlé to support the joint venture and to service and maintain the machines.

By 1988, it was clear that the new product was not living up to its promise. Sales were well below budget, and costs were escalating due to quality problems. Nestlé executives were considering halting the operation when Jean-Paul Gaillard was chosen to decide whether and how to strategically reposition the subsidiary. At the top of Gaillard's list were questions such as

▼ Should Nespresso continue targeting offices and restaurants as customers or focus on upper-income households and individuals?
▼ Should Nespresso continue focusing activities in Switzerland or expand into other espresso-friendly countries?
▼ Should Nespresso adhere to its strategy of selling the coffee and machines as a system or concentrate solely on coffee?
▼ Did Nespresso's distribution policy make sense or should the company choose an alternative distribution method, such as mail order?

THE HEART AND SOUL OF STRATEGY

The answers to these questions were not immediately obvious, and several possible alternatives were put forward. Debates and disagreements ensued. Yet out of this debate and uncertainty, specific choices were made and specific decisions implemented. In fact, this process of asking questions, generating alternatives, and making choices that may prove to be the wrong ones is what strategy is all about.

This is because, in every industry, there are several viable positions that companies can occupy. Therefore, the essence of strategy is selecting *one* position that a company can claim as its own. A strategic position is simply the sum of a company's answers to the following questions:

▼ *Who* should the company target as customers?
▼ *What* products or services should the company offer the targeted customers?
▼ *How* can the company do this efficiently?[1]

Strategy involves making tough choices on three dimensions: which customers to focus on, which products to offer, and which activities to perform. Strategy entails *choosing,* and a company will be successful if it chooses a *distinctive* strategic position that differs from those of its competitors. The most common source of strategic failure is the inability to make clear and explicit choices on these three dimensions.

As it turned out, Jean-Paul Gaillard chose correctly for Nespresso—whether by luck or foresight. Nespresso targeted high-income households as its main customer and chose mail order (the "Nespresso Club") for distributing the coffee capsules. As a result of these choices and other strategic decisions, Nespresso grew tremendously during the next five years. The main point of the Nespresso story is simple: The heart and soul of strategy is asking the *"who"-"what"-"how"* questions, developing alternatives, and selecting specific goals and actions.

To substantiate this point further, consider the example of Edward Jones. With 1997 revenues of $1.1 billion, the St. Louis, Missouri-based partnership of Edward Jones is the thirty-fourth largest brokerage firm in the United States. However, the firm is one

of the most profitable in the volatile securities industry and is growing rapidly. Since 1981, it has expanded its broker force 15 percent
annually without making any acquisitions. It now boasts more than
2,500 partners—up from a 1981 count of eight.

As described by many outside observers, including management guru Peter Drucker, the firm is a federation of highly
autonomous entrepreneurial units bound by a strong set of values
and beliefs. The entrepreneurial units are Edward Jones brokers,
who are scattered across the United States. They operate out of one-
person offices located in small communities, selling selected financial products to people living in their communities. They are united
by the strong cultural belief that their job is to offer sound, long-
term financial advice to their customers, even if that does not generate short-term fees. The "customer-first" value is ingrained in every
broker working in the Jones system.

It wasn't always like this. During the past fifty years, the firm
passed through three evolutionary stages. It was originally set up by
Edward Jones Sr. to be a financial department store able to satisfy
all the financial needs of a customer. In the 1960s, the department
store concept slowly evolved into a "delivery system" for the rural
areas of the United States, as a result of Ted Jones (the owner's son)
setting up small offices in rural communities and expanding the firm
into a network of 200 offices. At that time, Edward Jones began
assigning brokers to small towns (instead of sending them there
every week or two). The idea was to convert Edward Jones into a
distribution network to sell mutual funds in rural areas.

The third stage in the evolution of Edward Jones took place in
1970 after the firm's managing principal, John Bachmann, arrived.
In what he describes as a "defining moment" for the firm, he began
to convert Jones into a "merchant"—an informed buyer for the end
customer. According to Bachmann, the distinction between a distributor and a merchant is crucial: "A distributor is structured
around the product and tries to sell only profitable products. A merchant, on the other hand, is structured around the end consumer.
He acts as an informed buyer for the investor, selecting only the

products that are good for the investor, as opposed to products that generate fees for the brokers. Most investment firms look at brokers as their customers. We don't. For us, the customer is the individual investor that signs the checks."

This vision of being a merchant for the individual investor has guided every move of Edward Jones since 1980. It also has shaped the company's currently successful strategy, the main elements of which are as follows (see Table 10.1):

▼ Edward Jones targets and sells its products only to individual investors, never to institutional investors.
▼ The firm sells only selected products—often transparent, long-term products such as large-cap equities and highly rated bonds. It avoids selling risky initial public offerings, options, or commodity futures.
▼ Edward Jones does not manufacture the products it sells, unlike its major competitors (e.g., Merrill Lynch, Smith Barney) that sell their own in-house mutual funds. Jones acts only as a distributor for the products of a few selected manufacturers, such as Capital Research, Putnam, and Morgan Stanley.
▼ The firm sets up one-person offices in selected areas—usually small communities or specific areas within cities where there is a "sense of community."[2]
▼ Edward Jones remains a partnership so that individual brokers feel and think like owners, not employees.
▼ The company behaves like a family whose mission is to help ordinary people invest their money wisely. The glue that holds everything together is Jones's strong culture.

These are the main elements of the successful Jones strategy. John Bachmann likes to point out that each element involved some kind of trade-off for the company: "We target individual investors, not institutional ones. We buy good securities and keep them a long time instead of trying to maximize transaction fees. Rather than have big offices in large cities, our offices are small and are placed in small communities

Table 10.1. Strategic Choices of Edward Jones.

Who are the company's targeted customers?	Individual investors rather than institutional investors. Individuals living in areas that have a "sense of community."
What products or services should the company offer?	Transparent, long-term products, such as large-cap equities and highly rated bonds. No risky initial public offerings or commodity futures.
How can the company efficiently conduct business?	Never manufacture products. Act only as a distributor. Buy only from a few reputable suppliers, such as Capital Research and Morgan Stanley. Establish one-person operations in community-based offices. Remain a partnership. Focus on the end customer, not the brokers

to be convenient to the customer. Our offices are one-person operations, not multiperson ones. We do not manufacture our products, and we showcase the products of a limited number of leading houses. We do not sell all products—we select transparent and safe products to promote. We remain a partnership rather than try to go public."

The company has remained faithful to these judicious choices for more than twenty years. As John Bachmann phrases it: "These principles are cast in stone. We don't debate these things."

UNIQUENESS IS TRANSITORY

Edward Jones built its success on finding and exploiting a singular strategic position in its industry. It did not try to imitate the strategic position of other competitors or try to beat its competitors at their specialties. Instead, Jones's unique position allowed it to play an entirely different game. Although no position is truly unique, the idea is to create as much differentiation as possible.

Unquestionably, success stems from exploiting an unparalleled strategic position. Unfortunately, a position's uniqueness will not last forever! Aggressive competitors will not only imitate attractive positions, but perhaps more importantly, new strategic positions will be emerging continually. A novel strategic position is simply another viable who-what-how combination—perhaps a new customer segment (a new "who"), a new value proposition (a new "what"), or a new way of distributing or manufacturing a product (a new "how"). Gradually, such new positions may challenge the domination of existing positions.

This happens in industry after industry: Once formidable companies with seemingly unassailable strategic positions find themselves humbled by relatively unknown companies that base their attacks on creating and exploiting *new* strategic positions in the industry. The rise and fall of Xerox from 1960 to 1990 highlights this simple but powerful point.

In the 1960s, Xerox dominated the copier market by following a well-defined and successful strategy. Having segmented the market by volume, Xerox decided to win the corporate reproduction market by concentrating on copiers designed for high-speed, high-volume needs. This inevitably defined Xerox's customers as big corporations, which in turn determined its distribution method: a direct sales force. Xerox also decided to lease rather than sell its machines, a strategic choice that had worked well in the company's earlier battles with 3M.

The Xerox strategy was clear and precise, with sharp boundaries. Undoubtedly, lively debates and disagreements within Xerox preceded the firm's discerning strategic choices. Yet difficult decisions were made and actions taken. The company prospered because of its distinctive strategic position with well-defined customers, products, and activities. Throughout the 1960s and early 1970s, Xerox maintained a return on equity of around 20 percent.

In fact, Xerox's strategy was so successful that several new competitors, including IBM and Kodak, tried to enter this huge market by adopting the same or similar strategies. Fundamentally, their strategy was to grab market share by being better than Xerox. For example, IBM entered the market in 1970 with the IBM Copier I, which the IBM sales force marketed on a rental basis to the medium- and high-volume segments. In 1975, Kodak entered the market with the Ektaprint 100 copier-duplicator, a high-quality, low-price substitute for Xerox machines that was aimed at the high-volume end of the market.

Neither of these corporate giants made substantial inroads into the copier business. They failed for many reasons, but their inability to create a distinctive position was undoubtedly one of them. Unlike Xerox, both IBM and Kodak failed to identify or create a distinctive strategic position in the industry. Instead, they tried to colonize Xerox's position and fought for market share by trying to outdo Xerox. Given Xerox's first-mover advantage, it is not surprising that IBM and Kodak failed.

In contrast, Canon chose to play the game differently. After diversifying in the 1960s beyond cameras into copiers, Canon segmented the market by end user, targeting small- and medium-sized businesses while producing personal copiers for the individual as well. Canon also decided to sell its machines through a dealer network rather than lease them. Whereas Xerox emphasized the speed of its machines, Canon elected to concentrate on quality and price as its differentiating features. Unlike IBM and Kodak, Canon successfully penetrated the copier market, emerging as the market leader in terms of volume within twenty years. Canon succeeded for many reasons, but particularly because it established a distinctive, well-defined strategic position rather than trying to beat Xerox at its own game.

CONTINUALLY EMERGING NEW POSITIONS

Canon challenged Xerox by creating a new strategic position in the copier business that undermined Xerox's position and destroyed its basis of profitability. Such attacks are common (see Table 10.2). The "dominant" competitors establish unique strategic positions in their respective industries. Over time, "traditional" competitors imitate their

Table 10.2. Undermining Established Strategic Positions.

Industry	Dominant Competitor	Traditional Competitor	Strategic Innovator
U.S. airline	American	Delta, United, Northwest	Southwest
Car rental	Hertz	Avis, Europcar, National	Enterprise Rent-A-Car
U.S. television broadcasting	NBC	CBS, ABC	CNN
U.K. banking	Natwest	Lloyds, Barclays	First Direct
Earth-moving equipment	Caterpillar	International Harvester, John Deere, J.I. Case	Komatsu
Steel	U.S. Steel	Bethlehem, Inland, National	Nucor
U.K. supermarket	Sainsbury's	Tesco, Asda, Waitrose	Flanagan's
Coffee	General Foods (Maxwell House)	Procter & Gamble (Folger's), Nestlé (Nescafé), Sara Lee (Douwe Egberts)	Starbucks
U.K. insurance	Norwich Union	Prudential, Royal Sun Alliance	Direct Line
Photocopier	Xerox	IBM, Kodak, Ricoh	Canon
U.K. airline	British Airways	Virgin Atlantic, British Midlands, other European carriers	EasyJet
Securities	Merrill Lynch	Smith Barney, Dean Witter, Paine Webber	Edward Jones
Computer	IBM	NCR, Control Data	Microsoft

predecessors in an attempt to wrest market share from them. Increasingly, though, "strategic innovators" emerge that run away with huge chunks of the market—often a new market that they helped to create.

Incursions into established markets by strategic innovators have resulted in the following notable outcomes:

▼ Canon's market share in the copier business jumped from zero to 35 percent in about twenty years.

▼ Komatsu increased its market share in the earth-moving equipment business from 10 percent to 25 percent in less than fifteen years.

▼ Launched in 1982, *USA Today* had become the top-selling U.S. newspaper by 1993, selling more than 5 million copies per day.

▼ Dell Computer Corporation emerged from its college-dorm beginnings in the mid-1980s to capture more than 10 percent of the global personal computer market in less than ten years.

▼ Started in 1989 as the United Kingdom's first dedicated telephone bank, First Direct had nearly 700,000 customers within seven years—an achievement that the business press described as a miraculous cure for the stagnant banking industry.[3]

▼ Starbucks Coffee grew from a chain of eleven stores and sales of $1.3 million in 1987 to 280 stores and sales of $163.5 million in five years. The store total now tops 1,600.

▼ Direct Line was launched in 1985 and, within ten years, became one of Britain's biggest motor insurers (2.2 million policyholders).

These companies achieved their hard-earned successes in a similar way, namely, by proactively breaking the rules of the game in their industries. The hallmark of their success was strategic innovation: proactively establishing distinctive strategic positions that were critical to shifting market share or creating new markets.

As industries change, new strategic positions arise to challenge existing positions. Changes in industry conditions, customer needs or preferences, demographics, technology, government policies, competition, and a company's own competencies generate new opportunities and the potential for new ground rules. Existing niches expand while others die, new niches appear, mass markets fragment into new segments (or niches), "old" niches merge to form larger markets, and so on. This dynamic occurs in every industry.

Now imagine your company as it tries to compete in its industry. Let's say that your company has carved out a nice position in the mass market. It has several competitors in the mass market, and several niche players exist on the periphery. While you are competing with your primary competitors, you know that new niches are developing, and you want to ensure that your company does not miss these new opportunities. But from among hundreds of new niches, identifying a productive one is difficult; so is predicting its growth rate and eventual size. Meanwhile, though your company's sales are increasing, a winning niche arises—its growth resulting from the creation of an entirely new market. Such developments complicate your ability to understand the magnitude of the problem confronting your company. What can you do in this situation?

After a niche becomes a huge market, hindsight confirms that you should have done something earlier. But it is hard to know which threat to respond to and when! For example, it is only with hindsight that we can say IBM should have responded to the Dell threat long ago. But in the early 1980s, even if IBM had spotted this new entrant, should it have worried about a tiny niche player with 1 percent of the market? How about when Dell's market share grew to 5 percent? Or 10 percent? When did Dell really become a major worry for IBM? Even if IBM wanted to respond to the Dell challenge now, what could it do? Can it play two games simultaneously?

PREPARING FOR THE UNKNOWN

No company has perfect foresight in predicting emerging strategic innovations. However, lack of certainty is no excuse for inactivity. A company can face up to all this uncertainty by adopting one or both of the following generic options.

Option One: Become the Innovator

Established competitors can proactively develop the next strategic innovation in an industry. Just as cannibalizing existing products when creating next-generation products is acceptable, companies should not hesitate to cannibalize an existing strategic position to create the "next generation" position. This is difficult, but not impossible.[4]

Practically speaking, a company must cultivate the "right" attitude but also organize itself to compete effectively in its existing business while simultaneously experimenting with new technologies and ideas. How can the old and the new coexist harmoniously?[5] This calls for creating an ambidextrous organization, which is a formidable task. As Tushman and O'Reilly point out: "This requires organizational and management skills to compete in a mature market (where cost, efficiency, and incremental innovation are key) *and* to develop new products and services (where radical innovation, speed, and flexibility are critical)."[6]

Utterback also forcefully makes this point:

> Firms owe it to themselves to improve and extend the lives of profitable product lines. These represent important cash flows to the firm and links to existing customers. They provide the funds that will finance future products. At the same time, managers must not neglect pleas that advocate major commitments to new initiatives. Typically, top management is pulled by two opposing, responsible forces: those that demand commitment to the old and those that advocate for the future. Unfortunately, advocacy tends to overstate the market potential of new product lines and understate their costs. Management, then, must find the right balance between support for incremental improvements and commitments to new and unproven innovations. Understanding and managing this tension perceptively may well separate the ultimate winners from the losers.[7]

Option Two: Exploit Someone Else's Innovation

Chances are that an established company will not be the source of the next new strategic innovation. For every established competitor, hundreds of new entrants or entrepreneurs are trying to concoct the next "great" innovation, and it is likely that one will succeed. Nevertheless, an established competitor should be poised and ready to take advantage of emerging innovations. But what does "being ready" imply?

BEING READY

Research shows that most established companies fail when a technological innovation invades their market—even when they actually adopt a new technology. Several reasons for this have been identified:

▼ They lack the necessary core competencies to take advantage of the innovation.

▼ They are late adopters and abandon an innovation at the first sign of trouble.

▼ They are trapped in their customary ways of competing, their core competencies having become core rigidities.

▼ They do not effectively manage the organizational transition from the old to the new when adopting a new technology.[8]

This implies that to prepare for the inevitable strategic innovation that will disrupt a company's market, an organization should

1. *Build an early monitoring system to identify turning points before a crisis occurs.* Firms must develop the capability to recognize early whether a new strategic position is emerging that will unsettle their markets. The most effective way to do so is to regularly monitor indicators of *strategic* rather than *financial* health—that is, leading indicators of a company's performance such as employee morale, customer satisfaction, and distributor feedback. Also track and benchmark maverick competitors that operate in small niches or appear to be breaking the rules of the game in the industry. In

addition, encourage people close to the market to actively monitor and proactively report changes in the market to the appropriate decision makers. Alternatively, build a strong sense of direction, establish the parameters within which people can maneuver, and then empower them to take action. In short, develop the capability to identify changes early.

2. *Prevent cultural and structural inertia.* Cultivate a culture that welcomes change and is ready to accept a new strategic innovation even if it disrupts the status quo. Established companies often wait too long to adopt an innovation. Reasons for this are many—not the least of which is the uncertainty of whether the innovation will be a winner. By developing a culture that welcomes change and encourages experimentation and learning, obstacles to innovation may be overcome. Such a culture may be further enhanced if top management uses "shocks to the system" to acclimate employees to change.

For example, cultural inertia at Raychem is challenged every day. Company founder Paul Cook says:

> Raychem is working to make its own products obsolete every day. Right now, we are in the process of making one of our best products obsolete, a system for sealing splices in telephone cables. Now, we could have kept on improving that product for years to come. Instead, we've developed a radically new splice-closure technology that improves performance tremendously, and we're working very hard to cannibalize the earlier generation. Our old product wasn't running out of steam. Our customers had virtually no complaints about it. But because we knew the product and its applications even better than our customers did, we were able to upgrade its performance significantly by using a new technology. Why are we doing it? Because we understand that if we don't make ourselves obsolete, the world will become more competitive.[9]

3. *Develop processes that allow experimenting with new ideas.* New innovations are not adopted quickly because they are not recognized to be winners. If experimentation were to reveal the poten-

tial of a new innovation, a company would be more likely to adopt it. Experimentation is the process that Intel's Andrew Grove terms "let chaos reign"—when people explore novel ideas until enough information is collected to allow the firm to make a decision. Grove further describes the process:

> When danger comes, the adrenaline starts flowing and you want to pull the reins in and take control. But the opposite is what is needed. The reason you need to do the opposite is that, in this phase of the curve, you do not know enough to take charge. The fragmented information will come with fragmented suggested directions. You let things develop, and the way you let things develop is to relinquish control and let people—division heads, geography heads, engineers—pull in various directions. . . . This is the only way to get enough information to really build up a basis on which to decide whether to go for one option or the other.[10]

4. *Be prepared with the required competencies.* Prepare to exploit the company's new position by building the appropriate competencies and skills. Unfortunately, this is easier said than done. Utterback makes the point succinctly:

> There is no easy answer as to how firms should choose the core competencies that will assure their progress and survival. Certainly, it is essential to anticipate discontinuities and to try to act in advance of their full impact. Doing so requires constant monitoring of the firm's external environment to notice forerunners of significant change. We have seen that most firms look in exactly the wrong places for vital signs of technological change: namely, their universe of traditional rivals. . . . Looking toward more obscure new entrants and unconventional sources of competition is more fruitful, although these sources are more diffuse and difficult to monitor. Technological and market uncertainty, however, implies that no one can act with clear anticipation or forecasts. Among equally capable generals, the one with the best contingency plans will usually win the battle. Unexpected departures from the anticipated plan are almost certain to arise and in the best of cases, they

will open the way to greater opportunities than at first imagined. This is crucial in the choice of capabilities to foster.[11]

In the face of uncertainty, the best a firm can do is build internal variety (even at the expense of efficiency), and let the market mechanism determine what wins. By nurturing variety, a company also builds the competencies needed in the future. Creating and managing internal variety is intrinsically difficult—but it is achievable if learning is allowed to flourish in the organization.

5. *Manage the transition.* Finally, a firm must manage the transition to the new strategic position. Two issues are involved.

First, the organization must clearly decide whether to adopt the new position. As Grove puts it: "At last, you have got through the strategic inflection point. In this second phase, it is time to rein in chaos. The phase for experimentation is over. Now is the moment to pull the reins in and to take charge again. At this point, you must be completely explicit in stating the direction of the new business. When you get out of pursuing multiple architectures, you must be completely explicit that the experiment is stopping, that all resources are being put into one option. No ifs or buts: explicit clarity."[12]

Second, the company must ensure that the "old" and the "new" coexist harmoniously. Any innovation, by virtue of being small in scope relative to the existing company, will receive little attention and limited resources unless it is protected. The solution is to develop a separate organizational unit for the new position to prevent its suffocation. Dedicated people who consider it "their baby" will fight for it.

To summarize the general approach, a company can prepare to take advantage of a strategic change by developing the ability to recognize an innovation early, promoting a corporate culture that welcomes change, developing processes that allow experimenting with new ideas, and developing skills that allow exploitation of the new position. After introducing an innovation, the company must protect it in a separate organizational unit and nurture it by means of consistent investments.

ELEMENTS OF A DYNAMIC STRATEGY

Given the analysis so far, we can now begin to view strategy in a more dynamic way (see Figure 10.1). In thinking about its strategy, a company must first identify and colonize a *distinctive* strategic position in its industry. It should then excel at playing the game in this position, thus making it the most attractive position in the industry. While competing in its current position, a company also must search continuously for new strategic positions. After identifying another viable strategic position in its industry, the company then must attempt to manage both positions simultaneously—no easy task. As the old position matures and declines, the company must slowly make a transition to the new, at which point it must start the cycle again: While fighting it out in the new position, it must again search to discover another viable strategic position to colonize.

Of course, at any time during this dynamic process, a company could opt to jump into a new technology or industry. This could happen while the company is still competing in its first strategic position, later while the company is striving to balance the demands of two strategic positions, or at any time during the evolution of a firm's strategy. Notice, however, that after jumping into another industry, the firm must go through the same dynamic process as in its original industry. Moving into another industry does not alter the strategic tasks that a company must undertake in *each* business—it just makes management more complicated in that the firm faces additional challenges, such as how to manage a diversified portfolio and how to exploit synergies among its businesses.

Hence, designing a successful strategy is never-ending. A company needs to continuously revisit and challenge its answers to the who-what-how questions in order to remain flexible and ready to

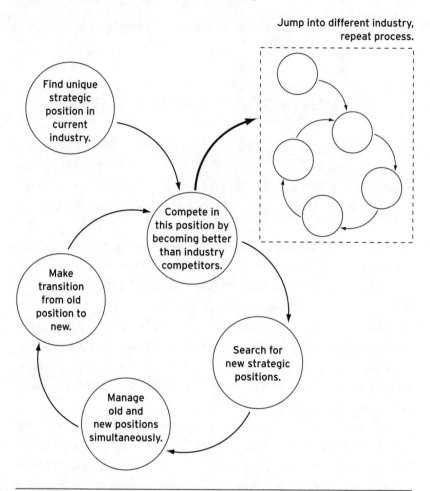

Figure 10.1. Elements of a Dynamic Strategy.

adjust its strategy if feedback from the market is unfavorable. Changing industry conditions and customer needs or preferences, countermoves by competitors, and a company's evolving competencies give rise to new opportunities and the potential for new ways to play the game. A strategy adopted a decade ago on the basis of prevailing industry conditions is certainly not a guaranteed game plan for the future.

Even (or perhaps, especially) successful companies must continuously question the basis of their business and the assumptions behind their successful formulas. Because new who-what-how positions spring forth from the mass market almost ceaselessly, established companies must be on the lookout for these new positions. Like modern-day pioneers, corporate executives must set out to explore the evolving terrain of their industries in search of unexploited strategic positions. Only the intrepid who abandon the safety of the familiar to venture into the unknown will have a future worth discussing.

NOTES

1. The "who-what-how" framework was introduced in D. Abell, *Defining the Business: The Starting Point of Strategic Planning* (Englewood Cliffs, New Jersey: Prentice Hall, 1980), chapter 2.

2. In nearly all cases and contrary to traditional wisdom that emphasizes exploiting economies of scale in such offices, a Jones office is a one-person operation. Each Jones broker has extraordinary autonomy in managing his or her office, and every branch is a profit center. A satellite communications network that broadcasts "home-grown" TV programming ties brokers to the home office.

3. P. Weever, "Growing Call of Telephone Banks," *Sunday Telegraph* (London), 22 December 1996, p. 2; and A. Bailey, "Telephone Banking—It's for You: The Service Has Scope for Great Popularity," *Financial Times,* 3 April 1996, p. 18.

4. See C. Markides, "Strategic Innovation," *Sloan Management Review,* Spring 1997, *38,* 9–23; and C. Markides, "Strategic Innovation in Established Companies," *Sloan Management Review,* Spring 1998, *39,* 31–42.

5. This same point is also discussed in M. Tushman and C. O'Reilly, "The Ambidextrous Organization: Managing Evolutionary and Revolutionary Change," *California Management Review,* Summer 1996, *38,* 8–30; and R. Burgelman and A. Grove, "Strategic Dissonance," *California Management Review,* Winter 1996, *38,* 8–28.

6. Tushman and O'Reilly (1996), p. 11.

7. J. M. Utterback, *Mastering the Dynamics of Innovation* (Boston: Harvard Business School Press, 1994), p. 216.

8. A. Cooper and C. Smith, "How Established Firms Respond to Threatening Technologies," *Academy of Management Executive,* May 1992, *16,* 92–120; R. Foster, *Innovation: The Attacker's Advantage* (New York: Summit Books, 1986), chapter 6, pp. 139–164; A. Cooper and D. Schendel, "Strategic Responses to Technological Threats," *Business Horizons,* February 1976, *19,* 61–69; and Utterback (1994), chapter 9, pp. 189–213.

9. W. Taylor, "The Business of Innovation: An Interview with Paul Cook," *Harvard Business Review,* March-April 1990, pp. 96–106.

10. A. S. Grove, "Navigating Strategic Inflection Points," *Business Strategy Review,* 1997, *8*(3), 11–18.

11. Utterback (1994), p. 220.

12. Grove (1997), p. 17.

CHAPTER ELEVEN

Transforming Internal Governance: The Challenge for Multinationals

C. K. PRAHALAD
JAN P. OOSTERVELD

The emerging competitive landscape poses a challenge to the internal-governance capacity of large, established firms. *Internal governance* refers to the wealth-creation processes inside diversified multinational corporations (DMNCs). Three main processes constitute internal governance: cultivating strong corporate business-unit relationships, fostering interunit linkages, and pursuing growth and innovation. First, it is easier to create wealth when frictions in the relationships between the corporate center and the business units (and the geographical units) are reduced. Eased frictions allow business units to be market oriented rather than embroiled in internal debates. Second, enhancing the quality of interunit linkages (for example, global account management) creates value. Internal corporate leverage of resources requires business units to collaborate to address new, emerging opportunities. Finally, growth and innovation are an integral part of a corporation's vitality.

The rate of change in the competitive environment exceeds the speed with which established DMNCs have been able to transform their internal-governance processes.[1] Consider Kodak, Matsushita, Toshiba, and other firms with great traditions, global scope, and established technological capabilities. As the dominant paradigms in their businesses shift, their ability to lead is severely compromised. Although leaders recognize the need for rapid transformation of their firms' internal governance, the problem lies in determining how to accomplish that transformation.

DMNCs are not constrained by a lack of knowledge about new technology; they often create new technologies. Philips is a technological leader in the optical media that gave the world CD and now DVD. Long before smaller start-ups, Xerox and IBM had all the technology needed to develop the personal computer. Kodak had the knowledge base to lead the development of the digital-imaging market. Nor are these organizations financially constrained. Their R&D budgets and capital spending run into billions of dollars per year. The malaise cannot be attributed to resource constraints.

OLD REMEDIES AND NEW PROBLEMS

At the first signs of competitive difficulty, managers assumed that the time-tested remedy of cost cutting would save them. All large, established firms bought time through the rituals of portfolio adjustment, reengineering, and head-count reduction. From 1991 to 1996, many leading firms attempted to restructure their way out of problems (see Table 11.1).

As late as 1998, Kodak and Xerox were undertaking restructuring efforts: In January, Kodak announced a reduction of 16,800 employees; in April, Xerox announced a reduction of 9,000 employees. Through restructuring activities, managers reduced inefficiencies accrued over decades. Yet these cost-cutting efforts failed to transform the firm as many had hoped. The competitiveness problems persisted because managers were applying old remedies to new problems.

In this article, we first describe the competitive discontinuities that DMNC managers face. From that description, we derive the new managerial challenges. We then examine the impediments to

Table 11.1. Restructuring, 1991–1996.

▼

		Number of Layoffs
AT&T	January 1996	40,000
Chemical/Chase	August 1995	12,000
Delta Airlines	April 1994	15,000
Digital Equipment	May 1994	20,000
GTE Corp.	January 1994	17,000
NYNEX	January 1994	16,800
IBM	July 1993	60,000
General Motors	December 1991	74,000

Source: A. Sloan, "The Hit Men," *Newsweek,* 26 February 1996, *127,* 44–48.

change that established firms must overcome. Finally, we argue that transformation of the internal-governance process—a capacity for corporatewide unlearning as well as learning—is at the heart of sustained wealth creation.

COMPETITIVE DISCONTINUITY

We define *discontinuity* as an abrupt change. An example is the Internet. Five years ago, no one could have anticipated its rapid proliferation and impact on consumers and firms. The rise of the Internet has forced a quantum jump in the rate of change in how firms do business. In an environment of rapid and discontinuous change, gradual evolution of the business model, and therefore of internal governance, is insufficient. Discontinuity arises from many sources:

▼ *Prosumerism.* During the past decade, multinational firms gained access to more than a billion new customers as formerly closed economies—in Eastern Europe, China, India, Brazil, and the Commonwealth of Independent States (former Soviet republics)—joined the free markets. As a result, the demographic composition of the global markets available to DMNCs has changed; for example, potential markets include an aging population in Europe and

Japan, a young population in China, Mexico, and India, and an aging and young population in the United States. Furthermore, customers spend their time and money differently. Lifestyles and fashions are evolving. The spread of television in emerging markets and the Internet worldwide gives consumers access to vast amounts of information. In many industries, such as software, consumers are actively involved in product design and development.

The changing nature of customers' expectations, age, income levels, regional spread, and knowledge base has profound implications. Consumers are in charge and have more choice than previously. The dramatic shift in the balance of power among manufacturers, distributors, and consumers is best described as the age of *prosumerism*. Businesses have to become "pro" consumers as they gain access to more information and start exercising their new options.

▼ *Disintermediation.* Traditional channel structures are being challenged. Manufacturers are more likely to be in direct contact with end users by eliminating intermediaries—wholesalers, dealers, and distributors. The Internet provides a new approach to customer access and distribution. Managers are gaining increasingly sophisticated knowledge of consumers and will be able to serve them better. While the quality of relationships between manufacturers and customers can improve through disintermediation, selling and administrative costs as a percentage of sales in most firms are likely to decline significantly. The mix of marketing investments will change as well.

▼ *Deregulation, Privatization, and Globalization.* Although the pace and timing vary in different parts of the world, deregulation and privatization are changing the character of globalization. A wide variety of industries are being deregulated and privatized; for example, financial services, power, telecommunications, water, airports, broadcasting, and postal services. Deregulation destroys local monopolies, allowing entrepreneurial firms to exploit global opportunities in industries that were, for most of the century, primarily local. The globalization of Enron (in power, gas, and water), Sprint (in telecommunications), and Schiphol Airport Authority are but a few examples of the dramatic shift in industry dynamics resulting from deregulation and privatization. Significant regional differences, however, persist, as beneath the veneer of global uniformity, differences lurk. For example, MTV can be seen as a uniform, global force. Yet as a manager in India told one of the authors, "If you only see the video, MTV in India is like it is anywhere else in the world. If you listen to the audio as well, you know it is India. The freedom of movement may be global but the soul is local."

▼ *Digital Convergence.* Many traditional industries are learning to harmonize traditional technologies with new ones. For example, traditional consumer electronics firms such as Philips and Sony will have to learn to harmonize what used to be the domains of telecommunications, computing, and software. The new high-volume electronics (HVE) industry is attempting to combine these capabilities seamlessly. Products like cellular phones, palm tops, and Web TV are the results of such integration. Similarly, electronic commerce may be forcing a convergence of traditional banking, retailing, database management, and communications industries. Plant and animal genetics is becoming an integral part of food processing. The pressures to converge are reshaping every industry—from auto dealerships to bookselling, education, government, and health care. Convergence results in industry structures that are fundamentally different from those that survived for a century. For example, in the financial services industry, there are megamergers (for example, Citigroup) and the emergence of nontraditional competitors such as Tesco, Sainsbury, and Virgin.

▼ *Indeterminate Competitive Landscape.* With convergence and deregulation, traditional industry boundaries among telecommunications, computing, and consumer electronics are disappearing. The personal computer serves as a bridge between those three traditional industries. The same transformation is taking place among the investment, insurance, and banking industries. These changes suggest that the business models developed to compete in a traditional industry structure are becoming irrelevant in the new, evolving industries.

▼ *Evolution to Open Standards.* Standards are important if new industries are to evolve. However, standards are emerging as much from market dynamics as from government imposition. Furthermore, most of the standards developing in new industries are open. No single vendor or government controls them, and they are available to anyone willing to license. As a result, technology investments may not be as critical for effective participation in an industry as they were thirty years ago. IBM benefited from a proprietary standard. Compaq, on the other hand, benefits from an open, de facto industry standard. The sources of competitive advantage are shifting from patents and technology to cost, quality, speed, and access to suppliers and distribution channels.

▼ *Zero Cycles.* The life cycles of products and services are becoming dramatically shortened, approaching months and weeks. Discontinuity is creating an era of close "zero cycles." Managers must expect competing products to appear almost immediately, which means that a firm has to gain volumes rapidly to amortize investments. Scaling up the logistics chain—supply, manufacturing, distribution, and marketing—is a critical capability. Because the market for a product can decline just as rapidly, the ability to scale down is equally important. This volatility imposes new demands on organizations. Access to a responsive supplier base, global logistics, and flexible manufacturing systems are becoming new sources of competitive advantage.

▼ *Ecological and Social Sensitivity.* Businesses are moving swiftly from a position of compliance to active involvement with environmental issues, a development that has a significant impact on packaging, product design, and technology choices (for example, nuclear energy versus coal). Social issues—child labor, family orientation, workers' rights, and consumers' rights—are becoming major topics of social and political debate. The attention that Shell got in offshore drilling and Nike in making shoes in factories with (by our standards) inappropriate labor standards are examples.

All established firms face these competitive discontinuities, but managers often misinterpret their effects. They regard loss of market share, unattractive products, profit declines, and new competitors as the result of inefficiencies rather than as the result of the rapidly changing competitive landscape. Hence, their first reaction to discontinuities is to "work harder" when what they really need is to "work differently." Competitive challenges demand an "out of the box" strategy, an attempt to operate in the zone of opportunity. Yet organizations make "in the box" operational improvements, attempts to stay in the zone of comfort. Once managers learn the futility of old solutions, they begin to recognize the new internal-governance issues that competitive discontinuities generate. This recognition is the first step toward transformation of the established firm.

NEW INTERNAL-GOVERNANCE CHALLENGES

Traditional wisdom dictated that managers think globally and act locally. The former chairman of Sony called it becoming "glocal"—global and local.[2] In our view, that rule is no longer valid, if it ever was. Managers must think and act globally (for example, deciding where to locate the next $1 billion semiconductor facility). Managers must think and act regionally (for example, determining how to exploit opportunities in the Latin American market). Regions of the world, such as greater China, the Indian subcontinent, and the North American market each have their own dynamics. For example, a European firm cannot manage, from Europe, the opportunities available in these diverse, fast-growing markets. Finally, managers must think and act locally. Each market has its own peculiarities, including regulation, local politics, local competitors, distribution channels, pricing pressures, quality of talent available, and company history in that market.

We believe that thinking and acting globally, regionally, and locally is a new capability for most established DMNCs. As we enter the new century, managers must become sensitive to what is outside their normal purview. Trends in Shanghai may be as important as trends in New York. In the video CD (a two-in-one product that combines audio and video players using CD technology) business, for example, the Chinese market is more important than the European and U.S. markets. Emerging markets do not suffer from the problems of an installed base.

Innovations can emanate from both the corporate center and the subsidiaries. Furthermore, local innovations can be exploited globally. In telecommunications, China and India are just starting to build their infrastructures and are not saddled with the traditional "copper wire" infrastructure. As a result, they can adopt new technologies more readily and may also become sources of innovation in how new products are used. For example, the Chinese, without universal access to telephones, use pagers to send one-way messages. This usage requires more display space, thus adding a new feature to the traditional pager. All markets with characteristics similar to China's are candidates for pagers used as one-way communication devices. The locus of innovation and the locus of exploitation of innovations can be global, regional, and local. The corporate environment must resemble a network of distributed intelligence. Multiple languages, perspectives, customs, and business environments must be incorporated into the firm's thinking and actions.

A different pace and rhythm will permeate all aspects of a firm's activities. As we have noted, for example, cycle times for product development in most industries are becoming shorter; to amortize R&D investments, firms must build volumes quickly. Exploiting global markets is one way to build volume. As product life cycles decrease, so do the life cycles of business models and management processes. As competitive conditions change, management processes must be constantly evaluated for their relevance. The global launch of products is a consequence of these pressures.

The convergence of technologies requires that managers rapidly absorb and integrate new knowledge with old as well as reconfigure that knowledge into new business opportunities. As the established firm acquires new knowledge, it confronts an intellectual heritage germane to that knowledge—which often means confronting a generation of managers with skills different from those of incumbents. Almost all firms must learn to accept and harmonize technologies that are new to them. Although the convergence of chemical with electronic technologies (for example, Kodak), pharmaceuticals with fashion (Revlon), plant genetics with commodity processing (Cargill), and hardware with software (Philips) are obvious, the process by which multiple intellectual disciplines are commingled to create new knowledge is not. We often lack adequate labels to describe hybrid knowledge and use clumsy labels such as "cosmeceuticals" to describe the harmonization of pharmaceutical and cosmetics knowledge. In today's DMNCs, geographic distance may be less worrisome than cognitive distance. Harmonizing different intellectual traditions (for example, between software engineers and chemical engineers) is often more demanding culturally than coping with cultural differences among nations and races.

In a rapidly evolving competitive environment, it is natural for managers to disagree on direction, priorities, and timing of actions such as market entry. For example, a manager at Kodak USA or Japan might believe that the development of digital photography products is urgent. A manager at Kodak Germany or China may feel less pressure. These managers may not even have access to the same data on the importance of digital photography. If dissent is legitimate, consensus building becomes a critical element of internal governance. Consensus building across cultures and distances in a DMNC is a tall order. IBM and Hewlett-Packard are developing information technology systems that supply all managers involved in making complex trade-offs with the same information and knowledge base. Their debate focuses on interpretation of data rather than disagreement over data. Candor, openness, and intellectual challenge must characterize the debate within the organization, and top management sets the tone. Information cannot be merchandised and used as a source of private power, but must be seen as a corporate resource.

Firms need to form a wide variety of alliances—for setting standards, for market entry, and for gaining access to technology. Managers will have to prepare their organizations to learn from these alliances. Simultaneously, they have to protect their organization from unanticipated leakage of intellectual property. Becoming selectively open and opaque is a new skill for most firms.

Managers must allocate financial and human resources in an increasingly ambiguous world. No one can fully predict the implications of discontinuities. Different firms may pursue varying approaches to the future. For example, Disney, Microsoft, IBM, Sony, and Compaq may each develop different strategies for exploiting the opportunities presented by digital convergence. Each firm starts from its base of experience and moves forward. Multiple migration paths in an evolving industry such as multimedia are equally legitimate. Strategy in this evolving environment involves convincing customers of what the future could be and then shaping that future. Its goal is to create a new competitive space.

At the same time, managers cannot ignore the current businesses. With all the discussion surrounding PC-TV, for example, companies still have to sell televisions and personal computers. Discontinuities do not happen overnight. Black-and-white TVs still account for more than 5 percent of the world market for televisions. The market for traditional color TVs is growing. The question is not whether color television will disappear in the next three to five years, but how fast the business's center of gravity will shift. How can managers migrate from one profit engine to the other?

In view of these pressures, why do incumbent managers in established firms hesitate to act? The impact of discontinuities on the established firm may not always be obvious, and the internal-governance implications of discontinuous change are even less so. Top managers may disagree on the time frames within which the changes will affect their firm. We have found, in most established firms, a sufficient sense of discomfort with the status quo. Managers agree that the changes in the competitive environment during the past decade are qualitatively different from those in the previous environment and see the pace of change as accelerating. What, then, prevents managers in established firms from being more proactive?

ZONE OF COMFORT VERSUS ZONE OF OPPORTUNITY

We believe there is a big gap between knowing the problem and knowing the solution. Faced with discontinuous change, most managers do not know where to start. Over many years, firms such as General Motors, Hitachi, or Siemens have developed a set of managerial routines. The more successful the firm, the more entrenched the managerial routines. Furthermore, the senior ranks of these firms are populated with managers promoted from within. All senior managers have been socialized in the same "village." They may not even have an intellectual understanding of (much less experience with) an alternate model of managing. As a result, there are several impediments that prevent rapid response to the discontinuous changes in the competitive environment.

In most established firms, managers do not distinguish between "social" and "task" performance. Having "grown up" together, managers have strong social ties. Discontinuities challenge the established social order within the company. Task performance—protecting the interests of the company and transforming it to meet the new reality—challenges social harmony. Senior managers, against all good advice and their better judgment, entrust the new tasks to old friends who may not be prepared for them. It is an age-old problem, illustrated delightfully in Tuchman's history, *The March of Folly*.[3]

Discontinuous change demands new knowledge. Hierarchical positions represent old knowledge. The people with power and authority to make things happen lack specific new knowledge. Senior managers must often manage business opportunities that they do not fully understand and are simultaneously burdened with the responsibility to make current businesses profitable. The resulting tensions are both administrative and personal. How much attention is the new business likely to get when folded administratively into the current business? What underlying business model will managers likely use to evaluate the new business opportunities? How will they allocate resources? These systemic problems are exacerbated by personal inadequacies of senior managers, their knowledge gaps, and an accompanying sense of personal vulnerability. The risks of the new opportunity are thus magnified.

Discontinuities create competitive problems; they are the "bad news" that top managers get tired of listening to. In a profit crisis, top managers are willing to listen to advice. But as soon as the firm's profitability starts to improve and reaches a minimum acceptable threshold, the appetite for continuing to make tough choices—pruning the portfolio, raising performance standards, or making personnel changes—is lost. Top managers' attitude is: "We have gone through a rough period. I do not want to hear more of the same. We'll be fine." This weariness expresses a lack of the intellectual and physical stamina that top managers need to be able to lead the transformation of a DMNC. The people who report to the top managers stop bringing up difficult issues or try to minimize the importance of persistent problems. Often the investment analysts and consultants become the firm's conscience. Over time, the momentum of the change process is lost. Performance deteriorates, and more restructuring becomes inevitable. Few CEOs are able to keep the pressure for higher performance at the top of the agenda. Jack Welch at General Electric may be the rare exception.

Traditionally, senior managers seek administrative clarity. Pressures to improve performance in current businesses reinforce the emphasis on accountability. For most managers, accountability equals administrative clarity. The popularity of the trend to break up DMNCs into defined SBUs with clear charters and performance measurements reflects the desire for clarity. As DMNCs march toward the goal of administrative clarity and accountability, competitive discontinuities are creating a need to articulate strategic direction for the entire corporation. Strategic questions—for example, the Internet's impact on marketing and logistics—transcend the domains of individual business units.

To exploit emerging opportunities, managers have to devise strategies that do not respect current business-unit charters. In an age of discontinuities, strategic clarity—the ability to create new businesses and business models—confronts administrative clarity—the ability to foster accountability for current business performance. Senior managers tend to postpone strategic questions because they impinge on administrative clarity. Paradoxically, the longer managers cling to administrative clarity to deal with the demands of current performance and avoid important strategic questions, the more performance will suffer. In a rapidly changing competitive environment, profitability demands a new strategy and a new approach to internal governance.

The intellectual demands of the new economy are at odds with those of the traditional businesses. For example, new customer demands are forcing managers to shift from selling "boxes"—discrete, stand-alone devices—to selling "solutions." The shift applies to diverse businesses, from financial services (for example, selling "financial freedom" in contrast to selling mortgages, insurance policies, credit cards, or checking accounts) to cleaning services (for example, selling "health and sanitation" in contrast to selling detergents, mops, and disinfectants). "Things" and "knowledge" have to be creatively bundled and sold as a package. Managers accustomed to pricing "boxes" and "things" find the costing and pricing of know-how and solutions difficult. Know-how is usually given away free as a basis for selling "boxes."

Until recently, in a variety of industries (for example, utilities, telecommunications) and in many countries (for example, China, Russia, India), customers did not have choices. Managers in these environments developed skills appropriate to markets characterized by no choice or shortages. In the new economy, customers have not only choices but information to facilitate those choices, for example, via the Internet. Price differences across markets for the same product are less likely to be defensible. The new reality is that customers benefit and managers face unprecedented margin pressures.

Relevant managerial knowledge may be related to age. In most established firms, the managerial ranks break down into clusters: age fifty-five years and older, forty-five to fifty-four, thirty-five to forty-four, and twenty-five to thirty-four. As a rule, the older managers are disconnected from the new reality of technologies and customers. The lower-middle and middle managers may be more in tune with marketplace realities. The resulting gap between authority and ability creates an obstacle to active debate on strategy formulation and implementation. The phenomenon has led to suggestions such as "middle-out" initiatives[4] and using lower-level executives in strategy formulation.[5]

The need to invent a new strategic direction for the DMNC, coupled with the need to manage current businesses, can lead to paralysis. The zone of comfort—the familiar—often wins over the zone of opportunity—the unfamiliar. For example, at Matsushita, moving away from the company's famous system of decentralized management has not been easy. Everyone in Matsushita grew up in the system; it is all they have experienced. At Philips, enforcing disciplines and accountability went against what senior managers recognize as the "mentality of the village and the social fabric." Poor performance was tolerated until a new management group, consisting primarily of outsiders, took over. The new CEO of Philips came from a performance-driven U.S. DMNC. We can attribute the dramatic improvement in the company's profitability during the past two years largely to his managerial style.

LESSONS IN MANAGERIAL TRANSFORMATION

Experience with organizational transformation during the past fifteen years has taught us several lessons. First, transformation is not just about reducing costs, improving profitability, or reengineering. Transformation is the invention of strategies and management processes. It must be driven by new ideas, a new concept of opportunity. Second, transformation must involve the whole organization. Top managers leading the transformation effort must dramatically change the worldview of the entire organization—the perception of the firm's opportunities. Only a new and shared perception of opportunity can lead to new ways to compete. Third, transformation must deal with deeply embedded and often tacit values and beliefs. They have a significant influence on how managers act. Fourth, transformation requires building a new portfolio of skills within the DMNC. New markets and businesses and new approaches to creating and sustaining competitive advantage inevitably demand changes in the skill sets at all levels. Finally, transformation must be cemented with new management processes; performance evaluations, rewards, career management, product development, and logistics must change.

The demands of transformation are complex, involving interrelated systemwide changes. Most top managers are unprepared, intellectually and emotionally, to cope with the task. Their managerial models and cognitive maps are conditioned by their experience.[6] The "bandwidth" of responses is limited. Managers must start with a blueprint to prevent transformation efforts from stalling or failing. A detailed road map is impossible because much learning takes place as the effort unfolds and the competitive situation evolves. However, managers must be clear about the elements of the transformation effort; if they cannot imagine the future, they cannot create it.

HOW TO CHANGE AN ESTABLISHED DMNC?

Needless to say, without restoring the firm to an acceptable level of profitability, no management group will have a chance to attempt a long-term transformation. Restoring profitability creates confidence among employees inside the firm. It soothes the anxieties of suppliers, customers, and investors. Without their support, no long-term transformation effort is likely to succeed. However, top managers must recognize that *restoring profitability is but a necessary condition.* Too often, regaining profitability in existing businesses is equated with transformation.

Based on our experience, we suggest the following process for managing the transformation of an established DMNC.

CREATING AN AGENDA
FOR TRANSFORMATION

Transformation cannot be initiated without an explicit recognition among top managers that the environment of discontinuous change presents risks and opportunities. Transformation is a voyage beyond the known. Discomfort and anxiety are, therefore, normal reactions in embarking on transformation. Managers can create the future only if they have a point of view. Therefore, the first step should be to create on paper a transformation agenda consisting of two components: the firm's strategic architecture and its social architecture. The purpose of developing a strategic architecture is to assess the trends, drivers, and discontinuities that are likely to influence the evolution of the various businesses and the new opportunities that the firm can expect to create over the next decade. It provides a framework for how the businesses, competencies, and the business model(s) within the firm can be transformed.[7] Based on the strategic architecture, managers must then develop a social architecture, or blueprint, of how the organization's social fabric—its beliefs, values, management processes, skill sets, workforce, and geographical distribution—will change. The purpose of the transformation agenda is to create a framework—a set of new ideas—that can mobilize the entire organization.

Once the framework for transformation is ready, top managers must fight organizational inertia. They must initiate actions that get attention and jolt the entire organization. Major divestments (for example, of the very profitable chemicals business at Unilever), significant alliances and mergers (Citicorp and Travelers, for example), or major shifts in key people tend to send the signal that "business as usual" is over. These signals followed by a significant and coordinated educational experience, such as the Centurion process at Philips, can create a sense of urgency and reinforce the need for deep change.

The organization is then ready for deployment of the new strategy. The goal is now to align the entire organization with the new direction. Each employee should be able to see where the firm is headed and why and be able to translate that vision into action. Deployment involves sharing the same big picture of the emerging competitive landscape with everyone, persuading people, and providing them with the new tools they need to contribute to the new strategic direction. Each employee can and must make a contribution. For transformation to take hold, work has to become meaningful at a personal level.

Individuals, groups, and the organization as a whole have to learn to operate differently. Deployment of strategy requires breaking the broad conception of the future into specific, bite-size projects that provide the basis for experimenting and learning. These projects not only provide learning opportunities but also generate small wins along the way.

In initiating projects, organizations must recognize the need for evaluation. Most organizations do not become efficient at transformation because they do not create processes for analyzing failures. They often blame individuals or business units. Yet most failures result from systemic problems. As the organization starts to invest in projects to support the new strategy, vestiges of the old organizational processes are still in place; failures and difficulties in the early stages are a natural outcome. Rather than abandon initiatives or change managers, top managers must create forums for examining the systemic reasons for failure. Analysis of successes is also critical.

Managers must analyze failure and success with the future in mind. They must base their inquiry on an assessment of future internal-governance needs. But for managers to assess why they failed or succeeded, they need to go back to the past. Looking back to move forward is the goal. We call this process *forward-reverse thinking*. For example, as Citicorp moves forward toward creating a billion consumer market for its services, it must look back on its history of how it created the consumer business using the credit card as the vehicle. What lessons can be carried forward? A culture of learning from failures and successes is a prerequisite for transformation. The analysis must move beyond easy explanations toward an understanding of the dynamics of success and failure. Failure analysis is more difficult in most organizations and requires candor and trust.

As organizations undertake new activities, their current skill base may be inadequate for executing the strategic architecture. Top managers often hire talent from outside at senior levels, assuming that they will be able to provide new knowledge. Unfortunately, in most established firms, managers at senior and middle levels are adept at neutralizing the one or two top managers from outside. As one top-level DMNC manager from outside said, "The natives have the map and are not willing to share it with the new kid on the block." The newcomers are naturally frustrated. Reskilling is a multi-level task. Top managers must create a critical mass of new skills on multiple levels to accomplish the transformation task.

Almost all top managers, reflecting on their own experiences of transforming their organizations, believe that they could have moved more quickly. A fast pace always seems risky at first. The CEO's hesitancy may reflect, in part, personal anxieties. Furthermore, CEOs have to balance current performance and transformation. It is natural to believe that if they stepped up the pace of transformation, the profit performance in the short term might deteriorate. In retrospect, however, CEOs believe that was not a valid concern.

CONCLUSION

Increasingly, the managerial task embraces innovations in how firms manage. These must precede innovations in how firms compete and create wealth. Managers must step out of their zone of comfort and move into the zone of opportunity. They must focus on the new internal-governance requirements—changing the relationships between the corporate center and business units, finding opportunities for creating new businesses outside traditional business-unit boundaries, and pursuing growth and innovation. As we look at the transformation process, we see strategy at its heart—identifying discontinuities, determining their impact on markets of today and tomorrow, and developing new business models. A successful transformation rests on both strategic thinking and flawless execution.

NOTES

1. For examples that demonstrate some of the problems established firms face, see C. Christensen, *The Innovator's Dilemma: When Technologies Cause Great Firms to Fail* (Boston: Harvard Business School Press, 1997); and D. Leonard-Barton, "Core Capabilities and Core Rigidities: A Paradox in Managing New Product Development," *Strategic Management Journal,* Summer 1992, *13,* 111–125.
2. S. Morita, "Global Localization," in *Genryn* (Tokyo: Sony, 1996), chapter 8.

3. B. Tuchman, *The March of Folly: From Troy to Vietnam* (London: Michael Joseph Ltd., 1984).

4. I. Nonaka and H. Takeuchi, *The Knowledge-Creating Company* (New York: Oxford University Press, 1995).

5. G. Hamel, "Strategy as Revolution," *Harvard Business Review,* July-August 1996, *74,* 69–82.

6. C. K. Prahalad and R. Bettis, "Dominant Logic: A New Linkage Between Diversity and Performance," *Strategic Management Journal,* November-December 1986, *7,* 485–501.

7. G. Hamel and C. K. Prahalad, *Competing for the Future* (Boston: Harvard Business School Press, 1994).

CHAPTER TWELVE

Three Strategies for Managing Fast Growth

GEORG VON KROGH
MICHAEL A. CUSUMANO

Many companies approach growth management with no strategy other than to do what they did when they were new. New companies begin with a flourish. They have certain capabilities and knowledge. As they get caught up in short-term survival, they may cling to the same capabilities and knowledge. Or they may acquire the wrong kind of new knowledge and fail to grow the right capabilities. In the end, they may pour on new capabilities and knowledge—when it's too late.

The key to a long, healthy corporate life is steady growth. According to a 1998 survey, of the companies that enjoyed greater than 10 percent sales growth per year, about 78 percent were still around six years after starting. Of the companies with flat or decreasing sales, only 27.5 percent survived for six years.[1]

GROWING STRATEGICALLY

To grow steadily and avoid stagnation, a company must learn how to scale up and extend its business, lengthen its expansion phase, and accumulate and apply new knowledge to new products and markets faster than competitors.

Managers can't leave growth to chance. They must choose a plan that renders consistent sales growth for years, not just in short bursts. A good growth plan captures the vision for expanding the company. It addresses the product and market combinations the company intends to pursue, the size it hopes to achieve in a particular time frame, and most important, the know-how and organizational structures that will support expansion or diversification.

Such planning has an internal focus—rather than a focus on what competitors might do or what type of technological change might transform an industry. It is designed to help a company exert more control over its fate as it tackles outside challenges.[2] Implementation is easier for start-up companies but possible for established enterprises, too. Company size should not drive the growth plan. Companies of all sizes need systems for creating, acquiring, and sharing knowledge. Consider Netigy, a San Jose–based e-commerce service provider. Netigy has only 650 employees, but it already has invested in a chief knowledge officer and a knowledge-management system for 20,000 people. Netigy is prepared to handle its vision for growth.[3]

What does drive the growth plan is the company's set of capabilities. Managers must choose a plan that fits with the knowledge, learning skills, and assets that the organization possesses or plans to develop. On the basis of the literature and our personal knowledge of fast-growing companies, we conclude that companies grow using three basic strategies: scaling, duplication, and granulation. (See box, "About the Research.") There is no one best strategy. A growth plan may end up tapping more than one. The important thing is to include principles of organizational learning, knowledge acquisition, and knowledge transfer.

▼

About the Research

We began our inquiry into growth strategies and capabilities by reflecting on cases of rapidly growing companies we knew. Michael Cusumano has written about Nissan, Toyota, Microsoft, and Netscape.[a] Georg von Krogh has addressed learning, capability building, and application of knowledge management in companies such as Skandia AFS, Sencorp, Shiseido, Sony, Siemens, Gemini Consulting, General Electric, and Phonak AG.[b]

We also considered what authors in management and organization studies had to say about expansion strategies, the management of start-ups and young firms, the processes of knowledge creation and knowledge sharing, and organizational learning in general. We found that very few authors addressed the topics in combination and none attempted to integrate ideas about growth strategy, knowledge management, capabilities, and organizational learning.

We concluded that companies must combine strategies for growth with explicit strategies for learning. They must base their growth strategies on their capabilities and market opportunities, then prepare their organizations to acquire or create specific knowledge about new technologies, customers, and industries.

[a] M. A. Cusumano, "The Japanese Automobile Industry: Technology and Management at Nissan and Toyota," *Harvard East Asian Monographs* no. 122 (Cambridge, Massachusetts: Council on East Asian Studies, Harvard University, 1989); M. A. Cusumano and R. W. Selby, *Microsoft Secrets* (New York: Free Press, 1995); and M. A. Cusumano and D. B. Yoffie, *Competing on Internet Time* (New York: Free Press, 1998).

[b] G. von Krogh, K. Ichijo, and I. Nonaka, *Enabling Knowledge Creation: How To Unlock the Mystery of Tacit Knowledge and Release the Power of Innovation* (New York: Oxford University Press, 2000); and G. von Krogh and J. Roos, *Organizational Epistemology* (London: Macmillan, 1995).

SCALING: DOING MORE
OF WHAT YOU'RE GOOD AT

Scaling starts with a coherent vision of products, technologies, and customers. The vision is the foundation for growth, at least until circumstances change significantly. The vision should reflect the company's commitment to growth, be brief and clear, and be understood by all employees. The focus should be on a concrete product, technology, and customer segment.[4]

Netscape's founders believed that the Internet would revolutionize the way people worked and interacted.[5] Their vision was to build infrastructure software that would put the company at the heart of the new, networked world and let it ride the Internet wave while experimenting with new products, technologies, and markets.

Scaling requires a company to implement its vision quickly. As co-founder Jim Clark observed, "An axiom of motorcycle racing applies precisely to the technology business: Move fast, keep going—or end up on your butt. Slow down on the throttle and you'll be off the road and into the trees."[6] In two years, Netscape (see box) went from a basic browser for surfing the Internet to more sophisticated browsers for corporate customers. It kept up the momentum by quickly adding a variety of servers, then opening up new markets for corporate intranets and extranets (the latter being intranets extended to select customers or suppliers). Next it moved to electronic commerce, adding new servers and applications tools and creating Netcenter.com—all within four years of starting. When America Online acquired it in fall 1998, Netscape had a value of more than $10 billion.

▼

Netscape

1994   Founded by Jim Clark and Marc Andreessen

1995 $80 million in sales

1998   Approximately $500 million in revenues and more than 3,000 employees

In our business, stability comes from doing things quickly.
    —JIM CLARK

Invest Aggressively

To grow by scaling, a company expands product development around core technologies and offerings, expands product lines, and increases the intensity of marketing by using existing distribution channels to reach new customer groups with related needs. It must increase manufacturing capacity and enlarge corporate infrastructure—for example, by building bigger and better information systems and setting up central human resource management systems to recruit and train employees quickly. (See box, "Is Scaling the Right Strategy?")

▼

Is Scaling the Right Strategy?

Growth by scaling works best when

▼ The market is potentially large enough for rapid growth in a focused product line

▼ The product creates unique value in the customers' view

▼ The company can distribute products widely at low cost

Netscape used the Internet to overcome traditional entry barriers that software producers faced, such as bundling software with hardware or relying on software retail stores. Customers simply downloaded software from the Netscape Web site.

Scaling requires a company to learn about mass manufacturing and new manufacturing techniques. If the product is related to software or services, the company must become expert in the latest relevant technologies and standards, information systems, and hardware trends. Knowledge of mass marketing is important, but when competition intensifies, individualized customer information becomes the strategic weapon. Learning how to offer technical support for an increasing customer group is critical for companies that are scaling. So are new routines (for procedures, quality standards, planning, milestones, and goals), without which a company can become increasingly chaotic and unprofessional and ultimately hurt product quality and service.

Companies must pursue aggressive investment—often *before* sales growth becomes apparent. Netscape invested in growth, knowing that without growth, it would face far more serious problems than overinvesting. And Netscape grew—even more quickly than it anticipated.

Specialize and Standardize

Companies that grow fast often centralize and standardize administrative areas such as finance and accounting to handle the increased transactions. Initially, they have simple functional structures, with manufacturing, marketing, sales, product development, finance, and accounting all separate. As they grow, they duplicate the functional departments within divisions tied to particular products or geographic markets. Smaller teams then focus on specific customer segments and control the resources they need. Netscape moved from one small research-and-development group to separate R&D divisions for its browser and server products—and later for its e-commerce tools and Web site.

Hire the Right Mix

To refine and exploit existing products, processes, and market know-how, key people must learn quickly and share their insights and technical knowledge. Netscape co-founder Marc Andreessen and a core group of programmers gained invaluable design experience and market insights from working at the University of Illinois on Mosaic, Navigator's predecessor. They distributed two million copies of Mosaic and learned how the networked world of the Internet could function, with hot links potentially connecting every computer and database worldwide.[7]

But although Andreessen and the other programmers had most of the essential concepts and technical skills, they lacked the money, managerial insights, and organizational skills needed. Jim Clark, who had founded Silicon Graphics a few years earlier and knew how to make a technology into a viable business, served as a pied piper in attracting other talent and resources.[8]

Netscape had to learn quickly. Its customers changed from savvy Internet users of a single product—the browser—to more conservative corporate users who wanted an array of products that were rock-solid reliable. Netscape had to figure out how to design, document, test, sell, and support mission-critical products in a more professional way.

At the same time, it had to absorb many new people. Clark hired young programmers who had worked on Web browsers and added seasoned managers, engineers, and sales and marketing experts from computer and telecommunications industries. Recruiting from a veritable *Who's Who* of U.S. high-tech companies, Netscape leveraged the experts' knowledge to train the less seasoned.

Adapt the Structures

For knowledge to be shared, a company must set up the right organizational structures, processes, and culture. As Netscape grew, it sought to maintain the creativity and innovative capabilities typical of small organizations; in late 1996, it reorganized the product divisions into minidivisions, or *divlets*. Each divlet reported to its own general manager and worked on a specific product release or server product.

The arrangement had certain flaws: poor cooperation, redundant work and mistakes that could have been avoided through collective brainstorming. In 1997, after Netscape failed to rewrite Navigator/Communicator in Java, Netscape president/CEO Jim Barksdale decided to make the divlets report directly to Andreessen. As chief technology officer, Andreessen had been without formal product responsibilities. Barksdale's move effectively centralized product planning and gave Andreessen authority to cancel projects and to force more knowledge sharing among the browser and server teams.

Find Ways to Learn from Customers Early

Netscape discovered the intranet market by learning from its customers. A major bank in Switzerland had begun using Netscape's browser and server technology for its internal corporate network to allow employees to share information easily by using the Internet communications protocols. Netscape quickly identified intranets as a new opportunity and extended the idea to create extranets.

Netscape also learned to cultivate lead users and to have them test early versions of its products and give rapid feedback to developers. It started internal initiatives to find new ways to apply its technology to corporate markets. It used its own technology to create extranets that linked Netscape engineers, sales, marketing, and support personnel to independent software vendors, content providers, Internet-service providers, and computer manufacturers.

DUPLICATION: REPEAT THE BUSINESS MODEL IN NEW REGIONS

Like scaling, *duplication* starts with a coherent vision of products, technologies, and customer segments. But unlike scaling, the vision must include goals for geographical expansion. The vision of IKEA (see box) founder Ingvard Kamprad was to go beyond Sweden and democratize the furniture industry throughout Europe by making new products affordable to the masses. Kamprad's vision relied on Swedish design skills and a store ambiance that could communicate an appealing lifestyle to young people everywhere. (See box, "Is Duplication the Right Strategy?")

Balance Standardization and Adaptation

Duplication typically involves packaging the company's entrepreneurial know-how for new geographic areas, for example, by setting up overseas subsidiaries or franchising a business concept.[9] A carefully orchestrated tension balances standardization (keeping processes and organizational details close to the way they are done in the original location) and adaptation (changing the organization and processes to address the needs of the local region).

Duplicating marketing in overseas markets is important, but responsiveness to local market conditions is key to long-term success. In new geographic areas, companies may choose to centralize manufacturing and administrative functions, duplicate the functions, or both. Centralized manufacturing reduces manufacturing costs, but duplicated manufacturing increases flexibility.

Duplicated businesses should follow similar human resource–management practices. By standardizing staffing, training, and remuneration plans, a company can rotate employees among subsidiaries instead of having to hire and train new people when work in one locale increases. With HR duplication, employees also share new ideas and experience smoothly while providing consistent service to customers.

Hire Flexible, Independent Managers

Companies must give managers the independence they need to balance adaptation to local markets with preserving what made the original business successful. IKEA did that well, although its senior

---

▼

IKEA

1954	Starts as a small, domestic furniture manufacturer and retailer in Sweden with sales of 2 million Dutch guilder.
1984	Sales grow to 2,679 billion guilder.
1999	Sales grow to 16,954 billion guilder. Is franchiser and direct owner of many stores; operates out of Denmark. Has a presence in 25 countries, with 50,000 employees worldwide; 80 percent of sales are in Europe and 14 percent in the United States.

Beautifully designed home furnishings are created for a small part of the population—the few who can afford them. We have decided to side with the many.

—INGVARD KAMPRAD, FOUNDER

▼

Is Duplication the Right Strategy?

Growth by duplication works best when

▼ The business requires physical presence and the company can repeat its business model in new geographic markets. Home furnishings, for example, include items that customers want to see before purchasing. For services such as consulting, architecture, and customized software development, personal contact and trust building are essential.

▼ There is a need for better distribution. A company might shift from a scaling to a duplicating strategy when distribution channels are under-developed or when it can build up a unique set of local distributors that would be costly for potential competitors to imitate.

▼ The company can adapt its experience in product development, manufacturing, and marketing approaches fairly easily. Unique information about local customers and new trends from foreign markets may lead to better market segmentation and targeted marketing than smaller local companies can offer.

Duplication requires several kinds of learning. To set up new subsidiaries abroad, a company must learn about local market conditions and apply the knowledge in adapting products, marketing, and operations. Duplicating, like scaling, may require learning about mass manufacturing or mass marketing, but it is also likely to require individualized communication to flow among central management and local management, product-development staff, local marketing staff, sales staff, and customers. Duplicating involves learning about new competitors, regulatory differences, the best ways to handle logistics, and currency-related risks. Alliances with local companies can expand knowledge because they provide access to local insights about marketing, manufacturing capacity, and product development. Acquisitions are an option, but integration into the existing organization may be problematic, especially if the acquired company is in another country.

country and regional managers often were Swedish or familiar with the Swedish language. Eventually, however, a truly global company must train foreign managers in its practices and values, as IKEA has been doing gradually in the United States and China.

Duplicate Key Parts of the Infrastructure

Geographical expansion calls for simple procedures and work processes robust enough to handle varied employee backgrounds. During expansion, informal sharing of experience usually is not the best learning mechanism. Senior managers have less control over local recruiting and human resource development than those using scaling. Growing by duplication requires that a company externalize, or transfer, key elements of its infrastructure.[10] Some companies use *black-boxing*—whatever mechanism they can set up to share their *black boxes* (critical data at various levels of detail in ready-to-use form, such as written or online manuals or video presentations).

Black boxes must be available at a moment's notice to help employees and managers worldwide accomplish important tasks. A single black box at one level of detail may help in establishing a new subsidiary in a new territory. It might include checklists on choosing a site, using legal counsel, selecting and training personnel, laying out a store, and purchasing manuals. A box at another level might include detailed instructions on how to service clients outside business hours or how to set up a store-maintenance program.

IKEA used black-boxing. The European expansion group it organized to jump-start its duplication in Switzerland, Germany, France, Italy, Denmark, Norway, and Austria bought land, hired people, constructed furniture outlets, and decided on the new outlets' decor. Two months before opening a new store, a first-year operations group would move in while the expansion group moved on to the next site. The first-year group would take charge, train people, arrange the store opening, and set up the operations. Then IKEA would establish a local country organization to run the operations.

The international expansion group, IKEA's "knowledge Marines," represented the ideal mechanism for accumulating know-how from each new site and spreading the knowledge to newer operations.

Duplicate Entrepreneurial Knowledge

IKEA learned how to black-box entrepreneurial knowledge, too. The preferred site for new stores was always relatively cheap land on the outskirts of a city. The stores were simple and functional, most often two-story buildings with displays on the second floor and warehousing on the first. IKEA standardized and documented products, catalog format, logo use (although in Norway the company used red and white instead of the traditional blue and yellow), and personnel selection and training. The custodian of the entrepreneurial knowledge was the international expansion group.

IKEA also used *devoted practice* to duplicate its corporate vision. Local employees would devote themselves to learning certain tasks by studying manuals and attending training courses. Kamprad acted like a field commander, communicating the vision to new employees, visiting new stores, taking notes on store operations, and discussing procedures and improvements directly with employees. Through such attention to detail, the black box can become a local routine. Employees then use it as a foundation for devising new and better solutions.

Be Aware of the Limitations

It would be naive to expect black-boxing to be consistently successful. Customer tastes and employee backgrounds are too diverse for one set of processes and programs to fit all situations. When IKEA expanded to the United States in 1986, it found that U.S. customers had subtle but important differences in tastes and shopping habits from Europeans. They wanted shelves, but for televisions, not books. European sheets did not fit American beds. European cups, plates, and drawers seemed small to Americans.[11]

In addition, black boxes may not be sensitive to new requirements. A company that grows through duplication must be able to learn quickly, fixing procedures and products that don't work and making the people who created them aware of the new requirements. That is especially true of young high-growth companies expanding abroad in highly competitive markets. Senior executives and central-management systems must have the openness and flexibility necessary for modifying a formula that was a winner back home.

IKEA had a slow start in the United States, but it learned quickly.[12] The company now adapts fully one-third of its product designs to U.S. tastes. Combining black-boxing and local learning has helped IKEA improve duplication of its business and remain competitive over time in many markets.

GRANULATION: GROWING SELECT BUSINESS CELLS

There are limits to scaling and duplicating. A company's product line may run out of steam, too many low-cost competitors may copy it, or there may be no new foreign markets to conquer. At that point, the best strategy could be *granulation*—distinguishing the cells, or smaller granules, of the business and growing them aggressively.

SAP (see box), now one of the largest software companies in the world, went through both scaling and duplication before attempting granulation. The company initially specialized in enterprise-resource-planning (ERP) systems that let clients track and plan financial and other resource flows. Its early product, R/1, supported only a few resource flows. In 1989, SAP launched R/2, which offered new features and more than doubled the company's sales over the next three years. In 1992, it launched R/3, which integrated resource planning across functions and customer-suppliers, allowing customers to manage more than 1,500 business processes. R/3 made SAP a global name in software.

▼

SAP

1972   Founded in Germany by former IBM Mannheim software engineers.

1992   Launches resource-planning software R/3 and makes its name.

1996   Begins developing industry-specific solutions. Introduces AcceleratedSAP methodology.

1998   Delivers services map for complete life-cycle solutions and support.
Has 22,000 employees in more than 50 countries. Hires 2,400
employees in this year alone.

1999   Delivers mySAP.com. Reports total sales of $5 billion, a one-year
increase of 18 percent.

*We must use the brainpower that we have in the company as much as
possible. We have to constantly reorganize ourselves, to rethink what
is best, not just celebrate 25-year anniversaries or quarterly results.*

—HASSO PLATTNER, SAP CO-FOUNDER

Toward the end of 1997, SAP embarked on duplication. In
1998 it reorganized into industry business units, with a core development unit for new technologies and services plus a global sales-
and-marketing unit. As custodians of specialized know-how in
industry-specific resource planning, the units transformed SAP from
a one-product company to a multiple-product company. SAP now
builds on the R/3 platform whatever the customer needs, while integrating component software from other suppliers.[13] It continues to
improve R/3 and shares knowledge by training in-house personnel
and representatives from local IT consultancies. Approximately 150
instructors now teach more than 200 courses at 85 training centers
worldwide. SAP is adding remote training programs, too. Such
enhancements and SAP's extensive implementation expertise have

enabled it to add Chevron, Eastman Chemical, and Microsoft to its long customer list.

BALANCE THE OLD AND NEW

Granulation is like the other strategies in starting with a strong, coherent vision for growth, but its focus is on developing unique capabilities and creating new businesses. A company uses its resources and knowledge to explore new territory with new, autonomous business units, independent subsidiaries, or corporate spinoffs. Granulation is risky; business units may not leverage fully the company's existing knowledge and asset base. Although individual entrepreneurs learn from working on local technologies with local customers and local staff, they work better when they have access to information, expertise, and resources from other parts of the company.[14] Each new cell, therefore, should reuse existing product technologies, manufacturing processes, organizational processes, and consumer information but combine those assets in new ways. (See box, "Is Granulation the Right Strategy?")

In 1996, SAP released R/3 Version 3.1, which had Web interfaces. The launch inspired further exploration of e-business solutions at SAP and led to a new growth strategy. The company began developing new business groups to create technologies for both individuals and small to midsize firms. It then launched mySAP.com, a portal-based marketplace that facilitates transactions among customers with different transaction volumes. In March 2000, SAP formed SAP-Markets, a separate venture for electronic market activities.

Balance the Informal and Formal

Both informal and formal methods are required for knowledge to flow between entrepreneurial cells. Informal personal ties help people in different groups establish trust and share experiences. SAP

▼

Is Granulation the Right Strategy?

Growth by granulation works best when

▼ Growth through scaling and duplicating has clear limits. The company has conquered all relevant markets, product demand is flattening out, customers are changing their preferences, or increasing competition for market share makes further growth too expensive.

▼ A new technology is flourishing that could become a substitute for the company's products or a new business opportunity. Companies must explore and experiment with new technologies that are adjacent but outside current knowledge areas, routines, and capabilities.

▼ The company is sufficiently mature to monitor new business activities, share knowledge internally, and learn effectively about new markets and competitive scenarios.

Granulation requires that a company obtain knowledge outside itself and its operations, especially about its industry. Initially, a new cell, or business unit, might benefit from employees' internal experiences, but as it ventures into an unknown market with new products and learns from the experience available to the industry at large, it will move away from the parent company's core know-how.[a] Skill at acquiring industry experience rapidly should become a generic skill for entrepreneurs throughout a company.

[a] P. Ingram and J.A.C. Baum, "Opportunity Constraint: Organizations' Learning from Operating and Competitive Experiences of Industries," *Strategic Management Journal*, 1997, *18*, 75–98.

---

favors a "football team" style of work over hierarchies. Communication frequently occurs spontaneously, making SAP seem almost like a university.[15]

However, informal ties generally center on short-term issues.[16] Fast-growing companies need to complement informal mechanisms with more-formal knowledge sharing, such as strategic-planning processes that encourage regular discussions among managers and employees from different cells. Companies also can hold periodic conferences or rotate experienced personnel among company units.

Evaluate and Monitor

Companies benefit from selectively evaluating and monitoring new business opportunities the way venture capitalists do. First, local entrepreneurs conceive business ideas, draft business plans, organize a venture team and form entrepreneurial cells. Then senior management representatives act as investors, with both a monitoring and advising role. The entrepreneurial model also lets companies invest successfully in outside enterprises with attractive technologies, products, services, or customer bases.

Learn from Customers, Partners, and Competitors

At SAP, the business units' chore is to dig up industry knowledge. Often knowledge comes from customer feedback or lead users. SAP has gathered interested customers to work with company developers on some fifty projects. A strategic alliance with Nokia—to extend mySAP.com to a wireless mobile workforce—is likely to generate useful learning, too.

When a company grows through granulation, its competitors may be unknown but they are probably not inactive. The company must establish systems to gather and analyze intelligence on existing and potential competitors—and speed it to decision makers.

Acquiring smaller companies with expertise in the new technology and forming alliances are two ways to acquire external knowledge. Both need routines for sharing knowledge between the acquisition or alliance partner and the rest of the company. Sharing mechanisms may include integration teams (for acquisitions), shared management responsibilities, periodic conferences and meetings, or shared access to databases and knowledge bases.

COMBINING STRATEGIES

To identify the strategy with the best fit, a company should start with a bird's eye view of the comparative strengths of scaling, duplicating, and granulating. (See Table 12.1.) The scaling strategy is

Table 12.1. Strategies for Growing and Learning.

Means of Learning	Scaling	Duplicating	Granulating
Experience sharing	Sharing the core business knowledge	Sharing the know-how of selecting e-entrepreneurs and managers	Sharing entrepreneurial knowledge in new business cells for new markets
Externalization: Making experiences explicit	Making entrepreneurial know-how in product development, manufacturing, marketing, and sales explicit	Black-boxing entrepreneurial know-how and applying it across new markets	Making the knowledge of entrepreneurs in new cells explicit
Formal sharing of knowledge	Sharing within and between functions, such as product development or marketing	Sharing knowledge about procedures that work and those that don't work	Building on and recombining explicit knowledge across cells in order to enhance creativity and generate new business
Devoted practice: Learning by doing	Developing different routines, practices, functions, and disciplines	Applying black-box procedures and knowledge	Devoting attention to evaluating and monitoring new business opportunities
External knowledge acquisition	Establishing formal market connections to ensure customer feedback to product development	Acquiring knowledge about the appropriateness of products, services, and processes in the local context	Developing procedures for industry learning
	Netscape	**IKEA**	**SAP**

simplest: A company merely learns how to do more of what it already does. Duplication is more complex, requiring a company to learn how to apply what it knows to new geographical markets. The most demanding in terms of knowledge acquisition, granulation requires a company to gather substantial information about new competitors and new product and market opportunities. But it also enables gradual diversification from related businesses into unrelated technologies, products, and markets.

Johnson & Johnson, with its emphasis on creating subsidiaries, is a classic example of granulation.[17] Founded to provide surgical supplies to doctors, the company grew by expanding into related health care markets for hospitals and home consumers. Early on, management created separate companies (usually wholly owned by J&J) for each distinct market and allowed them considerable independence. When necessary, the separate companies collaborate; for example, in providing joint distribution services to the hospital industry. By 1999, the company had 190 subsidiaries, 98,000 employees, operations in 51 countries, and approximately $24 billion in sales (divided among the hospital, pharmaceutical, and consumer health care sectors). It remains one of the fastest-growing large companies in the world.[18]

Large companies with business units or subsidiaries in different growth stages may want to tackle scaling, duplication, and granulation simultaneously. For most early-stage companies, though, it is best if managers implement the three growth strategies sequentially, with some overlapping, as SAP did. A successful firm might first try scaling up its basic business. As it reaches the limits of scaling, it might start duplicating its successful business model abroad, while still emphasizing scaling as much as possible. Eventually the company should be able to pursue granulation, using new business units or spinoffs to diversify in its home market and, later, abroad.

The road will not always be smooth. SAP learned from early customer feedback that it had overengineered R/3. Implementation at customer sites required considerable time, effort, and money. The company responded by launching its AcceleratedSAP rapid-implementation technology, which speeds up the introduction and use of its software systems. It also started to provide best-practice cases of business processes so that its clients could benchmark and improve their own operations.[19]

Managing and sharing knowledge is vital. Both IKEA, with its "knowledge Marines," and SAP, with its aggressive training program, worked hard to mobilize local staff to sell and implement products in different markets. But however a company chooses to apply its knowledge and whatever strategy it chooses, it must be committed to continued growth. It can't afford to become complacent. Companies that aren't steadily growing might very well be on their way to steadily dying.

Acknowledgments

For their helpful comments, we wish to thank three anonymous reviewers; also Simon Grand, Peter Gomez, Yvonne Wicki, and Mark Macus of the University of St. Gallen, and Harbir Singh of the University of Pennsylvania's Wharton School. In addition, we thank participants at the Conference on Knowledge and Innovation (Helsinki School of Economics and Business Administration, Helsinki, Finland, May 26–27, 2000), including James G. March, Ikujiro Nonaka, Patrick Reinmoeller, and Giovanni Dosi. Andreas Seufert at the University of St. Gallen assisted in the research on SAP.

Additional Resources

Many companies have deep corporate knowledge but are not sure how to use it to competitive advantage. *Working Knowledge: How Organizations Manage What They Know,* by Thomas Davenport and Laurence Prusak (Cambridge, Massachussetts: Harvard Business School Press, 1997) and *Enabling Knowledge Creation: How To Unlock the Mystery of Tacit Knowledge and Release the Power of Innovation,* by Georg von Krogh, Kazuo Ichijo, and Ikujiro Nonaka (New York: Oxford University Press, 2000) provide ample guidelines. The KnowledgeSource Web site (www.knowledgesource.org) offers additional links and information.

Reading about lessons learned from successful companies is a good way to avoid pitfalls and duplicate what works. *Competing on Internet Time: Lessons from Netscape and Its Battle with Microsoft,* by Michael Cusumano and David Yoffie (New York: Free Press, 1998), and *Microsoft Secrets: How the World's Most Powerful Software Company Creates Technology, Shapes Markets and Manages People,* by Michael Cusumano and Richard Selby (New York: Free Press, 1995) capture lessons from rapidly growing companies. Robert Spector tells Amazon.com's story in *Amazon.com—Get Big Fast: Inside the Revolutionary Business Model That Changed the World* (New York: Harper Business, 2000).

John Nesheim's *High Tech Start Up: The Complete Handbook for Creating Successful New High Tech Companies* (New York: Free Press, 2000) gives good pointers, particularly on how to deal with risk.

NOTES

1. J. Timmons, *New Venture Creation* (Burr Ridge, Illinois: Irwin, 1998), p. 14.
2. We concur with S. L. Brown and K. M. Eisenhardt's notion in *Competing on the Edge: Strategy as Structured Chaos* (Boston: Harvard Business School Press, 1998) that growth should be organically driven by the internal pace of the company rather than external factors.
3. Chuck Salter, "Built to Scale," *Fast Company,* July 2000, pp. 348–354.
4. J. R. Baum, E. A. Locke, and S. A. Kirkpatrick, "A Longitudinal Study of the Relation of Vision and Vision Communication to Venture Growth in Entrepreneurial Firms," *Journal of Applied Psychology,* 1998, 83(1), 43–54.
5. M. Cusumano and D. Yoffie, *Competing on Internet Time: Lessons from Netscape and Its Battle with Microsoft* (New York: Free Press, 1998).
6. J. Clark, *Netscape Time: The Making of the Billion-Dollar Start-Up That Took on Microsoft* (New York: St. Martin Press, 1999), p. 60.
7. Marc Andreessen often jumped from one topic to another during conversations but showed a remarkable ability to connect seemingly diverse ideas. As chief legal counsel of Netscape, Roberta Katz,

commented, "The browser is a map of his brain." Cusumano and Yoffie, *Competing on Internet Time,* p. 18.

8. Clark, *Netscape Time.*

9. S. G. Winter and G. Szulansk, "Replication as Strategy," working paper 98.10, Wharton School, Philadelphia, Pennsylvania, 1999.

10. G. von Krogh, K. Ichijo, and I. Nonaka, *Enabling Knowledge Creation: How to Unlock the Mystery of Tacit Knowledge and Release the Power of Innovation* (New York: Oxford University Press, 2000); and M. Boisot, *Knowledge Assets: Securing Competitive Advantage in the Information Economy* (New York: Oxford University Press, 1998).

11. "IKEA: Furnishing the World," *The Economist* (Nov. 19, 1994), pp. 79–80.

12. www.ikea.com/about_ikea/timeline/fullstory.asp

13. J. Rieker, "Die drei von der Baustelle," *Manager Magazine,* April 1998, pp. 114–126.

14. R. N. Yeaple, "Why Are Small Research and Development Organizations More Productive?" *IEEE Transactions on Engineering Management,* 1992, 39(4), 332–346.

15. "Die Regeln der SAP," *Manager Magazine,* May 1998, p. 238.

16. M.W.H. Weenig, "Communication Networks in the Diffusion of an Innovation in an Organization," *Journal of Applied Social Psychology,* 1999, 25(5), 1072–1092.

17. Another is Thermo Electron, whose growth is described in C. Y. Baldwin and J. Forsyth, "Thermo Electron," Harvard Business School case no. 9–292–104 (Boston: Harvard Business School Publishing Corp., 1992). Unlike Johnson & Johnson, Thermo Electron generally sold public stock in its subsidiaries to take advantage of the capital markets—an important tactic for raising money.

18. "Dusting the Opposition," *The Economist,* April 29, 1995, pp. 71–72; and www.jnj.com/annual/99_annual/jj_99_ar.pdf

19. www.sap.com/service/asap_rm.htm; and A. Seufert, "SAP: The German Software Giant" (presentation at the MIT Sloan School of Management, Cambridge, Massachusetts, Nov. 5, 1999).

THE AUTHORS

Christopher A. Bartlett is Daewoo Professor of Business Administration and chair of the Program for Global Leadership at Harvard Business School. He served as faculty chair of the International Senior Management Program from 1990 through 1993, and as area head of the school's General Management Unit from 1995 to 1997. He is a fellow of both the Academy of Management and the Academy of International Business, and maintains ongoing consulting and board relationships with several large corporations. Prior to joining the faculty of HBS in 1979, he was a marketing manager with Alcoa in Australia, a management consultant in McKinsey and Company's London office, and general manager of Baxter Laboratories' subsidiary company in France.

His interests have focused on the strategic and organizational challenges confronting managers in multinational corporations, and on the organizational and managerial impact of transformational change. He is the author, co-author, or editor of seven books, including *Managing Across Borders: The Transnational Solution* (Harvard Business School Press, 1989, 1998, with Sumantra Ghoshal), and *The*

Individualized Corporation (Harper Business, 1997), winner of the Igor Ansoff Award for the best new work in strategic management.

Eric D. Beinhocker is a principal at McKinsey & Company, Inc., an international management consulting firm, where he serves clients in the telecommunications, e-commerce, and biotechnology sectors. He is also co-leader of McKinsey's Worldwide Strategy Practice, where he conducts research on topics in economics and strategy. Prior to working at McKinsey, he was a venture capitalist with Summit Partners, focusing on software and communications investments, and was co-founder and CEO of Fulcrum Technologies, Inc., a start-up software company.

Beinhocker holds an AB in Economics and Engineering Sciences from Dartmouth College and an MS in Management Science from the MIT Sloan School of Management, where he was the Henry Ford II Scholar. He has held academic research positions at the Harvard Business School and the MIT Center for Organizational Learning, and has been a visiting scholar at the Santa Fe Institute.

Michael A. Cusumano is the Sloan Management Review Distinguished Professor at MIT's Sloan School of Management. He teaches courses on strategic management and the software business, and has been a visiting professor at Hitotsubashi University and Tokyo University in Japan, the University of St. Gallen in Switzerland, and the University of Maryland. He received a BA from Princeton University in 1976 and a PhD from Harvard University in 1984.

Cusumano is a consultant in software development, strategic planning, and technology strategy, and has worked with major companies around the world, including AT&T, Cisco, Ford, General Electric, IBM, and Intel. He serves on several corporate boards of directors and advisors, and is chairman of the board of the *MIT Sloan Management Review*.

Cusumano is the author of five books. His latest, *Competing on Internet Time: Lessons from Netscape and Its Battle with Microsoft* (Free

Press, 1998, with David Yoffie), was named one of the top ten business books of 1998 by *Business Week* and Amazon.com, and *Microsoft Secrets* (Free Press, 1995, with Richard Selby) is an international best-seller. He has also written *Thinking Beyond Lean: How Multi-Project Management Is Transforming Product Development at Toyota and Other Companies* (1998, Free Press, with Kentaro Nobeoka), *Japan's Software Factories: A Challenge to U.S. Management* (Oxford, 1991), and *The Japanese Automobile Industry: Technology and Management at Nissan and Toyota* (Harvard, 1985). He writes periodically for *The Wall Street Journal, Computerworld, The Washington Post,* and other business publications.

Kathleen M. Eisenhardt is Professor of Strategy and Organization at Stanford University. Her research centers on complexity and evolutionary theories with a focus on their application to corporate strategy in the new economy. She has won the Pacific Telesis Foundation Award for her ideas on fast strategic decision making, the Whittemore Prize for her writing on organizing global firms in rapidly changing markets, and the Stern Award for her work on strategic alliance formation in entrepreneurial firms. She is currently studying effective acquisition strategy among networking and Internet companies, and the creation of synergies in multibusiness corporations.

Eisenhardt is co-author of *Competing on the Edge: Strategy as Structured Chaos* (Harvard Business School Press, 1998), winner of the George R. Terry award for outstanding contribution to management thinking, and one of Amazon.com's top ten business and investing books for 1998. She has also published in journals including *Administrative Science Quarterly, Harvard Business Review, Sloan Management Review, Strategic Management Journal, Academy of Management Review, Red Herring, Academy of Management Journal,* and *Organization Science.*

Eisenhardt has worked with firms in the computing, telecommunications, networking, software, biotech, and semiconductor industries. She is a member of the Strategic Management Society and INFORMS, and a fellow of the Academy of Management and the World Economic Forum. She serves on the editorial boards of *Administrative Science Quarterly* and *Strategic Management Journal.* She received a BS in Mechanical Engineering (Brown University) and also holds an MS in computer science. Her PhD is from Stanford's Graduate School of Business.

Sumantra Ghoshal holds the Robert P. Bauman Chair in Strategic Leadership at the London Business School, where he is a member of the Strategy and International Management faculty. Prior to joining LBS, he taught at INSEAD, in France, and at MIT's Sloan School of Management. He is also the founding dean of the Indian School of Business in Hyderabad, India.

Ghoshal's research focuses on strategic, organizational, and managerial issues confronting global companies. He has published nine books, over fifty articles, and several award-winning case studies. *Managing Across Borders: The Transnational Solution* (Harvard Business School Press, 1989, with Christopher Bartlett) has been called one of the fifty most influential management books of this century by the *Financial Times*; *The Differentiated Network: Organizing the Multinational Corporation for Value Creation* (Jossey-Bass, 1997, with Nitin Nohria) won the George Terry Book Award in 1997; *The Individualized Corporation* (Harper Business, 1997, with Christopher Bartlett) won the Igor Ansoff Award in 1997.

With doctoral degrees in management from both MIT and the Harvard Business School, Ghoshal serves on the editorial boards of several academic and professional journals. He speaks frequently at management conferences in Europe, North America, and Asia on strategy and organization of transnational companies, the changing roles and tasks of corporate leaders, and the challenges of managing radical change. He maintains teaching and consulting relationships with companies around the world, and serves as the chairman of the supervisory board of Duncan-Goenka and as a nonexecutive member of the board of Mahindra-British Telecom.

Gary Hamel is visiting professor of strategic and international management at the London Business School and chairman of Strategos, an international consulting company. He has helped management teams create rule-breaking strategies and has changed the focus and language of strategy in many of the world's most successful companies, including Shell, Nokia, CGU, and Ford.

Hamel has published ten articles in the *Harvard Business Review* in fourteen years. Four of his articles have received the prestigious McKinsey Prize for excellence, and he is the most reprinted author in the history of the *Harvard Business Review*. He has also authored three cover stories for *Fortune Magazine* in the last three years. His landmark book, *Competing for the Future* (Harvard Business School Press, 1994, with C. K. Prahalad), was *Business Week*'s management book of the year and is the all-time best-selling book on business strategy. Among his other works are *Leading the Revolution* (Harvard Business School Press, 2000) and *Alliance Advantage: The Art of Creating Value Through Partnering* (Harvard Business School Press, 1998, with Yves L. Doz).

Hamel is a frequent speaker on strategy and innovation for the World Economic Forum in Davos, the Fortune 500 CEO Roundtable, Bill Gates's CEO Summit, and many others. In addition, he has spoken to hundreds of boards and senior management groups. He is on the boards of the Strategic Management Society and K.I.D.S. (Kids in a Drug-Free Society). He is a fellow of the World Economic Forum and is on the chairman's advisory board of Enron.

Arnoldo C. Hax is the Alfred P. Sloan Professor of Management at the MIT Sloan School of Management. He served as Deputy Dean from 1987–1990, and earned the school's Salgo Award for Excellence in Teaching and Dean's Award for Excellence. He is a native of Chile, where he received a BS in Industrial Engineering; he received an MS at the University of Michigan and his PhD at UC Berkeley. Previously, he was on the faculty of Harvard Business School and a senior consultant for Arthur D. Little, Inc.

Hax has published extensively in the fields of strategic planning, management control, and operations management and research. His books include *Strategic Management: An Integrative Perspective* (Prentice Hall, 1987), *The Strategy Concept and Process: A Pragmatic Approach* (Prentice Hall, 1996) (both with Nicolas Majluf), and *Production and Inventory Management* (Prentice Hall, 1984, with Dan Candea), which received the Institute of Industrial Engineers-Joint Publishers Book of the Year Award. He is Strategic Management Editor for *Interfaces,* former editor of *Operations Research* and *Naval Research Logistics Quarterly,* and an editorial board member for *The Journal of Manufacturing and Operations Research* and *The Journal of High Technology Management Research.*

Hax has consulted with companies worldwide in the development of formal strategic planning processes. He is the chairman of the Executive Program for the Americas at MIT, and was awarded an honorary doctorate degree by the Catholic University of Chile and the Ramon Salas Edwards Award by the Chilean Engineering Institute. He is a board member of Alpargatas.

W. Chan Kim is The Boston Consulting Group Bruce D. Henderson Chair Professor of International Management at INSEAD Business School, France. Previously, he was a professor at the University of Michigan Business School and has served as a board member as well as an advisor for a number of multinational corporations in Europe, the United States, and Pacific Asia. He has published numerous articles on strategy and managing the multinational corporation in journals such as *Academy of Management Journal, Management Science, Organization Science, Strategic Management Journal, Journal of International Business Studies, Harvard Business Review,* and *Sloan Management Review.*

Kim's current research focuses on strategy and management in the knowledge economy. He is a contributor to *The Financial Times, The Wall Street Journal, The Wall Street Journal Europe, The New York Times, The International Herald Tribune,* and *World Link,* and his research has also been featured in *The Economist*. He is a Fellow of the World Economic Forum at Davos, Switzerland, and the winner of the Eldridge Haynes Prize, awarded by the Academy of International Business and the Eldridge Haynes Memorial Trust of Business International, for the best original paper in the field of international business.

Joseph Lampel is professor of strategic management at the University of Nottingham Business School. He is also director of the school's PhD-DBA program, and head of the recently formed Centre for the Study of Emerging Industries. He obtained his undergraduate degree in physics from McGill University, and later pursued his MS on technology policy at the Institut d'Histoire et Sociopolitique des Sciences, Université de Montréal. After working for the Science Council of Canada and the Ontario government, he subsequently returned to McGill University to pursue doctoral studies in Strategic Management. His dissertation, "Strategy in Thin Industries," won the Best Dissertation Award from the Administrative Science Association of Canada in 1992.

Previously, Lampel was a reader at the University of St. Andrews and an assistant professor at the Stern School of Business, New York University, and taught at McGill University, Concordia University (Montreal), and the University of Illinois, Urbana-Champaign. He is the author of *Strategy Safari* (Simon & Schuster, 1998, with Henry Mintzberg and Bruce Ahlstrand), and has been published in *Strategic Management Journal, Sloan Management Review, Journal of Management, R&D Management,* and *International Journal of Technology Management*. He has also served as co-editor of the *Organization Science Special Issue on Cultural Industries* (May-June 2000).

Constantinos C. Markides is professor of strategic and international management and chairman of the strategy department at the London Business School. A native of Cyprus, he received his BA (with distinction) and MA in Economics from Boston University, and his MBA and DBA from the Harvard Business School. He has worked as an associate with the Cyprus Development Bank and as a Research Associate at the Harvard Business School.

Markides has done research and published on the topics of strategic innovation, corporate restructuring, refocusing, and international acquisitions. He is the author of *Diversification, Refocusing and Economic Performance* (MIT Press, 1995), and *All the Right Moves: A Guide to Crafting Breakthrough Strategy* (Harvard Business School Press, 1999). His work has also appeared in journals such as the *Harvard Business Review, Sloan Management Review, Directors & Boards, Leader to Leader, Long-Range Planning, Business Strategy Review, British Journal of Management, Journal of International Business Studies, Strategic Management Journal*, and *Academy of Management Journal*.

Markides has taught many in-company programs and is on the academic advisory board of the Cyprus International Institute of Management. He is also a nonexecutive director of Amathus (U.K.) Ltd., a tour operating company. He is the associate editor of *European Management Journal* and is on the editorial board of *Strategic Management Journal* and *Academy of Management Journal*. He is a member of the Academy of Management and the Strategic Management Society and a Fellow of the World Economic Forum in Davos, Switzerland.

Renée Mauborgne is the INSEAD distinguished fellow and affiliate professor of strategy and management at INSEAD, France, and fellow of the World Economic Forum in Davos, Switzerland. She has written many articles on strategy and managing the multinational corporation for journals, including *Academy of Management Journal, Management Science, Organization Science, Strategic Management Journal, Journal of International Business Studies, Harvard Business Review*, and *Sloan Management Review*. Her current research focuses on strategy, innovation, and wealth creation in the knowledge economy.

Mauborgne is also a contributor to *The Financial Times, The Wall Street Journal, The Wall Street Journal Europe, The New York*

Times, World Link, and *The International Herald Tribune.* Her research has been featured in *The Economist, The Times of London, Wirtschaftswoche, Global Finance, The Conference Board, L'Expansion,* and *Børsen Svenska Dagbladet,* among others. She is the winner of the Eldridge Haynes Prize, awarded by the Academy of International Business and the Eldridge Haynes Memorial Trust of Business International for the best original paper in the field of international business.

Henry Mintzberg is Cleghorn Professor of Management Studies at McGill University in Montreal, Canada, and visiting scholar at INSEAD in France. His research has dealt with issues of general management and organizations, focussing on the nature of managerial work, forms of organizing, and the strategy formation process. He is also working to develop a family of master's programs for practicing managers. He received his doctorate and MS degrees from the MIT Sloan School of Management and his mechanical engineering degree from McGill, having worked in between in operational research for the Canadian National Railways. He has recently been named an officer of the Order of Canada and of l'Ordre Nationale du Quebec and holds honorary degrees from nine universities. He has served as president of the Strategic Management Society and is an elected fellow of the Royal Society of Canada (the first from a management faculty), the Academy of Management, and the International Academy of Management. He was named distinguished scholar of 2000 by the Academy of Management.

Mintzberg is the author of ten books, including *The Nature of Managerial Work* (HarperCollins, 1973), *The Structuring of Organizations* (Prentice Hall, 1979), *Mintzberg on Management: Inside Our Strange World of Organizations* (Free Press, 1989), *The Rise and Fall of Strategic Planning* (Free Press, 1994), which won the Academy of Management's best book award, *The Canadian Condition* (Stoddart, 1995), and *Strategy Safari* (Simon & Schuster, 1998, with Joseph Lampel and Bruce Ahlstrand). He has written over a hundred management articles, including two *Harvard Business Review* McKinsey Prize winners.

Peter Moran is assistant professor of strategy and international management at the London Business School, where he teaches the school's core courses in strategy and general management. His degrees include a PhD in Management from INSEAD (France), an MBA from Cornell University, and a BS in Chemical Engineering from Clarkson University (Potsdam, New York). Before pursuing his career in academia he held process, research, and operations engineering positions in Conoco and was a management consultant, first with Booz Allen & Hamilton and later as an independent.

Moran's current research focuses on how organizations and their managers create value for themselves, their organizations, and society. Questions his research seeks to answer include, How does value creation differ from value capture, what gives rise to each, and how does the pursuit of either affect one's ability to achieve the other? His publications include "Bad for Practice: A Critique of the Transaction Cost Theory" and "Markets, Firms, and the Process of Economic Development," both co-authored with Sumantra Ghoshal and published in the *Academy of Management Review*.

Jan P. Oosterveld is senior vice president of corporate strategy and a member of the Group Management Committee at Royal Philips Electronics. He began his career with Philips in 1972, moving through various managerial positions in Spain and the Netherlands, and became a director in 1984. He founded Philips Key Modules in 1989. He is a member of the board of the Strategic Management Society, and a regular lecturer at Harvard and other business schools.

Born in Emmen, the Netherlands, Oosterveld studied mechanical engineering and factory automation at Eindhoven Technical University, and received an MBA from the Instituto de Estudios Superiors de la Empresa in Barcelona.

Richard T. Pascale was a member of the faculty at Stanford's Graduate School of Business for twenty years and taught the most popular course in their MBA program—a course on organizational survival. He is a leading consultant worldwide, a best-selling author, and a scholar. Over the past decade, he has worked closely with the CEOs and top management teams of many large corporations, including AT&T, General Electric, The New York Times, Intel, and Morgan Guaranty Bank. Recently, he has served as architect of several large-scale corporate transformations with major European and U.S. companies. He was a White House fellow, special assistant to the secretary of labor, and senior staff of the White House task force, which reorganized the executive office of the president. In 1991, BBC TV dedicated a prime-time broadcast to his work; the BBC is currently filming a video series on his ideas and methodology.

Pascale wrote the best-selling book, *The Art of Japanese Management* (Simon & Schuster, 1981, with Anthony Athos), as well as *Surfing the Edge of Chaos: The Laws of Nature and the New Laws of Business* (Random House, 2000, with Mark Milleman and Linda Gioja), and *Managing on the Edge: How the Smartest Companies Use Conflict to Stay Ahead* (Simon & Schuster, 1989). He has published numerous articles and received the *Harvard Business Review*'s McKinsey Award for the best article of 1984.

C. K. Prahalad, the Harvey C. Fruehauf Professor of Business Administration at the University of Michigan Business School, specializes in corporate strategy and the role and value added of top management in large, diversified, multinational corporations. He has been visiting research fellow at Harvard University, visiting professor at INSEAD in France, and professor and chairman of the Management Education Program at the Indian Institute of Management. He has consulted with the top management of many of the world's foremost companies; in addition, he serves on the board of directors of NCR Corporation.

Prahalad's works include the books *Competing for the Future* (Harvard Business School Press, 1994, with Gary Hamel), named the best-selling business book of the year in 1994, and *Multinational Mission: Balancing Local Demands and Global Vision* (Free Press, 1987, with Yves Doz), as well as numerous articles for journals such as the *Harvard Business Review, Sloan Management Review, Strategic Management Journal, Journal of Applied Corporate Finance,* and *Journal of Market Research.* His articles have won many awards, including the *Harvard Business Review* McKinsey Prize (1989, 1990, 1998), the ANBAR Electronic Citation of Excellence (1997), the European Foundation for Management Award (1993), the Maurice Holland Award as the best paper published in research technology management (1994), and *Strategic Management Journal's* best article of 1980–1988.

Prahalad studied at the University of Madras and the Indian Institute of Management, and received his DBA from Harvard University.

Georg von Krogh is visiting professor of strategic and international management at the MIT Sloan School of Management. Previously, he was professor and director of the Institute of Management at the University of St. Gallen in Switzerland, associate professor of Strategy at the Norwegian School of Management, and assistant professor at the SDA Bocconi University in Milan. He has also been a visiting professor at the Japan Advanced Institute of Science and Technology, the Hitotsubashi University in Tokyo, and the London School of Economics and Political Science. He was a visiting researcher at the Technical University Aachen and at the University of Munich, and earned his PhD at the University of Trondheim. He has written and edited numerous books and articles in strategy and knowledge management, including *Enabling Knowledge: How to Unlock the Mystery of Tacit Knowledge and Release the Power of Innovation* (Oxford University Press, 2000), *Knowledge Creation: A New Source of Value* (Macmillan, 1999), and *Knowing in Firms* (Sage, 1998). He has served on the editorial boards of several journals.

Dean L. Wilde II is a founding partner and chairman of Dean & Company, an international strategy consulting firm founded in 1993. Previously, he was a director and member of the board of directors at Mercer Management Consulting, where he headed the firm's worldwide communications and computing practice. He was an executive vice president of Strategic Planning Associates (SPA) and a member of its governing policy committee; he also founded and ran SPA's telecommunications and technology practice. He has twenty years of experience in consulting to companies on strategy, organization, and operations issues. He has worked across a broad range of industries, including financial services, manufacturing, food, distribution, and transportation. He has extensive experience in the technology and telecommunications sectors, including Internet, wireless, data services, cable, software, and hardware.

Wilde has served as a visiting lecturer at the MIT Sloan School of Management, where he teaches a course in strategy. He earned a physics degree from Iowa State University, where he graduated as top scholar in 1978, and an MS in management from the MIT Sloan School of Management in 1980. Mr. Wilde is co-author with Professor Arnoldo Hax of *The Delta Project*, which is due to be published by Macmillan in the Spring of 2001.

Peter J. Williamson is professor of international management and Asian business at the INSEAD in Fontainebleau, France, and Singapore. He was formerly dean of MBA programs at London Business School and visiting professor of global strategy and management at Harvard Business School.

Williamson's research and publications span globalization, strategy innovation, joint ventures and alliances, and competitive dynamics. His publications include *The Economics of Financial Markets* (Oxford University Press, 1995), *Managing the Global Frontier* (Trans-Atlantic Publications, 1994), *The Strategy Handbook* (Blackwell Publishers, 1992), and the upcoming *From Global to Metanational: How Companies Win in the Global Knowledge* (Harvard

Business School Press), as well as articles for *Harvard Business Review, Financial Times, Oxford Review of Economic Policy, Strategic Management Journal,* and *Academy of Management Journal.* He is currently undertaking major research projects on strategic innovation and how companies should approach the next round of competition in Asia.

Williamson has acted as consultant on business strategy and international expansion to numerous multinational companies in Asia, Europe, and North America as well as to the World Bank and to the Commission of the European Communities. He is a nonexecutive director of several listed companies.

INDEX